The Life of
William Jennings Bryan

BY

GENEVIEVE FORBES HERRICK
and
JOHN ORIGEN HERRICK
Nationally-known editorial writers

Illustrated

The last formal portrait of William Jennings Bryan, posed in Nashville, Tenn., en route to the evolution trial at Dayton.

FOREWORD

This Life of William Jennings Bryan is the simple story of a simple man, who was known to the people of America and the world as the Great Commoner because he found the Divine spark in the soul of the humblest of his fellow men. This biography tells the story of his life without attempting any searching criticism. His notable career and his death are too near at hand at this writing to make such an attempt productive of anything more than a very narrow view. In the perspective of the future his career will be viewed more truly, and the nation's progress will weigh his merits and his faults with a certain balance.

Much of the material in the closing chapters of this book was drawn from personal contact with the man and the events in which he so largely dominated. Other material has been garnered from the contemporary chroniclers of his activities—the newspapers of the country—where anything that had to do with Bryan was always sure of a "front page play." Facts concerning his early life have been drawn in part from a sketch written by his wife, to whom due appreciation is here made. Bryan's own book, entitled "The First Battle," was used as a source for certain facts concerning his terms in Congress and the convention and campaign of 1896.

The running story of his life largely found expression in his speeches, and extracts from these are frequently incorporated here as the best obtainable delineation of the character of this one of the most notable Americans of modern times.

GENEVIEVE FORBES HERRICK.
JOHN ORIGEN HERRICK.

Chicago, August 15, 1925.

DEDICATED

By the Authors

TO EACH OTHER

Companions in the work and play of marriage

PREFACE

At home on Sunday evening, July 26, we received over the radio the sad news of Mr. Bryan's death. After a few moments of silence my wife said "Why don't you publish a Biography of Mr. Bryan? There are millions of people who will want to read the story of his life in a more connected form than they have been able to get it through the newspapers."

I meditated on the suggestion for a few days and finally mentioned the subject to my good friend, John Herrick and his wife, Genevieve Forbes Herrick, the widely known feature writers on the Editorial Staff of one of Chicago's leading newspapers.

Mr. Herrick had just returned a few days before from Dayton, Tennessee, where he had seen and heard the Great Commoner defending "the faith of our fathers." He was so deeply impressed with Mr. Bryan's sincerity and earnestness, and with his determination to fight to the very last for principles he believed to be right, that it was no difficult task to persuade him and his able wife to burn the midnight oil for the next few weeks in preparation of this work.

It is doubtful if any biographers in the future, after years of thought and study, will be able to write a story of Mr. Bryan's life with more of the human interest element in it than this volume contains. No attempt has been made to eulogize Mr. Bryan nor to emphasize his manly virtues beyond their just deserts.

If this biography will help those who read it get a clearer vision of the principles of right and justice for which the Great Commoner lived and fought and died, the authors and publishers will feel that their purpose has not failed. It is hoped and believed that a study of this Life will stimulate a greater devotion to the ideals and principles for which he gave his life.

Grover C Buxton

Immortality

God may be a matter of indifference to the evolutionists, and a life beyond may have no charm for them, but the masses of mankind will continue to worship their Creator and continue to find comfort in the promise of their Savior that He has gone to prepare a place for them. *Christ has made of death a narrow, starlit strip between the companionship of yesterday and the reunion of tomorrow;* evolution strikes out the stars and deepens the gloom that enshrouds the tomb.

—From Bryan's Posthumous Speech.

"He who, from zone to zone,
Guides through the boundless sky thy
certain flight,
In the long way that I must tread alone
Will lead my steps aright."

WILLIAM CULLEN BRYANT.

(Bryan's favorite verse of poetry.)

List of Illustrations

TABLE OF CONTENTS

TABLE OF CONTENTS

TABLE OF CONTENTS

Last Will and Testament
of William Jennings Bryan

"In the name of God, farewell.

"Trusting for my salvation to the blood of Jesus Christ, my Lord and Redeemer, and relying on His promise for my hope of resurrection, I consign my body to the dust and commend my spirit to the God who gave it.

"I, William Jennings Bryan, a citizen of Dade county, Florida, being of sound mind and memory, but conscious of the uncertainty of life, and desiring to make just disposition of the worldly goods with which an indulgent Heavenly Father has seen fit to bless me, do make, publish, and declare this my last will and testament, hereby revoking and annulling all former wills by me made.

"First: I desire that all my just debts and funeral expenses shall be fully paid and satisfied, including the use of such sum as my wife and children may deem proper for the purchase of a monument to mark my grave.

"Second: I give and bequeath to my beloved wife, Mary Baird Bryan, my congenial comrade and companion and my faithful helpmate for more than forty years, all my household goods, jewelry, plate, library, automobile, etc., to use, distribute, or sell, according to her pleasure. I trust her to make such gifts to, or division among, our children, children-in-law, grand-children, relatives, and friends as we would make together if we joined in the distribution.

"Third: I give and bequeath to my said wife a life estate in our home, Marymont, in Cocoanut Grove, Florida, and I hereby authorize and direct the expenditure from my estate of such sums as may be necessary to pay taxes on said home, and keep it in repair. I hereby authorize my said wife to occupy, rent, or sell, said home according to her pleasure. If the house is rented the taxes and repairs shall be paid out of the rent. When the house is sold the proceeds shall be turned into the general fund of my estate.

"Fourth: I give and bequeath unto my said wife one-third of all the property, real, personal, and mixed, which I possess at the time of my death.

"Fifth: I give and bequeath to my beloved children, Ruth Bryan Owen, W. J. Bryan, Jr., and Grace Bryan Hargraves, one-fourth each of all the proceeds of my estate remaining after the payment of the bequest to my said wife and other bequests and expenses, but said bequests are made subject to the following provision—viz: if any child resort to the courts to break the provision of this will, the bequest to such child will be revoked by said act and said child's portion will go into my estate to be divided among the other legatees. One-half of each child's portion shall be set apart for it as soon as distribution can be made; the other half shall be available for the children respectively when my said wife dies. The second half held until my said wife's death shall be kept in the hands of my executors and invested in bonds of the United States government, state governments, city governments, and school districts.

"Sixth: I give and bequeath unto each of my beloved grand-children and great-grandchildren now living or that may be born before the final distribution of my estate, the sum of $2,000, said sum to be used for the education of the child, or, if not needed for that, paid to the child when said child is of age, unless the parent desires it paid to the child at an earlier date, my wife to decide as to John's needs in the payment of this sum to him.

"Seventh: I hereby bequeath to my said wife and my said children, Ruth, William and Grace, all my copyrights, manuscript letters, et cetera, and I hereby authorize them to prepare and publish my official biography, with a full sketch of my wife's life and details as to the important aid she has rendered me in all my work, and such other volumes of life and letters as they may deem wise. They shall share equally in all the profits and royalties derived from the books they publish.

"Eighth: I give and bequeath to my beloved sister, Frances Bryan Baird, the house in East Lincoln (near Fairview), Neb., where she now lives, together with the lot on which it stands with a frontage of seventy-five feet unless a different frontage is agreed upon before I die, to hold, use or rent, with remainder over in fee simple to her three children, Laura, Frank and Will. My sister is to pay taxes on it while she occupies it or rents it.

"I give and bequeath to my beloved brother and sister, Charles W. Bryan and Mary Bryan Allen, $2,000 each. My wife will, in the distribution of souvenirs, remember Essie, my brother's wife; Jim Baird, sister Fannie's husband; T. S. Allen, sister Mary's husband; and Roy Spangler, Laura's husband; A. R. Talbot, my former law partner, and W. F. Schwind, my companion in the army. They have all been very dear friends. I appreciate their affection and companionship with them.

"Ninth: I give and bequeath $1,000 each to the First Presbyterian church of Miami and Grove Temple of Cocoanut Grove, the two churches with which I am now connected, and $500 each to the following churches with which I have been connected—namely: The Cumberland Presbyterian church of Salem, Ill.; the First Presbyterian church of Jacksonville, Ill.; the First Presbyterian church of Lincoln, Neb.; the Westminster Presbyterian church of Lincoln, Neb.; the Normal Methodist church near my former Nebraska home, Fairview; the Lincoln, Neb., Y. M. C. A.; the Miami, Fla., Y. M. C. A.; the Bryan Bennett library, Salem, Ill.; the public library, Lincoln, Neb.; the public library of the Woman's club, Miami; the public library of Cocoanut Grove, and $250 each to Sigma Pi society, Illinois college, Jacksonville, of which I was a member; Philosophian society, McKendree college, Lebanon, Ill., of which my father was a member, and the Baptist church at Salem, Ill., of which my parents were members.

"Tenth: I give and bequeath to my private secretary (at the time of my death) a sum to be calculated at $100 for each year or part of a year he has been with me, and to the man who is taking care of my wife at the time of my death—driving car and carrying her—a sum calculated in the same way. To my gardener and each one of the female help a sum calculated at $50 for each year or part of year.

"Eleventh: I have saved for the last my bequest for religious education. While I have devoted a large part of my time to the study and discussion of political questions and have found an abundant reward in the reforms adopted with my humble aid, I feel more interested in religion than in politics, because religion is the only influence that can control the heart, out of which are the issues of life.

"Next to religion I am most interested in education, because education can and should increase one's capacity for service. But education will not be a benefit to its possessor and a blessing to society unless it is wisely used. I am very anxious that each intellectual ship shall be equipped with a moral rudder sufficient to control its course on life's stormy sea. My chief interest is, therefore, in Christian education—the entwining of the spiritual with the intellectual. I had hoped to aid in the establishing of an academy that would embody my idea and serve as a model. Fearing that I shall not be able to carry out this plan during the years that remain, I am setting aside a fund equal to each child's share in my estate.

"After taking out the bequest to my wife and other bequests I desire to divide the remainder in four equal parts. One part, as I have provided above, shall go to each of my three children, the fourth part, less $50,000, will be set apart for Christian education. As I have recently given our Nebraska home, known as Fairview, to the Methodist church for a hospital, I feel that its value, conservatively estimated at $50,000, should be deducted from the one-fourth set apart for Christian education and divided equally between my three children and my wife.

"With the amount left for this purpose—I estimate it at about $50,000—$100,000 less the $50,000 deduction above mentioned—I would like to have it used to establish an academy for boys, which shall be under the control of some unit of government, of some Evangelical church, Presbyterian preferred but not absolutely necessary, so that it can be controlled by a recognized religious organization. I would like to have it cover the junior and senior years of the high school and the freshman and sophomore years of the college—these being the years when the student most needs religious supervision.

"I would like special attention given to citizenship and applied Christianity so that the graduates may be prepared for leadership in both state and church. It should not be conducted for profit; board should be furnished students at actual cost, tuition should be as low as possible, room rent should be same for all rooms so as to discourage classification according to wealth. Assignments of rooms should be made on basis of classes, senior, junior, sophomore and freshman, and in classes according to scholarship where possible, and by lot until scholarship is tested.

"I would like the boys to wear a uniform made of blue and gray to symbolize the reunion of the north and south. If it is impossible to establish such an academy then the trustees of this fund shall distribute it among boys' schools, selecting schools as nearly like the one described above as possible, care being taken to see that the money is given only to schools that are firmly committed to Orthodox Christianity, including the making of man by separate act in God's image, the Virgin Birth and the Bodily Resurrection of the Savior.

"I regard supernatural and revealed religion as given in the Bible as the only religion that exerts a controlling influence on our lives. If this money is divided among several colleges, I would like to have it invested and the income loaned to needy students—not over one-half his annual college expenses, so that he will earn the other half—and when collected returned to the revolving fund.

"I hereby appoint as trustee of this religious fund my beloved wife, my son, my two daughters, my brother, C. W. Bryan; my brother-in-law, T. S. Allen; my former law partner, A. R. Talbot and the pastors of the First Presbyterian church of Miami and Grove Temple of Cocoanut Grove—the pastors, to serve while pastors. If any of the life trustees die their places shall be filled by the survivors, preference being given to my personal friends who are also sympathetic in matters of religion.

"It witness whereof, I have hereunto set my hand and seal, this fifth day of July (1925), nineteen hundred and twenty-five, at Marymont, Cocoanut Grove, Fla.

"WILLIAM JENNINGS BRYAN."

"Signed, published, and declared by said testator as his last will and testament in the presence of us, who at his request and in his presence and in the presence of each other, have hereunto subscribed our names as witnesses.

"Signed W. E. Thompson (Seal), Cocoanut Grove.

"William H. McCartney (Seal), Cocoanut Grove."

CHAPTER I

Bryan and His Greatness

Leader in Politics, Social Reform, and Religion—Likened to Henry Clay—Courage, Sincerity, Ambitions, Honesty—Fought for Religion and High Morals—Appealed to Heart, Not Intellect—Wilson and Roosevelt Aristocrats; Bryan, the Democrat—Friends and Enemies—Greater Than the Bosses—Lover of Peace, Not a Pacifist—Died in the Battle for His Faith.

When history records the closing years of the nineteenth and the opening years of the twentieth centuries in the United States, and lists therein the great men who have helped mould the fortunes of their nation, she will fill a dramatic chapter with the career of William Jennings Bryan.

She will say that this man, whom his fellow citizens learned to entitle the Great Commoner, was a leader in three fundamental phases of the times in which he lived—in politics, in social reform, and in religion. Whatever else she says, we have no means of knowing now; for it is too soon after his passing to forecast how the future will evaluate his words, his deeds, and the mighty reactions he evoked among his people.

Three times candidate for the highest office in the power of his countrymen to give him, once Secretary of State during the crystallization of the most potent crisis in America's history, esteemed one of the most eloquent men of his times, prophet of great social changes, and to millions of his fellow men the champion of their religious faith—surely the name of William Jennings Bryan will be writ large.

His life demonstrated the ends to which immovable moral convictions may bring a courageous man.

Friends were fond of likening him to Henry Clay, who also was

27

thrice nominated for the Presidency, who also was as many times defeated, and who, like Bryan, was once Secretary of State. The simile is apt in another way, for the proud declaration of the famous Whig might properly have come from the lips of Bryan: "I would rather be right than be President."

So closely are some great men linked with national events that their death means more than the loss of an individual leader. It means the placing of a period at the conclusion of a national epoch. Bryan was one of these men.

He was a man of unwavering purpose and unflinching spirit. When convinced that he was in the right he gave ground to no assault. He was sincere; no man who was not sincere could have withstood the attacks on his sincerity which were directed at Bryan throughout his life. He was ambitious not only for himself, but for the causes he had decided were right and beneficial to mankind. He was honest; he might have capitalized his power over people and have made millions, but he preferred to use that power to bring about results that he believed would aid the nation.

Throughout his career, religion and high morals were the motivating forces behind his actions. His was the fight on the side of his God and the God of millions of others, against the devil and the powers of darkness. The spirit of the crusader burned always fiercely within him.

Bryan was not a highly intellectual man. He led his people not by an appeal to their intellects but by an appeal to their hearts. Of himself, the progress of events has shown that intellectually he was often wrong; but his heart was always right. No other man in generations has had the power to sway an audience as had Bryan; it was not his argument that did it. It was not his logic, but his emotional appeal.

Into the solution of political and economic problems Bryan carried both his unchangeable moral beliefs and his emotional reactions.

Of every cause he made a moral issue; in every issue he found his position emotionally rather than logically. It was this disposition which found him, at the settlement of the question, morally always right, politically and economically sometimes wrong.

In thinking of Bryan, the memory that comes uppermost concerning his political career is that of the free silver issue in 1896. Time has shown he was wrong there, though he persuaded 6,500,000 people that he was right. But how many realize what a number of other measures advocated by the Commoner have been accepted? Prohibition, woman suffrage, the income tax, the direct election of senators, all were issues on which he was taking definite stands years ago. As it was always the other candidate who won the Presidency, so it was always someone else who put these measures over. Bryan never received his fair share of credit.

Bryan must occupy a place with Theodore Roosevelt and Woodrow Wilson in the annals of the period in which this triumvirate of great men lived. Totally unlike in so many ways, these three men had qualities in common. Objectively, no other three have left such a deep mark on the political history of their day, as did these men. All three won the esteem and confidence of an immense following; all three, with religious zeal, found in spiritual rather than worldly progress the measurement of a civilization; all three had the courage to do battle for the principles in which they believed.

Roosevelt and Wilson attained the highest office in the land. Bryan fell short of winning this supreme honor. It is a tribute to his intrinsic worth that in his defeat he found scarcely a diminution of his leadership of a great section of the American people. If old followers of one campaign deserted after a battle lost, new ones came and filled the ranks.

In one thing Bryan differed fundamentally from his famous contemporaries. They were essentially aristocrats. Bryan was, at heart as in political name, a democrat. Instinctively he understood the common people. He felt as they felt, and from his silver tongue fell the words that expressed to them their unphrased sentiments.

Few men in American public life have been so hated and despised, yet at that same time so beloved and esteemed, as William Jennings Bryan. Himself, a man who could conceive of no compromise between his beliefs and those of another opposing them, he inspired no half way reaction in those with whom he or his ideas came in contact. Bryan undoubtedly had more warm friends and more bitter enemies than any other man of his time. It is to be remembered to his credit that he was heedless of the counsels of the one or the invectives of the other if they meant changing in the slightest the path of what he believed the right thing to do.

Those who did not idolize him regarded him as a plague. They hated him because he smashed party totem poles and raised up in their stead issues that caught the heart of the people even though they did not always stand the test of thoughtful analysis. Bryan dismayed his enemies, but his friends always knew where to find him.

Political bosses with their backroom conferences, the political pilots who cared nothing for the well-being of their ship if they could safely get to shore, envied him and feared him. They envied him because he could dispense with political intrigue, go over the heads of bosses, and, in defiance of tradition, make his appeal to the people themselves in open forum. They feared him because of the popular tides that followed those appeals.

Bryan was a lover of peace but he was not, in the commonly understood sense of the word, a pacifist. He believed war was un-Christian and a crime upon the face of humanity; he hated war. But he wore the uniform of his country in the war with Spain. When the World War came on and was threatening to engulf the United States, he opposed the idea of conflict with all the powers at his command. When he realized that Wilson's policy, which differed radically from his own, would eventually lead to the entanglement of the United States in the war, he quit the highest office he had ever held rather than compromise his ideals. Yet when war was declared, he offered to serve as a private soldier. For all his pacifistic utterances, no one rightfully accused him ever of wearing the white feather.

In the last great phase of his career, standing in the little Tennessee town of Dayton, upright against the onslaughts of those whom he believed to be undermining the faith of the nation, Bryan rose to his supreme height. Baring to the taunts of the unbeliever the faith that had carried him through life, proclaiming publicly the simple beliefs that had steadied him through the storms of his career, he was at his best. Admitting his limitations, admitting some of the arguments of those who disagreed with him, he was a valiant figure.

For nearly thirty years the leader and dominant figure in a great political party, down among the hills of the Cumberlands he achieved an even greater leadership. Party lines were swept aside; voting qualifications made no difference.

He died there as he would have liked to have died could he have chosen; with the trumpets of battle still sounding; with the sword of a righteous cause in his failing hand, and with the buckler of his faith about him.

Surely his followers will carry him to a place of fame on the shield of his integrity.

CHAPTER II

In the Beginning

Ancestry—Judge Silas L. Bryan, the Father—Mariah Elizabeth Jennings Bryan, the Mother—Political and Religious Heritage— Born in Salem, March 19, 1860—"Lawyer just like father"— Father's Campaign Fires Political Ambitions—Prepares for the Academy.

Love of religion, love of politics and love of the common man: These three dominant characteristics of Bryan, throughout the sixty-five vigorous years of his life, can all be traced with a nicety of parallel to those sturdy pioneer folks who didn't know the meaning of the word "compromise"—folks whom the world calls Bryan's "ancestors," but whom scientists might term Bryan's "inheritance."

William Jennings Bryan, statistics tell us, was born on the 19th of March in the year 1860, in a tiny house of perhaps five or six rooms, on the outskirts of the town of Salem, Illinois. But the forces that went into that mighty personality, had begun years and years before.

Let us, therefore, go back a bit.

Bryan's father traced the family back to Ireland. Bryan, himself, in jestful platform speech, spoke often of that second cousin of a name, "O'Brien." We have the name, too, weaving its way about English and Welsh history.

It is a good hundred years ago or more that we first hear of that name of Bryan, in relation to William Jennings, and it is in possession of one William Bryan, a hardy Blue Ridge mountaineer. Nothing very much is known of him, save that he had a large parcel of land in and about Sperryville, Virginia, and that he had five children.

William's second son, John, was born about 1790. The family sketch, written by Silas L. Bryan, father of William Jennings, is a bit vague as to the exact date. When still little more than a lad, John, the sketch tells us, married Nancy Lillard. Here again, the ancestry quotient for the Great Commoner was strenghtened. For Miss Lillard came from an American family which even then was ranked as "old."

Presently John took his family out west. Only in those days the term didn't mean San Francisco or the Pacific coast. No, going out west, while it was considerable of an adventure, meant geographically, simply removing to that region which is now West Virginia. His last residence was Mount Pleasant, and there he died in 1836. His wife had died two years earlier.

So their boy, Silas, and now we are getting within easy perspective of William Jennings Bryan, went still further west.

Education wasn't handed out on a platter by any manner of means in those days of abundant hard work. But Silas was determined to obtain an education. And he did. When he had completed the public school course, he made up his mind he'd like to go to college. He went. Sometimes a slim purse compelled him to drop his Latin and his Greek for a hoe and a plough. Then he would work for six months in order to earn sufficient money to enable him to return to the classroom.

Later in his course, he started a productive circle. He would stop and teach school long enough to earn money to return to college and learn more to go out and teach. And so on. In spite of these intermittent journeys into farm field and country school, Silas Bryan was able to graduate with high honors from McKendree College, Lebanon, Illinois, in the spring of 1849.

But that wasn't enough. Silas wished to become a lawyer.

More periods of school teaching, at larger schools now, and he went on to law school. And finally, one fall day, this young man of twenty-nine had his ambition realized. He was admitted to the bar at Salem, Illinois. But there was still another ambition, as yet unfilled. Silas wanted to get married.

Some thirty-two years later, his son, William Jennings, was to follow in his father's footsteps; that is, was to become a lawyer and a benedict almost simultaneously. Only with this difference. Where the son married a girl of approximately his own age, a girl who was attending a female seminary near the campus of his own college, the father chose a former pupil of his, a girl twelve years his junior.

In later life, with sprightly vein but in serious tribute, the older Mr. Bryan often said how glad he was his meager treasury had compelled him to work his way through college. For that had forced him to teach school, and in teaching school he met his future wife.

So it was on the 4th of November, 1852, when the paint was still fresh on his lawyer's shingle, that Silas L. Bryan married Mariah Elizabeth Jennings.

They weren't talking much about eugenics in those days. But that marriage might have been taken as a good example of it. For Miss Jennings had an equipment of old family traditions and pioneer virtues, of good common sense, moral preoccupation, and of an appreciation of the value of education, as well as of hard work.

The Jennings family came from England, but just when it came no chronicler has ever been able to determine. We can, however, go back, authentically, to Mariah Jenning's grandfather, one Israel Jennings, who was born about 1774. Originally New England colonists, his ancestors had braved the frontier, and Israel spent his youth in Mason county, Kentucky. Married at the age of twenty-five to a Mary Waters, the couple moved to Illinois and raised a family of eight children at Walnut Hill.

Bryan's father and mother, Judge Silas L. Bryan and Mariah Elizabeth Bryan.

The house in Salem, Ill.. where Bryan was born, March 19, 1860.

Bryan at the age of 11 (right), with his brothers, Robert, deceased
(left) and Charles (center) aged 4.

When the Commoner was 24 years old: at his left, his brother,
Charles W. Bryan, former governor of Nebraska, then 17.

One of the eight, Charles Waters, is the one who concerns us. He married Maria Woods Davidson, December 14, 1826, and built a home for his bride on the estate adjoining his father's farm in Walnut Hill. And like the father, the son had eight children. And, again, it is one of the eight who stands out to fame.

That one, of course, is Mariah Elizabeth Jennings, who was born at Walnut Hill, May 24, 1834. She went to the public schools in the neighborhood, did her lessons and said "good morning" and "good evening" to the teacher.

But one day came a new teacher, an earnest, studious youth with a passion for more education, and a pleasant teaching manner. He was Silas L. Bryan, the young fellow from over Salem way. There was no foolishness about him, and the youngsters had to work hard at their lessons. But what of that, when the teacher made them so vivid with living facts.

And what of the fact that the young pedagogue was twelve years older than one of his students. They formed a friendship that was real and firm. First it was based on English composition and geography. Later it grew more personal. And just as soon as he was made an attorney, her former teacher claimed Miss Jennings for his bride.

Miss Jennings had been brought up in the Methodist Episcopal church, the church of her parents. When quite a young girl she had elected to join that church, and she remained a member until about 1877, when she joined the Baptist church of Salem. Her husband had been brought up a Baptist, the faith of his fathers, and was a consistently devout man.

Here we see, shaping themselves with definiteness, some of those forces that were going to join themselves together so potently in the son, William Jennings. As to religion, the Silas Bryans observed the Sabbath strictly. They read the Bible much. Above everything, they believed in the efficacy of prayer.

Three times a day Silas Bryan prayed. And nothing was permitted to interfere with this rite. When he became a judge, if court were in session at the noon hour, he would bow his head, where he sat on the bench, and offer up his simple supplication.

Then there was that aptitude for politics in the elder Bryan, a characteristic that was to become one of the focal points of the son's life.

For the year 1852 in which Silas, the young lawyer, married Miss Jennings, also saw him elected to the state senate. He served four terms. And in 1860, the year of William Jennings' birth, the father was elected to the circuit bench. For twelve years he held that position.

The Bryans had nine children born to them, four of whom died in infancy. William Jennings was their fourth. The children who lived to grow up with him were his brother, Charles, Democratic candidate for Vice-President in 1924; and his sisters, Mary, Nannie and Fanny.

Of their heritage, Mrs. William Jennings Bryan, in her sketch of her husband's life, has this to say:

"The Bryan, Lillard. Jennings and Davidson families all belonged to the middle classes. They were industrious, law-abiding, God-fearing people. No member of the family ever became very rich, and none was ever abjectly poor. Farming has been the occupation of the majority, while others have followed the legal and medical professions and mercantile pursuits."

Into the pattern of this heritage the Great Commoner fitted with no rough edges. Only, it wasn't long before his own individuality, plus that heritage, began to shine out through the entire mosaic.

Politics from his father; comradship, diligence, discipline from his mother; religion from both; and the fundamentals of the Great Commoner from all those ancestors who had gone before. That was Bryan's background, and it projects itself forcibly into Bryan's foreground.

It is quite easy and ever so consistent, then, for Bryan, the little boy, to have had two mighty ambitions coming upon him in fervent sequence. First, he wanted to be a minister. Later, a lawyer, "like father." And this latter was the permanent actuating ambition. The other tapered off, if indeed it can be called tapering when it was such a vital, potent thing to the very day of his death, into a firm conviction which he used as a yardstick to judge every phase of life and all human relationships.

They tell a story of young Bryan's repartee to an aunt who urged upon him that first ambition, to become a minister, when he had already become firmly entrenched in the desire to become a lawyer.

When the aunt made remonstrance, Bryan, who had joined the Baptist church when he was fourteen and had been a constant reader of the Bible, turned lawyer for the moment and rebutted her argument by a Bible text. It came out of Proverbs:

"To do justice . . . is more acceptable to the Lord than sacrifice."

Half in fun, half in earnest, the boy then argued from this text thiswise: Sacrifice is the emblem of the function of the clergy; the doing of justice is the prerogative of the lawyer.

And history records no answer that the aunt made.

His father was a busy circuit judge, and his mother had much to do with the raising of the quintet of children. When William was six years old, there were so many youngsters tumbling their frisky way about the small house in Salem that Mr. Bryan bought a farm out a mile from the village. There were 160 acres, and the children could do all the tumbling they wanted, provided they didn't forget their responsibilities.

For their parents hadn't forgotten the struggles of their pioneer ancestors, and they saw to it that their children, severally and collectively, should assume a reasonable share of house and farm duties. It may have been done to develop their character, but it had a by-product result of developing their physiques. Indeed, it was this early outdoor life with its buoyant good health that was largely responsible for the stupendous energy which Bryan, years later, manifested during campaigns which fatigued other men.

As a youngster Bryan was well knit, "sturdy, roundlimbed and fond of play." So he probably enjoyed his duties. They went under the somewhat stern name of "chores."

But as a matter of fact, they would be considered quite a lark these days for a city lad. For example, he had to feed the deer which were kept in a small parked enclosure on the farm. Then there were chickens to feed, pigs to attend to, and dogs to care for.

And for favorite recreation, there was rabbit hunting with the dogs.

Up until the time he was ten years of age, young Bryan learned his lessons from his mother's knee. The school book lessons were interwoven with a deep religious and moral interpretation that dug deep into the lad's consciousness and forever remained there.

When the boy was twelve years old and eager for knowledge of history and politics, his father was nominated for Congress on the Democratic ticket, with the endorsement of the Greenback party. The district was preponderantly Republican, but Judge Bryan made a fine campaign. And when the votes were counted, in spite of that "hopeless" Republican handicap with which he had started out, he was defeated by General James Martin, the Republican candidate, by a plurality of only 240.

The campaign didn't make Judge Bryan a congressman. But it had a great deal to do with making his son a congressman, out in Nebraska, not so many years later. For young William Jennings followed every step of the fight. He astonished the schoolmates at the Salem public school with his knowledge of every ramification of the contest. It crystallized into one big, burning ambition all those vague political inclinations which he had inherited, and which had been developing beneath the surface. But they were awakened now. And they were never again put to sleep until, at the end of a zestful period at the close of his life, Mr. Bryan shifted the emphasis to an impassioned plea for recognition of moral values in all departments of government.

Defeated for Congress, Judge Bryan was soon made a member of the convention of 1872. It was this convention which framed the constitution for the State of Illinois. The judge's most conspicuous part in this assemblage was played in connection with the resolution which he introduced in behalf of the convention, stating that all offices, legislative, executive and judicial, provided for by the new constitution, should be filled by popular election.

Here again, we find a foreshadowing of some of those reforms which the younger Bryan was later to enunciate. Jumping forward a decade or so, we find William Jennings urging the direct primary in connection with the nomination and election of the United States senators.

Judge Bryan, always a pivot figure in local politics, died March 30, 1880, and was buried in the old cemetery at Salem. Sixteen years later, on the 27th of June, 1896, just about the time her son was making his immortal "Cross of Gold" speech on the platform of the Coliseum at the Chicago convention, Mariah Elizabeth Jennings Bryan died, after weeks of illness. They buried her beside her husband, in that Salem cemetery.

And so it was, that the fall of 1875 saw a fifteen year old youth, vigorous of body, firm in religious faith, eager for political experience, and passionately endowed with the attributes of the Great Commoner, saw this lad leave his mother and father and the Salem farm, and journey over to Jacksonville to enter Whipple Academy.

He was only fifteen, but already his personality had silhouetted itself so definitely against that background which we have just traced, that it would not have been difficult to chart out at least some of the steps that the lad was to take in the next six years' progress through academy and college.

CHAPTER III

The Student

Whipple Academy—Lives at Home of Dr. Hiram K. Jones—
Sigma Pi Literary Society—Illinois College—Period of Skepti-
cism—College Oratory—Wins Prizes—Valedictorian—What They
Thought of Him.

If anything were needed to gather up all the loose ends of
any fugitive ambitions Bryan may have had, and to tie them
up securely into a definite factor in his life, that thing was his
experience at Whipple Academy and at Illinois College, Jacksonville, Illinois. And so it was both logical and fortunate that
this youth of fifteen, with a strong political heritage, a latent passion for oratory, and a growing zeal for participation in politics,
should find himself, that fall day in 1875, matriculating at
Whipple Academy.

For Jacksonville had long been a political center. The little
boys at the Academy had heard politics discussed at home and
now, in essay and debate, they began to take a fling at it themselves. The young men at the college fought hot fights in
their societies over the issues that men throughout the country
were upholding or denouncing.

It was during these six years at school that Bryan developed
into an orator; that he was projected along his career of
politician; that a brief period of religious skepticism swung the
pendulum back even further in the way of deep religious conviction; and that he met the girl whom he later made his wife.

So it was an eventful sextette of years.

When he left his home on the farm near Salem that fall day,
young Bryan went to a lovely, rambling, comfortable house on
College avenue, Jacksonville, the home of Dr. Hiram K. Jones,

a cousin of Judge Bryan who had come up from Culpepper county, Virginia, in the early '30's. For the next six years, save for an occasional vacation spent back on the farm, this was to be William Jennings' home.

It was more than home. It was a powerful influence in the young man's life.

A student, a philosopher, and the host to every distinguished scholar who passed through the town, Dr. Jones was a splendid influence on the lad who later paid him deep tribute, when he reckoned his influence up along side of that which his father, the judge, had exerted on him.

The Jones' library, with its statuette of Plato, and its volumes on that philosopher; with its book of Carlyle, of Homer, of Dante and of Sophocles, supplemented the lessons which Dr. Jones gave his youthful relative. Informal lessons they were, given of an evening round the library table, and they consisted in reading a bit from this philosopher; talking a bit of personal reminiscences with distinguished scholars; and, most of all, in thinking things out in an independent and un-selfconscious manner.

When he entered the Academy young Bryan had a slight difference of opinion with his parents. They were sure that a classical course was best for their son. Their son wasn't so sure, especially when he had a look at Greek verbs and Latin adjectives. But the parents won out, and a classical course it was.

Presently Bryan grew to like Latin, at least better than Greek. He liked mathematics and found geometry an amusing brain stunt. Political economy, too, attracted him.

Of course it was oratory, and the allied branches of debate and speech-writing which wooed and won the youth's deepest affection. But his career in this was not like the career of the little boy in the story-book, a sky-rocket affair, with spectacular success shooting out on all sides. Not a bit of it! The drama of his oratorical success, as charted out in those six years on the campus, was the drama, rather, of slow success. But his consistent up-curve took him, at graduation, to the high point of class valedictorian.

Now the forum in which he won his oratorical spurs was Sigma Pi.

There were two literary societies at college, Sigma Pi and Alpha Phi. Both were open, apparently, to Academy students, for in the early days Bryan was elected to membership in Sigma Pi. And from the first he was an active member. While other boys were busy thinking up excuses to get off the programs, Bryan, early reports in the handwriting of the secretary inform us, was volunteering his services on this and that occasion.

The man, who later was to be catapulted to instant fame by the delivery of his famous "Cross of Gold" speech, is first recorded as having taken part in a debate on November 5, 1875. He upheld the negative side of the question: "Are mechanics more useful to society than professional men?"

Three months later the Jacksonville Journal tells that "W. J. Bryan recited 'McLean's Child' with fine effect." Indeed, this selection on which he was drilled for two weeks by S. S. Hamill, one of the college instructors in public speaking, seems long to have remained a favorite with the boy, for dusty clip after clip sets forth how he recited it again and again.

In her sketch of her husband, Mrs. Bryan says: "During his first year at the Academy he declaimed Patrick Henry's masterpiece and not only failed to win a prize but ranked well down in the list."

But that failure was only the beginning of the up-curve.

For the next year, 1876, he entered the contest with "The

Palmetto and the Pine" and walked away with the third prize. Along about this time, too, the Sigma Pi secretary writes: "Then came Wing's proxy, Bryan, who spoke well, as he always does."

And in the entry of February 16, 1877, the secretary comments thiswise:—"Bryan, the substitute of W. E. Williams, showed the manly qualities of St. Louis in giving aid and comfort to Chicago after the fire."

It is an interesting commentary that the Williams mentioned was the delegate from Illinois who seconded Bryan's nomination at the Denver convention.

The fall of 1877 saw Bryan a freshman at Illinois College.

Founded in 1829 by a group of Yale men, this college was one of the oldest in the middle west. Edward Beecher, brother of Henry Ward Beecher, gave up his pastorate of the Park Street church of Boston in 1830 in order to become its first president. Richard Yates, the war governor of Illinois, was its first graduate.

The roster of its students in those early days lists William Herndon, Lincoln's law partner; John Wesley Powell, the first explorer of the Grand canyon; Robert W. Patterson, first president of Lake Forest college; and George S. Park, founder of Park college, Missouri.

And, skipping many decades, the institution was a focal point of public attention not so many years ago when William Jennings Bryan, one of its famous alumni, resigned from its board of trustees because the college accepted a $50,000 Carnegie gift. Bryan maintained the money was tainted.

Oratory continued to fill an important part in Bryan's life at college. But let us, for a moment, turn to the religious aspect of this period. When he was seventeen Bryan had joined the Cumberland Presbyterian church. In Jacksonville he became a member of the First Presbyterian church.

As an example of the seriousness with which he took life and his obligations to it, they tell this story of recreation in the Jones household. Dr. Jones, it seems, disapproved of card-playing, while his wife was fond of it. By card-playing, however, they meant cribbage and checkers and chess and old-fashioned card games. Mrs. Jones would have friends in to play when Dr. Jones had retired to the recesses of his study.

But Bryan never joined them.

"Oh, I know that it's all right," he would reply to their queries, "but I can't play. Father asked me not to when I left home, and I promised him that I wouldn't."

And that was the end of the discussion so far as he was concerned.

Throughout his college days Bryan held his adherence to his opinions. and his adaptability in nice balance. He was staunchly intolerant of other ideals; broadly tolerant of those who held those ideals.

So it was, that while he didn't achieve any amazing popularity on the campus, he was liked; he was respected; and he was rewarded with some of the substantial college honors. His first such distinction came in his freshman year. In the initial issue of the College Rambler, of January, 1878, mention is made of William Bryan as vice-president of his class.

The February number lists a trio of prize winners. Bryan's name is there, for he won half of the second prize in the Latin prose contest. A few months later, in the close of his first year, he declaims "Bernardo del Carpio" and carries off the second prize. His sophomore year finds him entering the oratorical lists armed with an original essay on "Labor". First prize rewards him.

His first recorded oration was reproduced in the Rambler for

February, 1879. Sophomoric though it was in many respects, and a bit too flowery in some places, the speech has, nevertheless, forensic foreshadowings of some of the later products of the silver tongued orator.

Here are a few sentences from it:

"That is not worth having which is not worth toiling for.

"There is no distinguished victory without hard fighting to win it. Great honors do not come without great exertions.

"It is possible to grow in size but strength comes only with exercise.

"Natural talent does not remove the necessity for labor.

"If it were possible to rise in the estimation of our fellowmen without an effort, honor would lose its charms."

The up-curve is now plotting its triumphant course with ease, but its progress has been gained by hard work.

The assiduous way in which the young man pegged away at that art of patterning words together effectively and then projecting the pattern forcibly, has been best described by Dr. G. A. Hulett, the Springfield historian who chummed with Bryan through academy and college.

Indeed, it was a strip of woods on the Hulett estate near the college that was Bryan's coliseum. And young Hulett was the audience. These rehearsals, out there in the woods, were daily events. When the rehearsal was done, the speaker and listener would hurry over to the athletic field to practice the broad jump. Theirs was a friendly rivalry here, for they were the two best broad jumpers in school.

Athletics had a certain appeal to Bryan, but they never edged out his love for debate. During his sophomore year he spoke often. Here are some of the debate questions, as listed by the scribe of Sigma Pi:

"Shall Garfield be the next President of the United States?"

"Shall the immigration of Chinese to this country be prohibited?"

But more significant, in the light of the reforms he was later to advocate so passionately, is the report that he took the affirmative in these two debates:

"Resolved: That intemperance is more destructive than war.

"Resolved: That the president of the United States should be elected by popular vote."

It was in February of this year, 1879, that Bryan was elected sergeant-at-arms of Sigma Pi, at the same election which put Richard Yates, Jr., in as president. Yates, who was to follow in his father's foosteps and become Republican governor of Illinois in 1901, had pleasant relations with the future leader of the Democratic party, through the debating society. There is no record of any great intimacy beyond that, for Yates was one year ahead of Bryan in school.

But then, with the exception of his close friendship for Hulett, contemporaries recall that Bryan made no very close friends on the campus. Living at Dr. Jones' home, he mingled as much, if not more, with the town boys, as with the college youths. "Phil" Dunlap, his greatest friend, did not attend college, but worked in a Jacksonville bank.

As a junior Bryan tried for and won first prize with an oration on "Individual Powers." Part of the prize was a volume of the poems of William Cullen Bryant. The college junior was delighted for the volume contained his favorite poem, "Ode to a Waterfowl," and he underscored his favorite passage, which might almost be used as the keynote theme of his life:

"He who, from zone to zone,
Guides through the boundless sky thy certain flight,
In the long way that I must tread alone,
Will lead my steps aright."

It was this book, with his beloved poem marked, that Bryan gave as his first gift to the girl who was to become Mrs. Bryan. But of that, more later.

This junior year victory qualified Bryan, in the beginning of his senior year, to represent his Alma Mater in the intercollegiate oratorical contest held in the fall of 1880 at Galesburg. He spoke on "Justice," and won the second prize. It was fifty dollars. There was a by-product of this success which made the winner happy. Gen. John C. Black of Illinois, one of the judges, marked Bryan 100 per cent on his delivery. And he asked the young man to drop around to see him at his hotel.

Bryan spent an hour or so with the general, learning, he said later, many valuable rules of oratory.

That steady but none too flashy success which had been working along for six years now reached out and got to the very top by commencement day, June, 1881. For he was elected class orator; and his high academic standing made him class valedictorian.

The class oration, on the class motto, "Ducamus, non sequamur" (Let us lead, not follow), which he had suggested to his fellow students, concluded with these words:

"Character is the entity, the individuality of the person shining from every window of the soul, either as a beam of purity, or as a clouded ray that betrays the impurity within. The contest between light and darkness, right and wrong, goes on—and this is the all-important question which comes to us in accents ever growing fainter as we journey from the cradle to the grave, 'Shall those characters be good or bad?'"

And the first paragraph of his valedictory, which has assumed a deeper significance since the Scopes evolution trial, contains these words:

"Beloved instructors, it is character not less than intellect that you have striven to develop. As we stand at the end of our college course and turn our eyes toward the scenes forever past . . . we are more and more deeply impressed with the true conception of duty which you have ever shown. You have sought not to trim the lamp of genius until the light of morality is paled by its dazzling brilliance, but to encourage and strengthen both."

The class day ceremonies did not leave Bryan out of the picture. One S. J. McKinney, class poet, recited how:

> "Comes Bryan on the stand,
> With many great orations in his hand.
> Accustomed to dispute, with all compete,
> He learned to act in victory or defeat."

And his good friend Hulett, the class historian, said: "Law and politics are his friends and he intends to court them as soon as other things permit."

The academic honors, the jolly and sincere tributes of his classmates, the praises of Dr. Jones, were all valuable and valued.

But the Great Commoner, for he was already beginning to be that, had made still other contacts, and had endeared himself to many others outside the path of his student life.

So it is appropriate that Bryan, the college graduate, about to leave for law school in Chicago, should receive the final tribute from J. A. Goltra, the Jacksonville hatter for whom he had worked.

Mr. Goltra, in earnest reminiscence years later, said:

"Will used to work for me in the store Saturdays when he went to college. He was the most likable boy I ever knew. We all thought the world of him and we were sorry when he went."

CHAPTER IV

Blackstone and Orange Blossoms

Meets Mary Baird—Her Estimate of Young Bryan—Frequent
Caller—The Courtship—April Fool Joke—Chicago Union College
of Law—Lives in Home of Lyman Trumbull—Law Degree, 1883—
Returns to Jacksonville—Enters Law Practice—How He Asked
Mary's Father—Marriage, October 1, 1884.

The fall of 1881 saw William Jennings Bryan starting off
for Chicago to enter the Union College of Law and to pursue
a two-year course which was to project him far on his political
career.

That same fall saw the young man already making plans to
return to Jacksonville just as soon as he could get his law degree,
in order that he might marry Mary E. Baird, the schoolday
sweetheart who was to be his supreme companion to the very
last hour of his life.

Ever since that day, years before, when he had determinedly
announced that he purposed to be a "lawyer just like father,"
he had been shaping his plans to that end. But for the two
years before his college graduation he had been more than ever
anxious to become an attorney. And the reason was not so
much one of law as it was one of matrimony.

For in the beginning of his junior year Bryan had met Miss
Baird, the only daughter of a wealthy merchant from Perry,
Illinois. She was attending the Jacksonville Female Seminary.

The person who should know most about that first meeting and the impression it made on Miss Baird ought to be
that young lady, herself. Happily, in her sketch of Bryan's
life, Mrs. Bryan has included the following autobiographical bit:

52

Lawyer—Early days in Lincoln, Neb.

College Student — Valedictorian, class of 1881. and dandy

Colonel—Leader of the 3d Nebraska volunteers in '98.

Boy Orator of the Platte—Breaking into politics.

The Farm Home—To this house near Salem, Ill., Bryan's parents moved a few years after his birth in 1860.

First Home of His Own—In Jacksonville, Ill.

"My personal knowledge of Mr. Bryan dates from September, 1879. He was then entering upon his junior year. At the risk of departing from the purpose of this biography, I shall speak of my first impression. I saw him first in the parlors of the young ladies' school which I attended in Jacksonville. He entered the room with several other students, was taller than the rest, and attracted my attention at once.

"His face was pale and thin; a pair of keen, dark eyes looked out from beneath heavy brows; his nose was prominent—too large to look well, I thought; a broad thin-lipped mouth and a square chin completed the contour of his face. He was neat, though not fastidious in dress, and stood firmly and with dignity.

"I noted particularly his hair and his smile. The former, black in color, fine in quality, and parted distressingly straight; the latter, expansive and expressive."

The description concludes with this challenge to critics:

"In later years this smile has been the subject of considerable comment; but the well-rounded cheeks of Mr. Bryan now check its onward march, and no one has seen the real breadth of the smile who did not see it in the early days. Upon one occasion a heartless observer was heard to remark, 'That man can whisper in his own ear,' but that was a cruel exaggeration."

Bryan never made public his own reactions to that meeting. But it isn't difficult to speculate on them. For he immediately became a constant visitor at the seminary. In fact he was one of the "trusties" whom Principal Bullard permitted to make formal calls at the academy. And formal calls they certainly must have been, judging from his sartorial equipment. He wore a checked suit, with a heavy silver watch chain swinging back and forth ponderously. And, of course, he boasted a tiled white hat and carried one of those slender canes that were the vogue then.

But Bryan was not the only young person to whom Principal Bullard granted privileges. Miss Baird's good conduct and her general high standing, plus the intercession of Mrs. Jones, won for her permission to visit in the Jones home. The Jones' were childless, and it is not unreasonable to suppose that the kindly woman, in her motherly way, was not averse to acting the role of matchmaker.

But neither is it unreasonable to suppose that the youth who was to become the silver tongued orator was well able to chart out the steps of his own romance.

However that may have been, we know that the romance thrived. Here were two students, a boy and a girl, young, earnest, with not unlike heritages and with similar interests. And their friendship was silhouetted against a background of college life, of campus ambitions, and of the gentle atmosphere of the Jones home. Small wonder the romance prospered.

But it was no pale, sickly thing. It was full of study and full of fun. A visitor in the Jones home relates an anecdote which goes something like this:

Every morning Bryan used to step out on to the balcony leading from his room, and wave a handkerchief greeting across the campus to Mary Baird, who returned the salute, standing at the window in her room of the seminary dormitory. On April Fool's morning Bryan rigged up a life-like looking dummy, placed a handkerchief in its hand, and set it up in the corner of the balcony.

Mary Baird stepped to her window and waved. No reply. She waved again. And again. She was beginning to grow worried when another figure stepped out on the balcony, stooped down and picked up the handkerchief and waved an enthusiastic good-morning.

But more seriously, those days of wooing and winning left

a deep impress in the heart and mind of Bryan. Years later, in his famous speech in the concluding campaign of 1908, he paid this solemn tribute to his wife:

"When but a young man not yet out of college, I was guided to the selection of one who for twenty-four years has been my faithful helpmate. No presidential victory could have brought her to me, and no defeat can take her from me."

Even as early as the summer of 1880, less than a year after he had met her, Bryan seems to have been confiding in her all his boyish aspirations, and she seems to have known his every success and defeat. For instance, to choose but one of many examples, there is the story she has ever been fond of telling "for the encouragement of young speakers."

The story tells of Bryan returning to the outskirts of Salem to deliver a Democratic speech at a farmers' picnic in his old home-town community. Two speakers were to precede him on the program. When he arrived at the picnic grove he found the two speakers with an audience of four: the owner of the grove, the man who spun the wheel of fortune, and two men who had hopefully planned to sell lemonade to the throng.

Mrs. Bryan tells this with a deal of humor. But she never fails to add the serious postscript that later in the fall he made four political speeches for Hancock and English, the first of which was delivered in the court house at Salem.

So then, in the fall of 1881, Bryan went to law school in Chicago. Here again, events seem to have justified Bryan's oft-repeated remark that he was "a child of fortune from my birth," and that, "When I was in law school, I was fortunate enough, as I was in my college days, to fall under the influence of men of ideals who helped to shape my course."

The big influence in his life during these Chicago days was ex-Senator Lyman Trumbull, who had been a political friend of

Judge Bryan. Out of school hours the judge's son worked in the senator's law office. And in school hours he made friends with the senator's son, Henry Trumbull. It wasn't many days before William Jennings packed up his bags and moved over to his second foster home, the Trumbull house, where he was to live the next two years.

It was of Lyman Trumbull that Bryan, standing over his new made grave the Sunday after the "Cross of Gold" speech at the Chicago convention, said:

"Any distinction I have gained I owe in part to the man who is buried here."

Academically, too, Bryan was happy in Chicago. The study of constitutional law, his classmates tell us, engaged his zealous attention. There were debates, many of them, and Bryan took an active part in them. With a foreshadowing of some of his later speeches, he chose for his graduation thesis, a defense of the jury system.

But, by far the most important thing which happened to Bryan during those two years at law school happened many miles from the court room. It happened at the home of Miss Baird, where she cared tenderly for her blind father.

Here's the way the then Miss Baird recollects the event:

"Many persons have remarked upon the fondness Mr. Bryan shows for quoting Scripture. This habit is one of long standing as the following circumstance shows.

"The time came when it seemed proper for him to have a little conversation with my father, and this was something of an ordeal as father is rather a reserved man. In his dilemma William sought refuge in the Scriptures, and began: 'Mr. Baird, I have been reading Proverbs a good deal lately, and find that Solomon says, 'Whoso findeth a wife, findeth a good thing and obtaineth favor of the Lord.'

"Father, being something of a Bible scholar himself, replied:
'Yes, I believe Solomon did say that, but Paul suggests that
while he that marrieth doeth well, he that marrieth not doeth
better.'

"This was disheartening, but the young man saw his way
through. 'Solomon would be the best authority upon this point,'
rejoined Mr. Bryan, 'because Paul was never married, while
Solomon had a number of wives.'

"After this friendly tilt the matter was satisfactorily arranged."

Graduated from Union College of Law in the spring of 1883,
Bryan elected to return to Jacksonville rather than to Salem.
And the reason has already been made pretty plain. On the
Fourth of July, 1883, he hung out a shingle from the office of
Brown & Kirby where he had desk room, and for six months
at least not much else.

Bryan's father had died in 1880 and several times during
those first lean months his attorney's fees were supplemented
by drafts from Judge Bryan's estate. Along about January of
the new year, the young lawyer wrote to his old classmate,
Henry Trumbull, then practicing his profession in Albuquerque,
New Mexico, and asked about the possibilities for one more
lawyer in that territory.

But after the turn of the year things went better. That
spring Brown & Kirby turned over their collection department
to him. And that summer, William Jennings Bryan planned
and had built for him a house, not a large house, but large
enough for two.

And so they were married, on the first day of October, 1884.

CHAPTER V

Young Lawyer—Coming Politician

Chance Visit to Lincoln, Neb.—Removes There, 1887—Law Partnership with A. R. Talbot—Builds Home—Law Practice—Meeting
With Charles G. Dawes—His First Political Appearance—Speaks
at Democratic State Convention—Enters Politics, but Declines
Nomination for Lieutenant Governor—Congressional Timber.

It was the first of October, 1887, three years to a day following his marriage, that William Jennings Bryan arrived in Lincoln, Nebraska, full of plans for entering a legal partnership
there and for building a house to which he might soon bring
his wife and their baby daughter, Ruth.

Those first three years in Jacksonville had been happy, energetic, eventful. But the next three years were to be even happier, and certainly more energetic and more eventful.

During the Jacksonville period Bryan's law practice prospered well enough for the young couple to lay up a small reserve
fund and to provide adequately, though economically, for their
personal needs. Nor were oratory, politics, debate, brushed aside
in the duties of a lawyer. Every campaign found Bryan out
stumping the country, and winning more and more friends.

Three years after his graduation, his Alma Mater called him
back to deliver the master's oration and receive a master's degree
at Illinois college. He spoke on "American Citizenship."

While Bryan was busy taking care of his law practice, making speeches and receiving college degrees, Mrs. Bryan was not
permitting her early academic industry to taper off. Besides
taking care of the home and of the new baby, this enterprising
woman studied law, which was none too usual for a woman to
do in those days, and was admitted to the Nebraska bar.

60

She did not take up the law with any idea of practicing it. But rather, that she might, in still another department of his varied interests, be an understanding and helpful companion to her husband.

Referring again to Bryan's oft-repeated remark that he was "a child of fortune from birth," it is interesting to note how he chanced to remove to the west.

In the summer of 1887 Attorney Bryan was called out to Kansas and Iowa to attend to some legal business. His fondness for a law school classmate, one A. R. Talbot, drew him on to Lincoln to spend Sunday with his old friend. Almost ten years earlier, in his freshman year at college, he had met Horace Greeley when the editor had visited Dr. Jones' home. He had talked with him and mayhap had caught from that distinguished gentleman something of his fervor for the "Go west, young man" program.

At any rate Bryan was enthusiastic that Sunday afternoon over the beauties and merits of Lincoln, a young state capital pioneering its way forward. His enthusiasm carried over when he returned to Illinois. He thought often of the new city to the west and of its advantages for a young lawyer with ambition. Presently, after talking it over with his wife, he decided to move to Lincoln.

Bryan, character delineators will say, would have been Bryan no matter what geographic spot he had chosen. But certain it is that the title, "The Boy Orator of the Platte," and, more fundamentally, the reputation that he won as an obscure lawyer rising up, overnight almost, in a western city, would never have come his way had he not gone to Lincoln.

He went first to Lincoln alone, leaving his wife and baby back in their home at Jacksonville for eight months. It was well that he had, for the first six months were precarious financially. True, his name was linked with that of his friend, Talbot, in partnership. But where Talbot had a regular salary as a railroad attorney, Bryan, once again, had to begin at the bottom rung of the ladder.

In the spring of the year, however, the Bryan treasury grew sufficient for the lawyer to build a house in Lincoln and in a month or so Mrs. Bryan and Ruth joined him in it.

Later, at the Chicago convention, they were to say harsh things of this young candidate, hard words about his pecuniary difficulties; were to make charges about his inability to make a living as a lawyer.

In her sketch of her husband's life, Mrs. Bryan meets those charges this way:

"I might here suggest an answer to hostile criticism, namely that Mr. Bryan did not distinguish himself as a lawyer. Those who thus complain should consider that he entered the practice at twenty-three and left it at thirty, and during that period began twice, and twice became more than self-supporting. At the time of his election to Congress his practice was in a thriving condition, and fully equal to that of any man of his age in the city."

Politics had been no motive in Bryan's removal to Lincoln. In fact, he had moved into a preponderantly Republican territory. And so, for the first year, he was concerned largely with taking care of and building up his law practice, with making informal rather than political talks, and with enlarging his circle of friends and acquaintances.

On the first point there are numberless anecdotes told, testifying to his clean reputation. Friends tell that he had a more than average knowledge of the law for one of his limited experience, that he had a tremendous power over a jury, winning them by his argument as well as his oratory.

A musty old file of the court records of those days reveals

an amusing story of a law-suit in which Vice-President Charles
G. Dawes and Bryan were court opponents. The judgment was
for $1.27, and Dawes won.

On the second point—his oratory—the lad who used to practice speeches out in the woods at Jacksonville was now achiev-
ing considerable of a local reputation for his use of words.
The following is an excerpt from a speech which he delivered
at a Methodist church banquet, and presents his views on the
law as a profession:

"Next to the ministry I know of no more noble profession
than the law. The object aimed at is justice, equal and exact,
and if it does not reach that end at once it is because the stream
is diverted by selfishness or checked by ignorance. Its principles ennoble and its practice elevates. If you point to the petti-
fogger, I will answer that he is as much out of place in the temple
of justice as is the hypocrite in the house of God. You will find
the 'book on tricks' in the library of the legal bankrupt—nowhere
else. In no business in life do honesty, truthfulness and up-
rightness of conduct pay a larger dividend upon the investment
than in the law. He who fancies that mendacity, loquacity and
pertinacity are the only accomplishments of a successful lawyer,
is not only blind to his highest welfare and to his greatest good,
but also treading upon dangerous ground.

"You cannot judge a man's life by the success of a moment,
by the victory of an hour, or even by the results of a year. You
must view his life as a whole. You must stand where you can
see the man as he treads the entire path that leads from the
cradle to the grave—now crossing the plain, now climbing the
steeps, now passing through pleasant fields, now wending his
way with difficulty between rugged rocks—tempted, tried,
tested, triumphant. The completed life of every lawyer, either
by its success or failure, emphasizes the words of Solomon—'The

path of the just is as a shining light that shineth more and more unto the perfect day.' "

And as to the third point, the ever-widening arc of friendly contact with the "folks" the Commoner loved, the examples are legion.

Bryan was always a great mixer. He liked people. And they liked him. He never smoked, he never chewed tobacco, and he never took a drink; but he soon became one of the most popular men in the community.

A few months after his arrival in Lincoln he was one of eleven men to organize a combination literary and social club, known as the Round Table. Debates were held. But what the men liked best were the informal talks that led them in and about the paths of politics, religion, theology and history.

Bryan was one of the leaders. But nobody put him up on a pedestal and hesitated to disagree with him, never, even when the Round Table had grown to larger proportions; and when Bryan was a national figure, neither did his fellow members treat him as anything but Will Bryan. They called him down when they didn't like his logic, just as he called them down when he didn't like their logic.

For all his capacity for friendship, Bryan was not a "joiner." He belonged to few clubs. In Lincoln he joined Lincoln lodge No. 80, Benevolent and Protective Order of Elks. But although he frequently wore the Elk watch-charm he rarely went to the club-house. Later, he scorned the golf club to join the Farmers' club.

For about a year then, Bryan was out of politics. But he couldn't stay away much longer. Nor could the Democrats scattered here and there through the state afford to let this brilliant orator stay off the stump any longer.

Present day political tacticians who advocate ward politics as the basis for a sound political career as well as for reliable political organization might well take him for example.

The pebble of his voice and influence, small enough at first, was cast into the waters of the political fight in his own ward. Then the circle of ripples about this pebble widened out through the county, then the state, and finally, of course, to the nation and the world.

Of political hostility, and there was plenty of it in this Republican stronghold, Bryan made capital. They tell the story of his retort to an adversary who had twice given him the lie in Lincoln.

"I have your enmity," Bryan said, "and it is a benefit to me."

His first political speech was made, we are told, in the town of Seward in the spring of 1888.

A few weeks later, in May, he went as a delegate to the Democratic state convention in Omaha which was to choose delegates to the national convention at St. Louis. During an interlude, some of Bryan's admirers called on the young orator for a speech. He talked of the subject that was on every man's tongue just then, the subject that was long to be on his tongue— the tariff. He was the focal point of the convention, and when the speech was finished the crowd went wild.

Curiously enough, this experience, with far more heightened effect, with even more drama in it, was to be repeated eight years later when the "Cross of Gold" speech made a none too prominent delegate an internationally famous presidential candidate. The Omaha speech, in a lesser degree, did this. It took a promising Lincoln lawyer and made him the most prominent figure in Nebraska politics.

The following year Bryan declined the nomination for lieutenant governor of the state. But he gave every possible support to the campaign and stumped every county in Nebraska.

Which brings us to the year 1890. The Democratic party had just lost the First Congressional district of the state to the Republicans in a landslide that transferred the normal Democratic plurality of 7,000 in the district to a margin of 3,400 on the minus side. The Democrats had no candidate for Congress and the managers were casting about for a Moses who should lead them back to victory.

And their eyes all turned to Bryan.

CHAPTER VI

"Boy Orator of the Platte"

Nominated for Congress—Writes Silver Plank in State Platform—
Debates with Connell—Presents Him with Gray's "Elegy"—
Stumps District—Wins Election by 6.713 Votes—Fifty-Second
Congress—Member Ways and Means Committee—Free Wool
Speech—The "Cahoots" Story—Demonstration for the "Boy Ora-
tor of the Platte."

As these political managers looked at Bryan they all came
to the same conclusion. In February of 1890 they met together
quite informally at Omaha, and agreed to tender the nomination
to the lawyer who was not quite thirty. Then, equally informally, they went and told Bryan. He looked over the situation, found it pretty hopeless in view of the recent Republican
landslide in his district, but said he would accept the nomination "Because no one else would have it," and promised to
"make a good race and do my best."

The following July, the 30th of the month, the nominating
convention was held at Lincoln. He was tendered a unanimous
nomination.

Here is Bryan's first speech of acceptance:

"I accept from your hands and at your command the Democratic standard for this Congressional district, and whether I
carry it to victory, or as our President has gracefully expressed
it, 'fall fighting just outside the breastworks,' it shall not suffer
dishonor. You have nominated me knowing that I have neither
the means nor the inclination to win an election by corrupt
means. If I am elected it will be because the voters of this district have by their free and voluntary choice selected me as
their public servant. I cannot promise that my course will be

free from mistakes, but I will promise that if elected every duty
devolving upon me, whether great or small, as your representative on the floor or in the execution of the details of the office,
will be discharged as my judgment shall dictate and to the best
of my ability, so help me God."

The Republican candidate was W. J. Connell of Omaha, a
man brilliant and experienced, then representing the district at
Washington.   Bryan still had to win his spurs but he wasn't
afraid, and just about the first thing he did was to challenge
Connell to a debate.   Connell accepted.

The convention which nominated Bryan had stood rigorously
on the plank in its platform which Bryan himself had written,
a plank demanding free coinage and decrying "the effort of the
Republican party to serve the interests of Wall Street as against
the rights of the people."   But Connell had no quarrel with him
on the silver issue, so the debate was confined almost entirely
to an argument over the McKinley tariff act, for which Connell
had voted in Congress.

Mrs. Bryan declares she regarded this first debate, which took
place in Lincoln, as "marking an important epoch in Mr. Bryan's
life."   For days Bryan worked, and perhaps worried, over the
speech he was to make.   Rather, the two speeches he was to
make, for he was to open and close the debate.

The night came.   The hall was packed.   Statisticians will tell
you that before the speaking began the house was about evenly
divided between the young orator and the seasoned congressman.
And there are many, many who will tell you, that after the
speaking was over, the crowd gave a mighty demonstration for
the "Boy Orator of the Platte" who had weaved a word pattern,
now gentle and full of simile, now virile and full of impassioned
pleading, now a quotation from the Scriptures, now a passage
from one of his favorite authors, now a metaphor chosen from

the field, the garden, the nursery, and ever and always, the fervent pleading for the common man and his weal.

Eleven such debates were held in strategic points in the district. In addition, Bryan visited every city and village in the territory and spoke about eighty times. On the night of his eleventh and last debate with Connell, Bryan, who had always had friendly relations with his opponent, presented him with a copy of Gray's "Elegy."

Following are extracts from the remarks he made on that occasion.

"Mr. Connell, we now bring to a close this series of debates which was arranged by our committees. I am glad that we have been able to conduct these discussions in a courteous and friendly manner. If I have in any way offended you in word or deed I offer apology and regret, and as freely forgive. I desire to present you in remembrance of these pleasant meetings this little volume, because it contains, Gray's 'Elegy,' and in perusing it I trust you will find as much pleasure and profit as I have found. It is one of the most beautiful and touching tributes to humble life that literature contains. Grand in its sentiments and sublime in its simplicity, we may both find in it a solace in victory or defeat. If success should crown your efforts in this campaign, and it should be your lot, 'The applause of listening senates to command,' and I am left—

'A youth to fortune and to fame unknown,'
forget not us who in the common walks of life perform our part, but in the hour of your triumph recall the verse:

'Let not ambition mock their useful toil,
Their homely joys and destiny obscure;
Nor grandeur hear with a disdainful smile,
The short and simple annals of the poor.'

. . . But whether the palm of victory is given to you or

to me, let us remember those of whom the poet says:
> 'Far from the madding crowd's ignoble strife,
>   Their sober wishes never learned to stray;
> Along the cool sequestered vale of life
>   They kept the noiseless tenor of their way.'

"These are the ones most likely to be forgotten by the government. When the poor and weak cry out for relief they, too, often hear no answer but 'The echo of their cry,' while the rich, the strong, the powerful, are given an attentive ear. . . . The safety of our farmers and our laborers is not in special legislation, but in equal and just laws that bear alike on every man. The great masses of our people are interested, not in getting their hands into other people's pockets, but in keeping the hands of other people out of their pockets."

When the votes were counted Bryan was found to have won the battle by a plurality of 6,713. And his personal campaign expenses, in spite of the fact that he toured the entire district, are said to have been only $400.

About this time, Bryan wishing to give the maximum of time and attention to the Congressional duties that were soon to be his, retired from the practice of law although he still retained an affiliation with his firm.

When the thirty-year old Nebraskan took his seat in Congress that Monday in December, 1891, a cross section of the record of some of his famous contemporaries reveals this information.

Benjamin Harrison was President. Theodore Roosevelt was Civil Service commissioner in Washington. William H. Taft was there, too, as Solicitor-General for the United States. Warren G. Harding was getting out his paper in Marion, Ohio; Woodrow Wilson was lecturing to his classes on politics and jurisprudence at Princeton university; Charles E. Hughes was practicing law in New York city. So was Grover Cleveland.

Sincerely yours,
Mary Baird Bryan

His Favorite Portrait—Mrs. Bryan from a picture taken about 1900.

Early Lincoln Days—The first home in Lincoln. Neb., taken about 1896.

Elihu Root was head of the New York bar. And James M. Cox was a little boy out in Ohio.

Right at the beginning of the 52nd Congress, we are reminded once again, of Bryan's statement that he was "a child of fortune from birth." For the young Congressman from Nebraska met his old friend William M. Springer, the veteran representative of an Illinois district, who had never forgotten the way the college-boy, Bryan, had stumped for him back in the days when William Jennings was at Jacksonville.

Springer was hopeful of becoming speaker of the House. Bryan voted for him in the speakership caucus. He lost to Congressman Crisp. Bryan voted for Crisp in the House. The speaker appointed the defeated Springer as chairman of the ways and means committee. And Springer, remembering the debt of gratitude he owed Bryan, and remembering also the flair for oratory that had already begun to be evidenced back in Jacksonville, and recognizing his talent, gave him a place on that important committee.

There was hot criticism of this move. Veterans in the House took it ill that a youngster with no experience should be given this honor.

The position gave Bryan an early opportunity to win a name and a great deal of fame for himself, in his first term, by delivering a spectacular speech on the tariff and free wool.

During the early part of the session Springer's "popgun" tariff bills got nowhere. The Democrats didn't like them; the Republicans laughed at them.

Presently came a great day, March 16, 1892. One by one the Democrats got up full of enthusiasm, made their speeches, were worn down by the sarcasm of Congressman Reed, and confused by the sharp questions of the others. Speaker Crisp was desperate.

Almost completely routed, the Democrats finally sent young Bryan into the thick of the fray. He was a likable chap; already his personality had won for him many friends; he had a good voice and he knew how to use it. Above all, his whole soul seemed to be wrapped up in this question. So they sent him in.

"The Boy Orator of the Platte," they called him around Washington when they wanted to make fun of him, and Bryan was conscious of their mockery. Fourteen years later, in a speech during a campaign, he confessed: "When you first knew me they called me, in derision, 'The Boy Orator of the Platte.' But I have outlived that title."

So now, the "boy orator" plunged into the fight that March day.

Reed let loose his sarcasm. Bryan was unperturbed. Others let fall their shafts. Bryan picked them up and sent them back. When the speech was over his own partisans crowded about him in a frenzy of delight. His opponents crossed the room to shake his hand and congratulate him.

More than one hundred thousand copies of the speech were circulated by Congress. Bryan's reputation grew; word of him began to penetrate into national consciousness.

Here follow a few of the high spots of that speech:

"The reason why I believe in putting raw material upon the free list is because any tax imposed upon raw material must at last be taken from the consumer of the manufactured article. You can impose no tax for the benefit of the producer of raw material which does not find its way through the various forms of manufactured product, and at last press with accumulated weight upon the person who uses the finished product.

"Another reason for believing that raw material should be upon the free list is because that is the only method by which one business can be favored without injury to another. We are

not, in that case, imposing a tax for the benefit of the manufacturer, but we are simply saying to the manufacturer, 'We
will not impose any burden to you.' When we give to the
manufacturer free raw material and free machinery, we give
to him, I think, all the encouragement which a people acting
under a free government like ours can legitimately give to an
industry.

"It is in the record that protection is responsible for the
fact that sheep today produce more wool than they used to.
I have often thought how perplexed the sheep must have been
after the passage of the last bill, when they got together and
consulted among themselves as to how they were going to
increase the amount of their wool, now that the tariff had made
it necessary.

"But nobody has said to this House that protection would
reduce the price of pasturage in this country, nor has anybody
claimed that it would so moderate the climate as to do away
with the necessity for winter feeding. The theory upon which
this is justified might as well be met here as anywhere; and I
want to state, as emphatically as words can state it, that I consider it as false in economy and vicious in policy to attempt to
raise at a high price in this country that which we can purchase
abroad at a low price in exchange for the products of our toil.

"And that is the theory of our friends. When we buy something, we buy with the results of our toil; and they tell us that
we must not so arrange the laws of this country that we can
buy a great deal, but that we must so arrange them as to make
us work just as long as possible upon every piece of work we
undertake. It is the old theory—'The maximum of toil and
minimum of product.' If this is the true principle, then discard
your riding cultivators, go back to the crooked stick, and let

us plow in such a way that all the people of this country can find employment in plowing alone.

"I therefore denounce as fallacious, as unworthy of consideration, the only reason that can be given in support of the tariff on wool, as a protective tariff and for protective purposes.

*   *   *   *   *

"I am not objecting to a tariff for revenue. If it were possible to arrange a system just as I believe it ought to be arranged, I would collect one part of our revenues for the support of the Federal Government from internal taxes on whiskey and tobacco. These are luxuries and may well be taxed. I would collect another part from a tariff levied upon imported articles, with raw material on the free list—the lowest duties upon the necessities of life and the highest duties upon the luxuries of life. And then I should collect another part of the revenues from a graduated income tax upon the wealth of this country.

"But I am not complaining at this time of a revenue tariff. What I denounce is a protective tariff, levied purely and solely for the purpose of protection. It is false economy and the most vicious political principle that has ever cursed this country.

"I have said that the purpose of the protective tariff is to transfer money from one man's pocket to another man's pocket. I want to show to you and to this committee that it is the only purpose a protective tariff can possibly have. Why do you impose a tariff? You impose it upon the theory that you can not produce in this country the article which you protect as cheaply as it can be produced abroad; and you put the tariff on that article in order that the price of the article may be so much increased that American manufacturers can afford to produce it. You mean that the man who buys that article shall pay into the public treasury the tariff upon the article, and you expect that this, together with the price, will be sufficient to protect somebody else.

* * * * *

"I submit this proposition: Either a tariff is needed or it is not needed. If a tariff is needed it is in order to add the amount of the tariff to the price of the home article to enable the American manufacturer to compete with the foreign. If it is not needed, who is going to justify it? Now, which horn of the dilemma will you take? Will you say that this tariff is needed and used; or will you say it is not needed and ought to be abolished?

* * * * *

"Whenever you see the government, by operation of law, send a dollar singing down into one man's pocket, you must remember that the government has brought it crying up out of some other man's pocket. You might just as well try to raise a weight with a lever without fulcrum as to try to help some particular industry by means of taxation without placing the burden upon the consumer.

"Back in Illinois when we were repairing a rail fence, we would sometimes find a corner down pretty low in the ground, and not wanting to tear down the fence, we would raise that fence corner and put a new ground chunk under it. How did we do it? We took a rail, put one end of it under the fence corner, then laid down a ground chunk for a fulcrum. Then we would go off to the end of the rail and bear down; up would go the fence corner—but does anybody suppose there was no pressure on that fulcrum?

"That, my friends, illustrates just the operation, as I conceive it, of a protective tariff. You want to raise an infant industry, for instance; what do you do? You take a protective tariff for a lever, and put one end of it under the infant industry that is to be raised. You look around for some good-natured consumer and lay him down for a ground chunk; then you bear down on the rail and up goes the infant industry, but down goes the ground chunk into the ground."

It was getting late now, and Bryan paused to glance up at the clock. Spirited cries of "Go on, go on" urged him to continue.

"If it is difficult to defend this on principle, it is equally difficult to defend it as a policy. I make this assertion, that if it is wise to appropriate money out of the public treasury to aid a private enterprise, then it is wiser for a town than for a county. It is wiser for a county than for a state. For a Congress of restricted and delegated powers, whose members are far removed from the people, it is most unwise of all to vote away the public money for private purposes. So that if that policy is wise at all, this is the last place to apply the principle.

"We would not dare to trust that policy in our county or town. Why would you not trust it at home? Because you know that there would go before that council or before the county commissioners, only the men who want something, only those men and their paid attorneys would go there to represent the great advantage that the proposed industry would be to the community, while the other side would never be heard."

Another glance at the clock, and more yells to "Go on."

"I want to say that it is as difficult to defend the necessity for a tariff as it is to defend its principle or its policy. And this brings me to another contradiction which we often find in the arguments of our Republican friends. If you ask them why they need a tariff they at once tell you that we pay so much better wages in this country than are paid abroad that we can not compete, and that until we are willing to reduce the wages of our workingmen we never can compete.

*   *   *   *   *

"Now, to an 'untutored mind,' such as we are told new members possess, it would seem that if you need protection to labor in this country because labor is higher, that idea is hardly consistent, upon the Republican theory, with a cheaper product. Yet the gentleman who yesterday told you that we must have a tariff to protect the laboring men in this country told you that the laboring men of this country were producing articles cheaper than the laboring men of other countries.

* * * * *

"Mr. Chairman, the laborer has been used as a catspaw to draw chestnuts out of the fire for the manufacturer. The manufacturer comes here and pleads for a protective tariff in order that he may give employment with remunerative prices to labor. You give him the protection he asks; you make him a trustee for the benefit of his employe; you give to that employe no law by which he can enforce his trust. The manufacturer goes back to his factory and puts in his pocket the bonus you have given him. And then the employe pleads, and pleads in vain, for his portion of the promised benefits.

"I will tell you a story. A white boy said to a colored boy, 'Let's go into cahoots and go a coon hunting; you furnish the dog and climb the tree, and I'll do the hollering.' They went. The white boy hollered; the colored boy furnished the dog and climbed the tree. They caught three coons. When they came to divide the white boy took them all. The colored boy asked, 'What am I going to have?' 'Why,' said the white boy, 'you get the cahoots.'

"Now, the manufacturer has been making just such combination of partnership with his employe. The manufacturer says to his workman, 'You come on and furnish the dog and climb the tree; you bring out the votes; and I will do the talking.' They get their coons—they have been getting them. But the workmen have been compelled to put up with 'cahoots.' Yes, and when the employe asks for the higher wages that were promised him last year, you find Pinkerton detectives stationed to keep him off and foreigners brought in to supply his place.

* * * * *

"Now, there are two arguments which I have never heard advanced in favor of protection; but they are the best arguments. Why not say to the farmer, 'Yes, of course you lose; but does not the Bible say, "It is more blessed to give than to receive"— and if you suffer some inconvenience, just look back over your life and you will find that your happiest moments were enjoyed when you were giving something to somebody, and the most unpleasant moments were when you were receiving. These manufacturers are self-sacrificing. They are willing to take the lesser part and the more unpleasant business of receiving, and leave to you the greater joy of giving.'

"Why do they not take the other theory, which is borne out by history—that all nations which have grown strong, powerful, and influential, just as individuals, have done it through hardship, toil and sacrifice, and that after they have become wealthy they have been enervated, they have gone to decay through the enjoyment of luxury, and that the great advantage of the protective system is that it goes around among the people and gathers up their surplus earnings so that they will not be enervated or weakened, so that no legacy of evil will be left to their children. Their surplus earnings are collected up, and the great mass of our people are left strong, robust and hearty. These earnings are garnered and put into the hands of just as few people as possible, so that the injury will be limited in extent. And they say, 'Yes, of course; of course; it makes dudes of our sons, and it does, perhaps, compel us to buy foreign titles for our daughters, but of course if the great body of the people

are benefited, as good patriotic citizens we ought not to refuse
to bear the burden.'

* * * * *

"When some young man selects a young woman who is willing to trust her future to his strong right arm, and they start
to build a little home, that home which is the unit of society
and upon which our government and our prosperity must rest;
when they start to build this home, and the man who sells the
lumber reaches out his hand to collect a tariff upon that; the
man who sells paints and oils wants a tariff upon them; the
man who furnishes the carpets, tablecloths, knives, forks, dishes,
furniture, spoons, everything that enters into the construction
and operation of that home—when all these hands, I say, are
stretched out from every direction to lay their blighting weight
upon that cottage, and the Democratic party says, 'Hands off,
and let that home industry live,' it is protecting the grandest
home industry that this or any other nation ever had.

* * * * *

"It is said that when Ulysses was approaching the island of
the Sirens, warned beforehand of their seductive notes, he put
wax in the ears of his sailors and then strapped himself to the
mast of the ship, so that, hearing, he could not heed. So our
friends upon the other side tell us that there is depression in
agriculture, and a cry has come up from the people; but the
leaders of your party have, as it were, filled with wax the ears
of their associates, and then have so tied themselves to the protected interests, by promises made before the election, that, hearing, they can not heed.

"Out in the west the people have been taught to worship
this protection. It has been a god to many of them. But I
believe, Mr. Chairman, that the time for worship has passed.
It is said that there is in Australia what is known as the cannibal

tree. It grows not very high, and spreads out its leaves like great arms until they touch the ground. In the top is a little cup, and in that cup a mysterious kind of honey. Some of the natives worship the tree, and on their festive days they gather around it, singing and dancing, and then, as a part of their ceremony, they select one from their number, and, at the point of spears, drive him up over the leaves into the tree; he drinks of the honey, he becomes intoxicated as it were, and then those arms, as if instinct with life, rise up; they encircle him in their folds, and, as they crush him to death, his companions stand around shouting and singing for joy. Protection has been our cannibal tree, and as one after another of our farmers has been driven by the force of circumstances upon that tree and has been crushed within its folds, his companions have stood around and shouted, 'Great is protection!'

*   *   *   *   *

"Thomas Jefferson, that greatest of statesmen, and most successful of politicians, tersely expressed the true purpose of government when he said:

" 'With all these blessings that are necessary to make us a happy and prosperous people, still one thing more; a wise and frugal government which shall restrain men from injuring one another; shall leave them otherwise free to regulate their own pursuits of industry and improvement, and shall not take from the mouth of labor the bread it has earned.'

"That is the inspiration of the Democratic party. If it comes, Mr. Chairman, into power in all the departments of this government it will not destroy industry; it will not injure labor; but it will save to the men who produce the wealth of the country a larger portion of that wealth.

"The day will come when those who annually gather about this Congress seeking to use the taxing power for private purpose will find their occupation gone and the members of Congress will meet here to pass laws for the benefit of all the people. That day will come, and in that day, to use the language of another, 'Democracy will be king. Long live the king.' "

The speech was done. Senator Burrows of Michigan, who in 1908 was to be temporary chairman of the Republican National convention, called it the best speech on the tariff he had ever heard. Newspapers of all political complexions termed it a masterpiece. And Congressman William L. Wilson of West Virginia was so impressed with Bryan that he made him his chief lieutenant in his fight the following year over the Wilson tariff bill.

And as they crowded about him, after the speech, they still called him "The Boy Orator of the Platte," but the sting of derision was gone from the name.

CHAPTER VII

The Silver Tongue Talks Silver

Second Campaign for Congress—Debates with Judge Field—Wide Acquaintance—Wins by 140 Votes—Beginnings of Silver—Conference of '89—Western States Congress of '91—Anticipates Attack on Sherman Law—State Party and Bimetalic League Conventions—Fifty-third Congress—Speech Against Unconstitutional Repeal of Sherman Law—Lincoln Homecoming—Speech on Jefferson—Editorial Staff, Omaha World-Herald.

When Bryan returned home after the 52nd session of Congress, he went back to a readjusted political territory. For the Nebraska districts had been reapportioned so that Omaha was eliminated from the First district, and the district in its new shape, was conceded to be Republican by about 6,500. Bryan easily secured the nomination and began his campaign fight against Judge A. W. Field, who also was a Lincoln man. Judge Field resigned from the bench and was confident of victory.

Again there was a series of debates. This time there was much bitterness on both sides. McKinley, Foraker and others were sent into Nebraska to aid the Republican candidate. Again Bryan made a complete tour of the district.

Judge Field was able; he was well liked; the district was strongly Republican; and he was an old time resident of Lincoln, whereas Bryan had lived there only five years.

But the following story is an indication of Bryan's aptitude for friendship, and his desire to know more and still more people. It was the morning of election and the Commoner drove up to the polling place in the third ward in Lincoln just as a crowd of workingmen had come there to vote. All the men jammed

84

themselves around the buggy to shake Bryan by the hand.   He called them all by name.

Presently Judge Field's buggy drew up.   But the only persons he seemed to know personally were a few political leaders. The incident was typical.

The contest was so close that both sides claimed the victory. It was not until several days after the election that the official count showed that Bryan had won by a plurality of 140 votes.

Back in the 53rd Congress in 1893, Bryan was reappointed on the ways and means committee, and aided Congressman Wilson in the preparation of his tariff bill.   His particular function was to serve as a member of the subcommittee which drafted the income tax segment of the bill.   He spoke in defense of this phase of the question, and later defended the Wilson bill.

But the big speech, the famous speech was, of course, the one he made in opposition to the unconditional repeal of the Sherman law, in which he had his first big chance to advocate the free coinage of silver.

To get the full significance of this speech, let us go back a bit to see the beginnings of Bryan's espousal of the cause of free silver.

In November, 1889, St. Louis had been the scene of a National Silver Conference which formed the nucleus of the American Bimetalic league, although that association was not actually organized until May, 1892.

As we have mentioned in a previous chapter, Bryan had written the money question plank into the platform of the Nebraska Democratic party in 1890, at the convention at which he was nominated for Congress.   After the election he began to probe more deeply into the question.

In 1891 he attended the Western States commercial congress in Kansas City and voted for free coinage.   He did more than that. He secured the adoption of a declaration stating that all legal tender money of the United States should be made a full legal tender for all debts.

That same year, in September, as a member of the committee on resloutions at the Democratic state convention, he secured the adoption of a free silver plank. But the next year when he attempted to have a similar plank made part of the platform at the state convention held at Omaha to select delegates to the Democratic National convention, he was defeated.

That convention split the Democratic party in Nebraska into two wings. Bryan and his adherents opposed the nomination of Cleveland for President because of his attitude on the money question, and favored Horace Boies of Idaho. Bryan was nominated for Congress the second time, on the day before the meeting of the national convention on a silver platform, and the silver question was an issue of that campaign which he won by the slim margin of 140.

With a bit of prophecy in his soul, along about his time, Bryan began to fear that the next and inevitable move of the anti-free-silver men would be to repeal the Sherman bullion purchasing act.

So all during that second Congressional campaign of his he took a copy of the Sherman law with him as he stumped his way through his district. He pointed out the likely attempt to have its unconditional repeal brought about and he pledged himself to resist such action to the best of his ability.

He was a good political prophet, for in the summer of 1893 President Cleveland called an extra session of Congress to put through a repeal of the Sherman law.

While the repeal bill was under discussion in the Senate, Bryan went as a delegate to the Nebraska Democratic state convention. His own district in the convention was a friend of free silver. But the majority sentiment of the meeting was in favor of President Cleveland's policy.

Bryan's district selected him as its member for the committee on resolutions, but T. J. Mahoney of Omaha, chairman of the convention, refused to appoint him. One silver Democrat, Robert Clegg, did win a place on the committee, however, and he brought in a minority report for a silver plank. Thanks to Clegg, Bryan got the floor and spoke against the majority report. But the silver plank was defeated by a large margin.

Bryan then took the position that he would not support for president an advocate of the gold standard. At this the gold Democrats construed his speech as an indication of the bolt of his faction.

In August of that year Bryan, every day a more ardent free silver crusader, attended the national conference of the American Bimetalic league held in Chicago. When there, he served on the resolutions committee.

All of which in sketchy detail is an indication of the depth of feeling and passion, as well as an indication of the information and experience which Bryan brought to the question that August 16th afternoon of 1893, when he stood up in the House and began his speech that was to project him one step nearer the presidential nomination and a niche in the world's hall of fame.

All of the House and most of the Senate were there listening to him.

Following are excerpts from that vivid speech:

"Mr. Speaker: I shall accomplish my full purpose if I am able to impress upon the members of the house the far-reaching consequences which may follow our action, and quicken their appreciation of the grave responsibility which presses upon us. Historians tell us that the victory of Charles Martel at Tours determined the history of all Europe for centuries. It was a contest 'between the Crescent and the Cross,' and when, on that fateful day, the Frankish prince drove back the followers of Abderrabman he rescued the west from 'the all-destroying grasp of Islam,' and saved to Europe its Christian civilization. A greater contest than Tours is here! In my humble judgment the vote of this House on the subject under consideration may bring to the people of the United States, and to all mankind, weal or woe beyond the power of language to describe or imagination to conceive. . . . . .

"Let me call your attention briefly to the advantage of bimetalism. It is not claimed that by the use of two metals at a fixed ratio, absolute stability can be secured. We only contend that thus the monetary unit will become more stable in relation to other property than under a single standard.

* * * * *

"They say we must adopt a gold standard in order to trade with Europe. Why not reverse the proposition and say that Europe must resume the use of silver in order to trade with us? But why adopt either gold or silver alone? Why not adopt both and trade with both gold-using and silver-using countries? The principle of bimetalism is established upon a scientific basis.

"The government does not try to fix the purchasing power of the dollar, either gold or silver. It simply says, in the language of Thomas Jefferson: 'The money unit shall stand upon the two metals,' and then allows the exchangeable value of that unit to rise or fall according as the total product of both metals decreases or increases in proportion to the demand for money. In attempting to maintain the parity between the two metals at a fixed ratio, the government does not undertake the impossible.

* * * * *

"What is the prospect for the establishment of international

Bryan at his desk—Taken about the time he made his "Cross of Gold"
speech in the Chicago Coliseum, 1896.

© Underwood & Underwood photo.

Bryan's Regiment Lines Up—The 3rd Nebraska Volunteers, which Bryan recruited and commanded as Colonel, in formation line up at Camp Columbia, Havana, Cuba, during the Spanish-American war.

bimetalism? I would be glad to see the unlimited coinage of
gold and silver at a fixed ratio among the nations, but how is
such an agreement to be secured? The gentleman from Maryland (Mr. Rayner) says the unconditional repeal of the Sherman
law will bring England to terms. Is it impossible to extract a
lion's teeth without putting your head in its mouth? Is it not
a dangerous experiment to join England in a single standard
in order to induce her to join us in a double standard? International agreement is an old delusion and has done important
duty on many previous occasions.

*   *   *   *   *

"In fixing the ratio we should select that one which will
secure the greatest advantage to the public and the least injustice. The present ratio, in my judgment, should be adopted.
A change in the ratio could be made (as in 1834) by reducing
the size of the gold dollar or by increasing the size of the silver
dollar, or by making a change in the weight of both dollars.
A larger silver dollar would help the creditor; a smaller gold
dollar would help the debtor. It is not just to do either,
but if a change must be made the benefit should be given to the
debtor rather than to the creditor.

*   *   *   *   *

"But what of the mine owner's profit?

"When we see a wheel of fortune with twenty-four paddles,
see those paddles sold for ten cents a piece, and see the holder of
the winning paddle draw $2, we do not conclude that money
can be profitably invested in a wheel of fortune. We know that
those who bought expended altogether $2.40 on the turn of the
wheel and that the man who won only received $2; but our
opponents insist upon estimating the profits of silver mining
by the cost of the winning paddle. It is strange that those who
watch so carefully lest the silver miner shall receive more for

his product than the bare cost of production ignore the more fortunate gold miner.

* * * * *

"To recapitulate, then, there is not enough of either metal to form the basis for the world's metallic money; both metals must therefore be used as full legal tender primary money. There is not enough of both metals to more than keep pace with the increased demand for money; silver can not be retained in circulation as a part of the world's money if the United States abandons it. This nation must therefore either retain the present law or make further provision for silver. The only rational plan is to use both gold and silver at some ratio with equal privileges at the mint. No change in the ratio can be made intelligently until both metals are put on an equality at the present ratio. The present radio should be adopted if the parity can be maintained; and, lastly, it can be.

* * * * *

"Some of the advocates of a gold standard, in the defense of their theory, find it necessary to dispute every well-established principle of finance. We are told that as civilization increases, credit takes the place of money, and that the volume of real money can be diminished without danger. That recalls the experience of the man who conceived the idea that a fish could be made to live without water. As the story goes, he put a herring, fresh from the sea, in a jar of salt water. By removing a little every morning and adding rainwater he gradually accustomed it to fresh water. Then by gradually removing fresh water he accustomed it to air and finally kept it in a cage like a bird. One day, in his absence, his servant placed a cup of water in the cage in order that the fish might moisten its food. But alas, when the master came home he found that the fish had thoughtlessly put its head into the water and had drowned.

"From the arguments of some of our opponents we might be led to the conclusion that the time would come when money would not only be unnecessary but really dangerous.

*   *   *   *   *

"The President has recommended unconditional repeal. It is not sufficient to say that he is honest—so were the mothers who, with misguided zeal, threw their children into the Ganges. The question is not, 'Is he honest?' but 'Is he right?' He won the confidence of the toilers of this country because he taught that 'Public office is a public trust,' and because he convinced them of his courage and his sincerity. But are they willing to say, in the language of Job, 'Though he slay me, yet will I trust him?' Whence comes this irresistible demand for unconditional repeal? Are not the representatives here as near the people and as apt to know their wishes? Whence comes the demand? Not from the workshop and the farm, not from the workingmen of this country, who create its wealth in time of peace and protect its flag in time of war, but from the middlemen, from what are termed the 'business interests,' and largely from that class which can force Congress to let it issue money at a pecuniary profit to itself if silver is abandoned. The President has been deceived. He can no more judge the wishes of the great mass of our people by the expressions of these men than he can measure the ocean's silent depths by the foam upon its waves.

*   *   *   *   *

"This question can not be settled by typewritten recommendations and suggestions made by boards of trade and sent broadcast over the United States. It can only be settled by the great mass of the voters of this country who stand like the Rock of Gilbraltar for the use of both gold and silver.

"There are thousands, yes tens of thousands, aye, even millions, who have not yet 'bowed the knee to Baal.' Let the

President take courage. Muehlbach relates an incident in the life of the great military hero of France. At Marengo the Man of Destiny, sad and disheartened, thought the battle lost. He called to a drummer boy and ordered him to beat a retreat. The lad replied:

" 'Sire, I do not know how. Dessaix has never taught me a retreat, but I can beat a charge. I can beat a charge that would make the dead fall into line! I beat that charge at the Bridge of Lodi; I beat it at Mount Tabor; I beat it at the Pyramids; Oh, may I beat it here?'

"The charge was ordered, the battle won, and Marengo was added to the victories of Napoleon.

"Let our gallant leader draw inspiration from the street gamin of Paris. In the face of an enemy proud and confident, the President has wavered. Engaged in the battle royal between the 'money power and the common people' he has ordered a retreat. Let him not be dismayed.

"He has won greater victories than Napoleon, for he is a warrior who has conquered without a sword. He restored fidelity in the public service; he converted Democratic hope into realization; he took up the banner of tariff reform and carried it to triumph. Let him continue the greater fight for 'the gold and silver coinage of the constitution,' to which three national platforms have pledged him. Let his clarion voice call the party hosts to arms; let this command be given, and the air will resound with the tramp of men scarred in a score of battles for the people's rights. Let this command be given and this Marengo will be our glory and not our shame.

* * * * *

"Well has it been said by the senator from Missouri (Mr. Vest) that we have come to the parting of the ways. Today the Democratic party stands between two great forces, each inviting its support. On the one side stand the corporate interests of the nation, its moneyed institutions, its aggregations of wealth and capital, imperious, arrogant, compassionless. They demand special legislation, favors, privileges, and immunities. They can subscribe magnificently to campaign funds; they can strike down opposition with their all-pervading influence, and to those who fawn and flatter, bring ease and plenty. They demand that the Democratic party shall become their agent to execute their merciless decrees.

"On the other side stands that unnumbered throng which gave a name to the Democratic party and for which it has assumed to speak. Work-worn and dust-begrimed, they make their sad appeal. They hear of average wealth increased on every side and feel the inequality of its distribution. They see an over-production of everything desired because of the under-production of the ability to buy. They can not pay for loyalty except with their suffrages, and can only punish betrayal with their condemnation. Although the ones who most deserve the fostering care of government, their cries for help too often beat in vain against the outer wall, while others less deserving find ready access to legislative halls.

"This army, vast, and daily vaster growing, begs the party to be its champion in the present conflict. It can not press its claims 'mid sounds of revelry. Its phalanxes do not form in grand parade, nor has it gaudy banners floating on the breeze. Its battle hymn is 'Home, Sweet Home;' its war cry, 'equality before the law.' To the Democratic party, standing between these two irreconcilable forces, uncertain to which side to turn, and conscious that upon its choice its fate depends, come the words of Israel's second law-giver: 'Choose you this day whom ye will serve.' What will the answer be? Let me invoke the

memory of him whose dust made sacred the soil of Monticello
when he-joined—

    'The dead but sceptered sovereigns who still rule

    Our spirits from their urns.'

"He was called a demagogue and his followers a mob, but
the immortal Jefferson dared to follow the best promptings
of his heart. He placed man above matter, humanity above property, and, spurning the bribes of wealth and power, pleaded
the cause of the common people. It was this devotion to their
interests which made his party invincible while he lived and
will make his name revered while history endures. And what
message comes to us from the Hermitage? When a crisis like
the present arose and the national bank of his day sought to
control the politics of the nation, God raised up an Andrew
Jackson, who had the courage to grapple with that great enemy,
and by overthrowing it, made himself the idol of the people
and reinstated the Democratic party in public confidence. What
will the decision be today? The Democratic party has won the
greatest success in its history; standing upon this victory-
crowned summit, will it turn its face to the rising or the setting
sun? Will it choose blessings or cursings, life or death—which?
Which?"

        *   *   *   *   *

When Bryan finished speaking he was picked up by his
friends and by his enemies alike, and borne around the hall on the
shoulders of enthusiastic men who appreciated a dynamic speech
whether they subscribed to it or not. And nobody disputed that
it was the greatest speech of that extra session.

Other issues which brought forth Bryan's voice in the House
during the 53rd Congress included advocacy of revision of the
jury system so as to permit less than unanimous verdict in civil
cases; support of the anti-opium bill; espousal of the plan to elect

United States senators by a direct vote of the people; and opposition to the railroad pooling bill.

In the spring of 1894 he announced he would not be a candidate for re-election to Congress and a bit later he became the unanimous convention choice of the Nebraska Democrats for United States Senator, in spite of the fact that many of them disagreed with him on the free silver question.

Twice during the campaign he debated against John M. Thurston, the leading Republican candidate; once at Lincoln, once at Omaha. The tariff was the bone of contention, Bryan defending the Wilson tariff bill which he had helped to frame. At Lincoln, members of his enthusiastic audience carried him from the platform at the conclusion of the meeting, and bore him along down the street where hundreds of "overflow" admirers awaited him. Bryan made a canvass of the state. But Thurston was elected, and Bryan became a private citizen.

But a mighty busy one.

For when Congress had adjourned, the "Boy Orator of the Platte," on his homeward journey, had stopped off at six or seven cities to deliver lectures. In fact, this was the beginning of his career as a lecturer, per se.

He arrived home in Lincoln on the 19th of March, 1895, his thirty-fifth birthday and found the town out to do him homage. The Jefferson club gave him a reception. They packed the opera house that night when Bryan, the Commoner, not the office holder or the office seeker, was greeted by thousands. The theme of his address that evening was, "Thomas Jefferson still lives."

Jefferson had long been a hero of his. Of him he said:

"Let us, then, with the courage of Andrew Jackson, apply to present conditions the principles taught by Thomas Jefferson—Thomas Jefferson, the greatest constructive statesman whom the world has ever known; the grandest warrior who ever battled for human liberty! He gave apt expression to the hopes that had nestled in the heart of man for ages and he set forth the principles upon whose strength all popular government must rest. In the Declaration of American Independence he proclaimed the principle with which there is, without which there can not be, 'a government of the people, by the people, and for the people.' When he declared that 'all men are created equal; that they are endowed by their Creator with certain inalienable rights; that among these are life, liberty, and the pursuit of happiness, and that to secure these rights, governments are instituted among men, deriving their just powers from the consent of the governed,' he comprehended all that lies between the Alpha and Omega of democracy.

"Alexander 'wept for other worlds to conquer' after he had carried his victorious banner throughout the then known world. Napoleon 'rearranged the map of Europe with his sword' amid the lamentations of those by whose blood he was exalted; but when these and other military heroes are forgotten and their achievements disappear in the cycle's sweep of years, children will still lisp the name of Jefferson, and free men will ascribe due praise to him who filled the kneeling subject's heart with hope and bade him stand erect—a sovereign among his peers."

Busy, too, he was with his writing. For on the first of September, 1894, Bryan took a place as chief of the editorial staff of the Omaha World-Herald, and held it until the presidential campaign of 1896; in fact he went to the Republican National Convention of that year as a newspaper correspondent.

Returning to Lincoln in the early spring of 1895, Bryan had tentative plans for returning to his practice of law and confining himself to that, together with his editorial work. But the Democratic party needed him. The silver question needed him.

For the preceding two years Bryan had been having friendly relations with the Populist party, with which he had once advocated affiliation by the Democratic party. In 1893, when it became apparent that no Democrat could be elected to the legislature, he threw his support to Allen, a Populist, and aided in bringing about his election.

In 1894 he helped secure the nomination of a portion of the Populist ticket, including Holcomb for governor before the Democratic state convention.

So now, there was again a multiplicity of interests coming in upon Bryan, the private citizen. He was much in demand as a Chautauqua speaker; he was an editorial writer; he was a pivot figure, though not an office holder, in state politics, and he was still the passionate sponsor of free silver.

It was this last cause, bimetalism, which took him off on trips to the West and to the South to talk for it. But these trips had an important by-product. They were stepping stones leading up, along with a number of other things which we have discussed, to that climax moment at the Chicago Coliseum when Bryan made his "Cross of Gold" speech, and became the Democratic presidential nominee, at the age of thirty-six, just one year beyond the minimum age requirement for the chief executive of the United States.

CHAPTER VIII

The First Battle

Chicago Convention of 1896—Mrs. Bryan Hopeful—Silver Republicans Have Bolted—Split over Temporary Chairman—Platform Fight—Money Plank—Bryan In Charge Silver Debate—Answers Senator Hill with "Cross of Gold" Speech—Victory—Silver and People's Parties Also Nominate Him—Notification at Madison Square Garden—Speech of Acceptance.

Bryan went to the Democratic convention of 1896 in Chicago with the silver delegation from Nebraska. He went with the half-formed ambition in mind that he might be his party's nominee for the Presidency.

Mrs. Bryan was urging him on. She could see nothing humorous in the proposal that her thirty-six year old husband should attempt to win the nomination. During their stay in Washington she had kept abreast of him in his political advancement. Her womanly instinct advised her that, with the convention split over the silver question, the inspiring oratory of Bryan might serve exactly to turn the delegates in his favor.

She was certain that her husband would stand a good chance of winning, could he only have the opportunity of taking the floor. She advised him to prepare a speech; and from old material used in previous debates on the silver question, from material gathered afresh, and, with confidence that his tongue would take advantage of the opportunity when it presented itself, he made up a rough draft of the classic oration that became known in political history as the "Cross of Gold" speech.

Bryan was very much in earnest over the money question, but, despite Mrs. Bryan's prophecies, he was none too confident of his ability to swing the convention his way. A fellow editorial writer on the Omaha World-Herald inquired of him jokingly one day whether he was a candidate for the nomination.

"I've got my lightning rod up," replied Bryan, and grinned a bit sheepishly.

It was largely due to Mrs. Bryan that the Nebraska delegation became solidly in favor of the nomination of their colleague. They went to Chicago with the side of their railroad coach decorated with a banner which read:

"Keep Your Eye on Nebraska."

The common understanding of the Chicago convention of 1896 seems to be that Bryan went there, plunged in, declaimed his famous speech, and was promptly elected by acclamation. The true case was far different. It is necessary first to turn to the convention of the opposing party to obtain the proper alignment of the forces as they stood.

The Republicans met in St. Louis. They too were troubled by a split over the money question. The money plank of their platform was the only important matter of dispute. Bryan was there as a correspondent for his paper, looking on with interest at the fight between the eastern gold men, the western free coinage adherents, and some from the central states who wanted gold in the platform but who hesitated to use the word outright.

The majority report of the platform committee was a compromise favoring gold. It opposed the free coinage of silver "except by international agreement with the leading commercial nations of the world."

Senator Henry M. Teller of Colorado was leading the silver faction. On behalf of the minority of the committee he brought in a report supporting the free coinage of gold and silver at 16 to 1. The minority silver plank was voted down ten to one; the compromise gold plank, adopted.

At the announcement of the vote, Teller and his adherents

left the convention and formed themselves into the Silver Republican party. They met a few days later and Teller was placed before the people as their candidate for the Presidency. But his candidacy lasted only a short time. Following the Democratic convention, Teller withdrew and the Silver Republicans threw their weight toward the support of the Democratic ticket.

This is why the Republican convention was important to Bryan. McKinley, of course, was finally chosen by the Republicans, with young Bryan, so soon to be his rival in the field, looking on from the press gallery. The Nebraskan was quick to seize that point in the Republican money plank concerning international consent. He was to make much of it in his "Cross of Gold" speech. On the strength of it he wired his paper suggesting the following plank for the coming Democratic convention:

"We are unalterably opposed to the single gold standard and demand the immediate restoration of the free and unlimited coinage of gold and silver at the present legal ratio of 16 to 1, without waiting for the aid or consent of any other nation on earth. We believe that the standard silver dollar should be a full legal tender, equally with gold coin for all debts, public and private, and we favor such legislation as is necessary to prevent the demonitization of any kind of legal tender money by private contract. We further insist that all government coin obligations should be payable in either gold or silver, at the option of the government."

Parts of that suggestion were bodily incorporated into the money plank of the Democratic platform as eventually adopted. That part of it referring to foreign nations was strengthened and much expanded.

In preparation for their convention in Chicago, the silver

Democrats met there at the Sherman House on June 30th. Richard Parks Bland, "Silver Dick" Bland, of Missouri was the logical heir-apparent to the nomination for President. The silver delegates determined that the gage of battle should be cast down immediately. A majority of the national committee were in favor of the single gold standard; they were sure to recommend as temporary chairman of the convention some delegate of their own persuasion. The bimetalists decided that battle should be joined on this issue.

The prophecy concerning the national committee's action came true. They placed before the convention the name of Senator David B. Hill of New York as temporary chairman. The silver faction promptly replied by naming Senator John W. Daniel of Virginia as a substitute for Senator Hill. In vain the committee protested that such a move cast humiliation upon them. The silver delegates answered their gold brethren by declaring that the committee should have respected the wishes of the majority of the convention in the first place. They stuck to their point and Daniel was chosen by a vote of 556, against 349 for Hill.

During this preliminary fight Bryan was forced to sit on the sidelines as a spectator, together with the other members of the silver delegation from Nebraska. The national committee, true to the majority within their membership, had seated the Nebraska gold delegates, who were sent by the "straight Democratic" party which had bolted the Nebraska state convention of 1894.

With the temporary organization ironed out, the contest between the two delegations was brought before the committee on credentials. By an almost unanimous vote the committee decided in favor of the silver delegation of which Bryan was a member, and he and his fellows were formally escorted to their seats. Senator Stephen M. White of California was proposed and chosen as permanent chairman of the convention.

As had been foreseen, the split over the election of a temporary chairman was widened when it came to the adoption of a platform. The committee on resolutions was hopelessly divided on the money plank. Bryan had been selected as a member of this committee, the majority of whom were delegates who had been sent with instructions to uphold a platform supporting the free coinage of silver. There was from the first no hope of reaching a compromise; feeling ran too high; convictions were rooted too deep. After some argument the question was taken before the convention.

The majority report was read by Senator James K. Jones of Arkansas. Its money plank read as follows:

"Recognizing that the money question is paramount to all others at this time, we invite attention to the fact that the Federal Constitution name silver and gold together as the money metals of the United States, and that the first coinage law passed by Congress under the Constitution made the silver dollar the monetary unit and admitted gold to free coinage at a ratio based upon the silver dollar unit.

"We declare that the act of 1873 demonitizing silver without the knowledge or approval of the American people has resulted in the appreciation of gold and a corresponding fall in the prices of commodities produced by the people; a heavy increase in the burden of taxation and of all debts, public and private; the enrichment of the money lending class at home and abroad; the prostration of industry and impoverishment of the people.

"We are unalterably opposed to monometalism, which has locked fast the prosperity of an industrial people in the paralysis of hard times. Gold monometalism, is a British policy, and its adoption has brought other nations into financial servitude to

London. It is not only un-American but anti-American, and it can be fastened on the United States only by the stifling of that spirit and love of liberty which proclaimed our political independence in 1776 and won it in the war of the Revolution.

"We demand the free and unlimited coinage of both silver and gold at the present legal ratio of 16 to 1 without waiting for the aid or consent of any other nation. We demand that the standard silver dollar shall be a full legal tender, equally with gold, for all debts, public and private, and we favor such legislation as will prevent for the future the demonitization of any kind of legal tender money by private contract.

"We are opposed to the policy and practice of surrendering to the holders of the obligations of the United States the option reserved by law to the Government of redeeming such obligations in either silver coin or gold coin.

"We are opposed to the issuing of interest bearing bonds of the United States in time of peace, and condemn the trafficking with banking syndicates, which, in exchange for bonds and at an enormous profit to themselves, supply the federal treasury with gold to maintain the policy of gold monometalism.

"Congress alone has the power to coin and issue money, and President Jackson declared that this power should not be delegated to corporations or individuals. We therefore denounce the issuance of notes intended to circulate as money by national banks as a derogation of the Constitution, and we demand that all paper which is made a legal tender for public and private debts, or which is receivable for dues to the United States, shall be issued by the Government of the United States and shall be redeemable in coin."

The sixteen minority members of the committee on resolutions presented their report and offered as a substitute for this money plank of the majority the following:

"We declare our belief that the experiment on the part of the United States alone, of free silver coinage and a change of the existing standard of value independently of the action of other great nations, would not only imperil our finances, but would retard or entirely prevent the establishment of international bimetalism, to which the efforts of the government should be steadily directed. It would place this country at once upon a silver basis, impair contracts, disturb business, diminish the purchasing power of the wages of labor, and inflict irreparable evils upon our nation's commerce and industry.

"Until international co-operation among leading nations for the coinage of silver can be secured, we favor the rigid maintenance of the existing gold standard as essential to the preservation of our national credit, the redemption of our public pledges, and the keeping inviolate of our country's honor. We insist that all our paper and silver currency shall be kept absolutely at a parity with gold. The Democratic party is the party of hard money and is opposed to a legal tender paper money as a part of our permanent financial system, and we therefore favor the gradual retirement and cancellation of all United States notes and treasury notes, under such legislative provisions as will prevent undue contraction. We demand that the national credit shall be resolutely maintained at all times and under all circumstances."

The minority report also stated that the platform of the majority failed to compliment the merits of the Cleveland administration. As an amendment to the majority report they offered the declaration that, "We commend the honesty, economy, courage and fidelity of the present Democratic national administration."

The majority platform was moved to adoption by the convention. The minority amendments came next in the order of busi-

About 1900—Bryan at his desk, taken about the time that he made his second run for the Presidency.

The Fairview Farmer—A picture of the Commoner taken with his horse on the farm at Fairview near Lincoln, Neb.

ness. Gold delegates and silver supporters lined up for the debate. It was William Jennings Bryan's chance. Just before the platform was reported to the convention, Senator Jones had asked him to take charge of the debate. We can imagine the elation of the young Nebraskan. Thanks to his wife, his speech was ready.. As speaker after speaker took the floor the points of his argument marshalled themselves in his brain.

Senator B. R. Tillman of South Carolina opened the debate in favor of the majority platform. Senator Jones followed him. On behalf of the minority, Senator Hill, Senator William F. Vilas of Wisconsin, and Former Governor J. E. Russell of Massachusetts, spoke long and powerfully.

The speech of Hill, especially, was a masterpiece, considered as a political brief. It was one of the closest and keenest arguments ever heard at a national convention. It dissected the platform recommended by the majority and picked it to pieces. Bryan's task, to make answer, was no easy one.

Added to his difficulty was the fact that everybody was tired. They had listened to hours of discussion; they were almost ready for compromise. But one advantage he did have. The convention was held in the old Chicago Coliseum on 63rd street near Stony Island avenue. The acoustics of the building were poor. Those in the back of the hall had diffculty hearing the speakers.

The delegate from Nebraska, the "Boy Orator of the Platte," mounted to the rostrum. Perhaps the others were ready for compromise; he was not. His eyes flashed with the fire of his zeal for the cause; he shook his thick black hair. He began to speak. It was the speech to be known later as his "Cross of Gold" speech, and it is printed in full in the next chapter. Sleepy delegates in the far seats, who had heard about half of the speeches of Bryan's predecessors, woke up with a jerk; for Bryan was called the "silver tongued" with reason. His full, rounded voice carried to every corner of the auditorium.

"It would be presumptous indeed," he began, and he went on to that famous peroration from which the speech took its name. The convention turned to him in a stampede. The prophecy of Mrs. Bryan was fulfilled. Word of the great oration spread outside the convention hall. Acclaimed by crowds who wanted to hear what he had said, Bryan was forced to make a second speech later that evening from the porte-cochère of the old Clifton House on Monroe street. His audience blocked the traffic for an hour.

The substitute for the money plank offered by the minority was defeated two to one. So too, the amendment, and two further amendments offered by Senator Hill. The majority platform with its original plank for the free coinage of silver in the ratio of 16 to 1 was adopted by a vote of 628 to 301. And two days later Bryan rode into the nomination on the tide of his own eloquence.

The balloting and the votes cast are detailed in the following chapter. Suffice it here, that Bryan had become, overnight almost, a figure of mounting national importance. He had jumped with one leap into the lead of the Democratic party and he was not to relinquish that leadership for years to come. It was almost undisputed from 1896 until 1916. And for the first time in many years he had thrown the weight of the Democratic party in favor of the man in whom he himself believed, the common man, not the man of privilege and wealth. For the first time since Jackson, the Democratic party was really democratic.

The Georgia delegate who nominated him called him a "Saul come to lead the Israelites to battle." Truly, Bryan lived up to the characterization.

On July 22, twelve days after Bryan's nomination at Chicago, the National Silver party and the People's party both met in convention at St. Louis. After conferences between the two meetings, both conventions nominated Bryan as their candidate for the Presidency. The Silver party followed the Democratic lead and selected Sewall for Vice-Presidential nominee. The Populists, however, nominated Thomas E. Watson of Georgia for the office. Their choice, which placed Bryan in the position of campaigning with two running mates, was embarrassing to him in the days to come. He hesitated for some time, but on Sewall's own urging, he finally accepted the Populist nomination.

Three days after the Chicago nomination, Bryan left for a visit to his old home in Salem, where he was called on to address a huge crowd of old neighbors and friends. There was another meeting in the evening at Salem and there he spoke briefly.

"If there is one lesson taught by six thousand years of history it is that truth is omnipotent and will at last prevail," he said. "You may impede its progress, you may delay its triumph; but after awhile it will show its irresistible power, and those who stand in its way will be crushed beneath it. You ask me if these reforms which we advocate will be accomplished. We who believe that they are right can only do our best and give such impetus to them as we are able to give, and then trust to the righteousness of our cause to prevail over those who oppose us."

To us in more modern days, the political passions that were aroused over the issue of monometalism versus bimetalism seem oddly out of joint with things as we know them. Those who lived and voted in those days thirty years ago know how real they were.

In later years Bryan declared that though free silver had been defeated, the ill that it sought to correct had been alleviated in another way. The free coinage of silver, he explained, was not an end in itself, but a means to an end—the relief of hard times through placing more money in circulation. And the end was accomplished by another means, by the unexpected increase in the production of gold.

From Salem, Bryan made a trip to Centralia, Illinois. From there he went to St. Louis, then to Kansas City, and on home to Lincoln, where he was received with a great welcome. On this trip, really the first swing of his campaign, he made several speeches and covered 830 miles.

It was decided that Bryan should receive formal notification of his nomination in New York at Madison Square Garden, in order that he might fire the opening gun of his campaign within the very country of the eastern enemy, the gold stronghold. Accordingly, on August 8, Bryan and Mrs. Bryan, accompanied by newspaper correspondents, began their trip eastward. They made many stops and Bryan spoke at Des Moines, Rock Island, Chicago, Canton, and Pittsburgh, among other places.

Governor William J. Stone of Missouri delivered to Bryan the letter of notification before a crowd which packed the famous New York convention hall to the doors. Thousands were turned away, unable to gain admittance.

Two paragraphs of the notification are quoted here:

"The circumstances attending your nomination cannot but afford you unqualified satisfaction, and must inspire enthusiasm throughout our country. You were selected by no clique, nor were you chosen as the result of any questionable combination. Those who nominated you were law-abiding, determined, and honest representatives of their countrymen, and preferred you because of your exalted integrity, patriotism, and ability. You are ripe in experience and judgment, in the prime of manhood, and enjoy the mental and physical characteristics essential to the great work which you have been required to undertake. You have been tried in public station. You have always done your entire duty.

"While you are a Democrat and have, during your political career, been an ardent advocate of Democratic principles, you are now the official head of an organization comprising not only those who have hitherto been Democrats, but also including within its membership numerous other patriotic Americans who have abandoned their former partisan associations, finding in our platform and candidate a policy and leadership adequate to save the Republic from impending danger."

Bryan's reply, careful piece of oration that it was, was a disappointment to many of his listeners. Quite contrary to his custom, he read the address, and those who had come to hear the fiery orator who startled the convention with the "Cross of Gold" speech heard a much more subdued candidate reading earnestly enough, but with no great eloquence, from his manuscript. The disappointment to his audience had been calculated on calmly. It was the first speech; it would be the center of immediate hostile attack. Therefore it must be concise and of air-tight logic. Also, it could be distributed to the press in advance if it was read, and Bryan wished to reach not only his immediate hearers, but the voters all over the country. So it was read with full understanding of the disappointed criticism that would follow.

The candidate centered his attack on the one question, the money question, and he championed the stand of his party for bimetalism. For days he had pondered on a closing for his speech. At last it had come to him, and Bryan concluded this first phase of his first great battle with the following words:

"I ask, I expect, your co-operation. It is true that a few of your financiers would fashion a new figure—a figure representing Columbia, her hands bound fast with fetters of gold and her face turned toward the east, appealing for assistance to those who live beyond the sea—but this figure can never express your idea of this nation. You will rather turn for inspiration to the heroic statue which guards the entrance to your city—a statue as patriotic in conception as it is colossal in proportions. It was the gracious gift of a sister republic and stands upon a pedestal which was built by the American people. That figure—Liberty enlightening the world—is emblematic of the mission of our nation among the nations of the earth. With a government which derives its powers from the consent of the governed, secures to all the people freedom of conscience, freedom of thought and freedom of speech, guarantees equal rights to all, and promises special privileges to none, the United States should be an example in all that is good, and the leading spirit in every movement which has for its object the uplifting of the human race."

CHAPTER IX

"The Cross of Gold"

Shot Into Fame by One Speech—Definition of a "Business Man"—
Need for a Jackson to Stand Against Organized Wealth—Gold
Standard More Deadly than Protective Tariff—Issue of '76 Over
Again—"Crown of Thorns; Cross of Gold"—Convention Stam-
peded—Five Ballots—Bryan Nominated.

There follows here Bryan's "Cross of Gold" speech delivered
at the Democratic national convention in Chicago, July 8, 1896.
By this half hour of oratory Bryan was catapulted to nation-
wide fame. It won him his first nomination for President of
the United States.

"I would be presumptuous, indeed, to present myself against
the distinguished gentlemen to whom you have listened, if this
were a mere measuring of abilities; but this is not a contest between persons. The humblest citizen in all the land, when clad
in the armor of a righteous cause, is stronger than all the hosts
of error. I come to speak to you in defense of a cause as holy
as the cause of liberty—the cause of humanity.

"When this debate is concluded, a motion will be made to
lay upon the table the resolution offered in commendation of the
administration, and also the resolution offered in condemnation
of the administration. We object to bringing this question down
to the level of persons. The individual is but an atom; he is
born, he acts, he dies; but principles are eternal; and this has
been a contest over a principle.

"Never before in the history of this country has there been
witnessed such a contest as that through which we have just
passed. Never before in the history of American politics has a
great issue been fought out as this issue has been, by the voters

115

of a great party. On the 4th of March, 1895, a few Democrats, most of them members of Congress, issued an address to the Democrats of the nation, asserting that the money question was the paramount issue of the hour; declaring that a majority of the Democratic party had the right to control the action of the party on this paramount issue; and concluding with the request that the believers in the free coinage of silver in the Democratic party should organize, take charge of, and control the policy of the Democratic party. Three months later, at Memphis, an organization was perfected, and the silver Democrats went forth openly and courageously proclaiming their belief, and declaring that, if successful, they would crystallize into a platform the declaration which they had made. Then began the conflict. With a zeal approaching the zeal which inspired the crusaders who followed Peter the Hermit, our silver Democrats went forth from victory unto victory until they are now assembled, not to discuss, not to debate, but to enter up the judgment already rendered by the plain people of this country. In this contest brother has been arrayed against brother, father against son. The warmest ties of love, acquaintance and association have been disregarded; old leaders have been cast aside when they have refused to give expression to the sentiments of those whom they would lead, and new leaders have sprung up to give direction to this cause of truth. Thus has the contest been waged, and we have assembled here under as binding and solemn instructions as were ever imposed upon representatives of the people.

"We do not come as individuals. As individuals we might have been glad to compliment the gentleman from New York (Senator Hill), but we know that the people for whom we speak would never be willing to put him in a position where he could thwart the will of the Democratic party. I say it was not a question of persons; it was a question of principle, and it is not with gladness, my friends, that we find ourselves brought into conflict with those who are now arrayed on the other side.

"The gentleman who preceded me (ex-Governor Russell) spoke for the State of Massachusetts; let me assure him that not one present in all this convention entertains the least hostility to the people of the State of Massachusetts, but we stand here representing people who are the equals, before the law, of the greatest citizen in the State of Massachusetts. When you (turning to the gold delegates) come before us and tell us that we are about to disturb your business interests, we reply that you have disturbed our business interests by your course.

"We say to you that you have made the definition of a business man too limited in its application. The man who is employed for wages is as much a business man as his employer; the attorney in a country town is as much a business man as the corporation counsel in a great metropolis; the merchant at the cross-roads store is as much a business man as the merchant of New York; the farmer who goes forth in the morning and toils all day—who begins in the spring and toils all summer—and who by the application of brain and muscle to the natural resources of the country creates wealth, is as much a business man as the man who goes upon the board of trade and bets upon the price of grain; the miners who go down a thousand feet into the earth, or climb two thousand feet upon the cliffs, and bring forth from their hiding places the precious metals to be poured into the channels of trade are as much business men as the few financial magnates who in a back room, corner the money of the world. We come to speak for this broader class of business men.

"Ah, my friends, we say not one word against those who live upon the Atlantic coast, but the hardy pioneers who have braved all the dangers of the wilderness, who have made the desert to blossom as the rose—the pioneers away out there (pointing to the west), who rear their children near to Nature's heart, where they can mingle their voices with the voices of the birds—out there where they have erected schoolhouses for the education of their young, churches where they praise their Creator, and cemeteries where rest the ashes of their dead—these people, we say, are as deserving of the consideration of our party as any people in this country. It is for these that we speak. We do not come as aggressors. Our war is not a war of conquest; we are fighting in the defense of our homes, our families, and posterity. We have petitioned, and our petitions have been scorned; we have entreated, and our entreaties have been disregarded; we have begged, and they have mocked when our calamity came. We beg no longer; we entreat no longer; we petition no more. We defy them.

"The gentleman from Wisconsin has said that he fears a Robespierre. My friends, in this land of the free you need not fear that a tyrant will spring up from among the people. What we need is an Andrew Jackson to stand, as Jackson stood, against the encroachment of organized wealth.

"They tell us that this platform was made to catch votes. We reply to them that changing conditions make new issues; that the principles upon which Democracy rests are as everlasting as the hills, but that they must be applied to new conditions as they arise. Conditions have arisen, and we are here to meet these conditions. They tell us that the income tax ought not to be brought in here; that it is a new idea. They criticize us for our criticism of the Supreme Court of the United States. My friends we have not criticized; we have simply called attention to what you already know. If you want criticisms, read the dissenting opinions of the court. There you will find criticisms. They say that we passed an unconstitutional law; we deny it. The income tax law was not unconstitutional when it was passed; it was not unconstitutional when it went before the Supreme Court for the first time; it did not become unconstitutional until one of the judges changed his mind, and we cannot be expected to know when a judge will change his mind. The income tax is just. It simply intends to put the burdens of government justly upon the backs of the people. I am in favor of an income tax. When I find a man who is not willing to bear his share of the burdens of the government which protects him, I find a man who is unworthy to enjoy the blessings of a government like ours.

"They say that we are opposing national bank currency; it is true. If you will read what Thomas Benton said, you will find he said that, in searching history, he could find but one parallel to Andrew Jackson; that was Cicero, who destroyed the conspiracy of Cataline and saved Rome. Benton said that Cicero only did for Rome what Jackson did for us when he destroyed the bank conspiracy and saved America. We say in our platform that we believe that the right to coin and issue money is a function of government. We believe it. We believe that it is a part of sovereignty, and can no more with safety be delegated to private individuals than we could afford to delegate to private individuals the power to make penal statutes or levy taxes. Mr. Jefferson, who was once regarded as good Democratic authority, seems to have differed in opinion from the gentleman who addressed us on the part of the minority. Those who are opposed to this proposition tell us that the issue of paper money ought to go out of the banking business. I stand with Jefferson rather than with them, and tell them, as he did, that the issue of money is a function of government, and that the banks ought to go out of the governing business.

"They complain about the plank which declares against life

tenure in office. They have tried to strain it to mean that which it does not mean. What we oppose by that plank is the life tenure which is being built up in Washington, and which excludes from participation in official benefits the humbler members of society. Let me call your attention to two or three important things. The gentleman from New York says that he will propose an amendment to the platform providing that the proposed change in our monetary system shall not affect contracts already made. Let me remind you that there is no intention of affecting those contracts which according to present laws are made payable in gold; but if he means to say that we cannot change our monetary system without protecting those who have loaned money before the change was made, I desire to ask him where, in law or in morals, he can find justification for not protecting the debtors when the act of 1873 was passed, if he now insists that we must protect the creditors.

"He says he will also propose an amendment which will provide for the suspension of free coinage if we fail to maintain the parity within a year. We reply that when we advocate a policy which we believe will be successful, we are not compelled to raise a doubt as to our own sincerity by suggesting what we shall do if we fail. I ask him, if he would apply his logic to us, why he does not apply it to himself. He says he wants this country to try to secure an international agreement. Why does he not tell us us what he is going to do if he fails to secure an international agreement? There is more reason for him to do that than there is for us to provide against the failure to maintain the parity. Our opponents have tried for twenty years to secure an international agreement, and those are waiting for it most patiently who do not want it at all.

"And now, my friends, let me come to the paramount issue. If they ask us why it is that we say more on the money question than we say upon the tariff question, I reply that, if protection has slain its thousands, the gold standard has slain its tens of thousands. If they ask us why we do not embody in our platform all the things that we believe in, we reply that when we have restored the money of the Constitution all other necessary reforms will be possible; but that until this is done there is no other reform that can be accomplished.

"Why is it that within three months such a change has come over the country? Three months ago, when it was confidently asserted that those who believe in the gold standard would frame our platform and nominate our candidates, even the advocates of the gold standard did not think that we could elect a President. And they have good reason for their doubt, because there is scarcely a state here today asking for the gold standard which is not in the absolute control of the Republican party. But note the change. Mr. McKinley was nominated at St. Louis upon a platform which declared for the maintenance of the gold standard until it can be changed into bimetalism by international agreement. Mr. McKinley was the most popular man among the Republicans and three months ago everybody in the Republican party prophesied his election. How is it today? Why, the man who was once pleased to think that he looked like Napoleon—that man shudders today when he remembers that he was nominated on the anniversary of the battle of Waterloo. Not only that, but as he listens he can hear with ever-increasing distinctness the sound of the waves as they beat upon the lonely shores of St. Helena.

"Why this change? Ah, my friends, is not the reason for the change evident to any one who will look at the matter? No private character, however pure, no personal popularity, however great, can protect from the avenging wrath of an indignant people a man who will declare that he is in favor of fastening the gold standard upon the country, or who is willing to surrender the right of self-government and place the legislative control of our affairs in the hands of foreign potentates and powers.

"We go forth confident that we shall win. Why? Because upon the paramount issue of this campaign there is not a spot of ground upon which the enemy will dare to challenge battle. If they tell us that the gold standard is a good thing, we shall point to their platform and tell them that their platform pledges the party to get rid of the gold standard and substitute bimetalism. If the gold standard is a good thing, why try to get rid of it? I call your attention to the fact that some of the very people who are in this convention today and who tell us that we ought to declare in favor of international bimetalism—thereby declaring that the old standard is wrong and that the principle of bimetalism is better—these very people four months ago were open and avowed advocates of the gold standard, and were then telling us that we could not legislate two metals together, even with the aid of all the world. If the gold standard is a good thing, we ought to declare in favor of its retention and not in favor of abandoning it; and if the gold standard is a bad thing why should we wait until other nations are willing to help us to let go? Here is the line of battle, and we care not upon which issue they force the fight; we are prepared to meet them on either issue or on both. If they tell us that the gold standard is the standard of civilization, we reply to them that this, the most enlightened of all nations of the earth, has never declared for a gold standard and that both the great parties this year are declaring against it. If the gold standard is the standard of civilization, why, my friends, should we not have it? If they come to meet us on that issue we can present the history of our nation. More than that; we can tell them that they will search the pages of history in vain to find a single instance where the common people of any land have ever declared themselves in favor of the gold standard. They can find where the holders of fixed investments have declared for the gold standard, but not where the masses have.

"Mr. Carlisle said in 1878 that this was a struggle between 'the idle holders of idle capital' and 'the struggling masses, who produce the wealth and pay the taxes of the country'; and, my friends, the question we are to decide is: Upon which side will the Democratic party fight; upon the side of 'the idle holders of idle capital' or upon the side of 'the struggling masses?' That is the question which the party must answer first, and then it must be answered by each individual hereafter. The sympathies of the Democratic party, as shown by the platform, are on the side of the struggling masses who have ever been the foundation of the Democratic party. There are two ideas of government. There are those who believe that, if you will only legislate to make the well-to-do prosperous, their prosperity will leak through on those below. The Democratic idea, however, has been that if you legislate to make the masses prosperous, their prosperity will find its way up through every class which rests upon them.

"You come to us and tell us that the great cities are in favor of the gold standard; we reply that the great cities rest upon our broad and fertile prairies. Burn down your cities and leave our farms, and your cities will spring up again as if by magic; but destroy our farms and the grass will grow in the streets of every city in the country.

"My friends, we declare that this nation is able to legislate for its own people on every question, without waiting for the aid or consent of any other nation on earth; and upon that issue we expect to carry every state in the Union. I shall not slander the inhabitants of the fair State of Massachusetts nor the inhabitants of the State of New York by saying that, when they are confronted with the proposition, they will declare that this nation is not able to attend to its own business. It is the issue of 1776 over again. Our ancestors, when but three millions in number, had the courage to declare their political independence of every other nation; shall we, their descendants, when we have grown to seventy millions, declare that we are less independent than our forefathers? No, my friends, that will never be the verdict of our people. Therefore, we care not upon what lines the battle is fought. If they say bimetalism is good, but that we cannot have it until other nations help us, we reply that, instead of having a gold standard because England has, we will restore bimetalism, and then let England have bimetalism because the United States has it. If they dare to come out in the open field and defend the gold standard as a good thing, we will fight them to the uttermost. Having behind us the producing masses of this nation and the world, supported by the commercial interests, the laboring interests, and the toilers everywhere, we will answer their demand for a gold standard by saying to them: You shall not press down upon the brow of labor this crown of thorns, you shall not crucify mankind upon a cross of gold."

Those final words, from which the speech popularly took its name, hurled by the little-known, dashing young Westerner, marked a high point in American politics.

The minority amendments were defeated; the majority platform for which Bryan spoke was adopted. The placing of candidates in nomination followed. They were, Richard P. Bland of Missouri, Governor Claude Matthews of Indiana, Former Governor Horace Boies of Iowa, Senator J. C. S. Blackburn of Kentucky, John R. McLean of Ohio, Robert E. Pattison of Pennsylvania, and Sylvester Pennoyer of Oregon.

Known to Millions—A characteristic speaking pose of the "Silver
Tongued Orator."

Around the World—Bryan, Mrs. Bryan, and their daughter, Grace, with native guides in Egypt during their circle of the globe.

Bryan left the convention hall at the close of the afternoon session and went to his hotel room. It had been arranged that the Nebraska delegation was to make no formal nomination, and it came as a surprise when word reached Bryan that Henry T. Lewis of Georgia had presented his name. Five ballots followed. In the first, Bryan received 137 votes. The fifth found him with 652 votes, only 768 out of the 930 delegates voting. On motion of Senator Turpie the nomination was made unanimous. Arthur Sewall of Maine was nominated for Vice-President.

Bryan was fond of adding, when he told of the convention and for the benefit of those who still believed that money was not necessary to secure a Presidential nomination, that his entire expenses while attending the convention were one hundred dollars.

CHAPTER X

The First Campaign

Campaign Tour Sets Record—First Campaign Speech at Madalin, N. Y.—West to Chicago—Labor Day Speech in Chicago—First Silver Horse-shoe—Crowds Night and Day—This Swing Totals 3,898 Miles—Third Trip Starts—Heckled by Yale Students— Takes Boston by Storm—From New England West Again—Last Speech at Chicago—Third Trip Ends, 18,009 Miles—Election Day —McKinley Wins—Beaten But Not Defeated.

No candidate before or since ever engaged in such a campaign as did Bryan in the campaign of 1896. No one ever traveled so many miles; no one addressed so many people; no one made so many speeches long and short, all in a period of two months and a half, as did Bryan. His total of 18,009 miles, 5,000,000 people addressed, 600 more or less formal speeches made, and no one knows how many informal talks, still stands as a political record.

In the middle of August, after his speech of acceptance at Madison Square Garden, he traveled northward through New York state.

The talk at Rhinebeck and the first real campaign speech at Madalin, extracts of which follow, are good examples of what he was telling the voters during that swing through hostile territory.

From the Rhinebeck, N. Y., Speech:

"I think I can go further even than the chairman of this impromptu meeting. He says that to be the President of the United States is to be greater than to be a Roman, or a king. But few can be President, and I rejoice that I live in a land where to be a citizen is greater than to be a king. I rejoice that I live in a land where those who exercise authority derive that authority from the consent of the governed and do not rule by the right divine.

"In this land, whether we live along the Hudson, or on the

128

Western prairies, we stand upon a common plane and we participate in a government which represents us all. We may belong to different parties, but I trust I may be able to express the desire of each of you, as well as of myself, when I say that we ought to belong at all times to that party which, in our judgment, will enable us best to serve our country.

"Parties are instruments, not ends. They are the means we use to secure that which we believe to be best for us, for our families, and for our fellows. Issues arise from time to time, and it is the duty of every citizen who loves his country, and who appreciates the responsibilities which rest upon him, to study each issue as it arises.

"I have visited some of your beautiful villas along the Hudson. I have been charmed with their beauty, but when you study this question, remember that those who, instead of occupying these magnificent places, must toil all day under the summer sun, have just as much interest in the money question as anybody else. Remember, that this question can not be viewed from the standpoint of any class of people.

"It reaches every man, woman and child in the land, and you should make your view broad enough to comprehend them all, because I believe I speak the truth when I say that the prosperity of the well-to-do rests upon the prosperity of those who toil, and that you can not have a financial policy which brings distress to those who create wealth without, in the end, reaching those who rest upon these toilers. And, more than that, you can not have a policy which brings prosperity to the masses without the prosperity proving of benefit to all mankind."

From the Madalin, N. Y., Speech:

"We are entering upon a campaign which is a remarkable one in many respects. Heretofore, at least during the last twenty-five or thirty years, each party has gone into the campaign practically solid, presenting a united front against the opposing party. But in this campaign there has been a bolt from practically every convention which has been held. What does this mean? It means that convictions are deeper this year than they have been heretofore.

"It means that people are not so willing now as they have been to allow the platform of a party to control their action. Men are thinking this year with more of earnestness and intensity than they have in recent years, and the results of this thinking will be manifested when the time comes to register the will of this great nation, and between that time and this hour we expect to present to those who must act upon the questions the issues of this campaign.

"When our party at Chicago wrote the platform which it did, we knew that it would offend some people.

"Do you remember the Good Book tells us that some 1,800 years ago a man named Demetrius complained of the preaching of the Gospel. Why? He said, 'It destroys the business in which we are engaged; we are making images for the worship of Diana, and these people say that they be not gods that are made with hands.'

"But Demetrius was much like men who have lived since his day. When he made up his mind that the preaching of the Gospel interfered with his business he didn't go out and say to the world, 'Our business is being injured and we are mad.' What did he say? He said, 'Great is Diana of the Ephesians.'

"We have some today who are very much like Demetrius. They know that the restoration of bimetalism destroys the business in which they have been engaged.

"But when they make public speeches they don't say that the Democratic party is wrong because it interferes with their business. What do they say? They say, 'Great is sound money; great is an honest dollar.'

"I assert that the people of the United States, those who produce wealth as well as those who exchange it, have sufficient patriotism and sufficient intelligence to sit in judgment upon every question which has arisen or which will arise, no matter how long our government may endure. The great political questions are, in their final analysis, great moral questions, and it requires no extended experience in the handling of money to enable a man to tell right from wrong.

"And, more than this, this money question will not be settled until the great common people act upon it. No question is settled until the masses settle it. Abraham Lincoln said that the Lord must have loved the common people, because He made so many of them. He was right about it.

"The common people are the only people who have ever supported a reform that had for its object the benefit of the human race."

The trip led south and west, through Pennsylvania, Ohio, Indiana, and then to Chicago, where Mrs. Bryan left the party to go to Lincoln. There were speeches all the way. No one can tell what Bryan said so well as Bryan, so let him speak for himself.

From the Erie, Pa., Speech:

"Offices cut no figure in this campaign. I believe my experience has been rather an unusual one. The people who have come to me have come with suggestions as to what can be done to help the cause and no one has come to ask me for the promise of an office in case of my election. I have not discussed patronage with anybody. I shall not discuss patronage with anybody during this campaign. A man who, in the midst of a great battle, stops to negotiate as to what official position he is to occupy when this battle is over is unworthy to hold any position."

From the Buffalo, N. Y., Speech:

"Our opponents tell us that they will try to secure an international agreement, and that they simply desire to maintain the gold standard until other nations will help us to let go. Can you expect the restoration of bimetalism from those who wrote the St. Louis platform? Never, until you can gather grapes from thorns and figs from thistles. Those who are responsible for the gold standard are not the ones to whom we must look for deliverance. As well might Pharoah have been expected to lead the children of Israel out of bondage, as to expect the Republican party to break the shackles of the gold standard."

From the Hornellsville, N. Y., Speech:

"It is the object, or at least should be, of public speakers to aid their audiences to understand the merits of disputed questions, and it is an evidence of sincerity of purpose when a person discusses public issues so plainly and clearly that one can understand just what is said and meant. When ambiguous language is used, when obscure expressions are employed, it is an indication that the person speaking has something to conceal. The Bible speaks of certain persons who love darkness rather than light, and it gives a reason for that peculiar affection. Do you remember what the reason is? We are told that they love darkness rather than light because their deeds are evil. Whenever I find darkness employed in the discussion of a question, or in the statement of a position, I am irresistibly reminded of that Bible passage, and conclude that the person who attempts to be obscure does so because he is not willing that the people should know what he believes and what he desires to accomplish. When I hear a man talking about 'sound money' without defining it, I think that, perhaps, he loves darkness rather than light because his deeds are evil.

"When I find a man talking about an 'honest dollar' without telling what he means by an 'honest dollar,' I am afraid that I have found another man who loves darkness rather than light because his deeds are evil."

From the Springfield, O., Speech:

"For a few moments only I shall occupy your attention, because a large portion of my voice has been left along the line of travel, where it is still calling sinners to repentance. I am told that in this city you manufacture more agricultural implements than are manufactured in any other city in the country. I am glad to talk to people who recognize their dependence upon the farmers. I have had occasion to talk to some who seem to imagine that the harder they could make the condition of the farmers the better would be their own. I am glad to talk to you who recognize that the dollars which you receive are earned first by those who convert the natural resources of this country into money, who till the soil and from its fertility bring forth this nation's primary wealth. As a matter of fact the farmers and the laboring men are the foundation of society. Upon this foundation the commercial classes rest, and the financier acts as a sort of a roof over the structure. You can take off the roof and put on another, but you can not destroy the foundation without destroying the whole building. Goldsmith well expressed it when he said:

'Princes and lords may flourish, or may fade;
A breath can make them, as a breath has made:
But a bold peasantry, their country's pride,
When once destroyed, can never be supplied.'

"The Democratic party, in its platform at Chicago, is pleading the cause of a nation's peasantry that must not be destroyed. Upon the prosperity of the great producers of wealth, whom we call the masses, as distinguished from the classes, depends all the prosperity of this city. If you have a gold standard you legislate the value of property down. Do you remember how, when we were young, we used to play on the teeter board? When one end of the board was up the other was down. It has remained for modern financiers to declare that you can keep both ends of the teeter board up at once. They seem to think that money can be dear and prices good at the same time.

"I understand that these gold standard Democrats have declared their emblem to be the hickory tree. We have heard about Satan stealing the livery of Heaven, but we have never before seen men try to use the name of that great hero, Jackson, to undo all that he tried to do. Talk about Andrew Jackson belonging to the gold Democracy! Go back to the time of Andrew Jackson, and who were arrayed against him? The very classes which, after having failed in their effort to use the Democratic party for private gain, are now trying to elect the Republican candidate for President by nominating a gold standard candidate. Take a hickory tree for their emblem? Why do they not take something more appropriate? Why do they not put upon their ballot the picture of an owl? Nothing could be more appropriate. It looks wise and does its work in the dark. Or, if they do not like the owl, let them take the mole. It is a smooth animal and works underground all the time. But they ought to spare the sacred memory of the man who was the hero of New Orleans, and whose resting place, the Hermitage, is the mecca of all who love Democratic principles still."

Bryan returned to Chicago for Labor Day and there addressed a huge crowd of working men. It was here that he received the first horseshoe. This one was of solid silver and was presented by a committee of horseshoers. It was the first of more than a score that were given him during his campaign.

From the Chicago Labor Day Speech:

"Labor Day has become a fixed event among our holidays, and it is well that it is so, because on this day, all over the nation, those who are engaged in the production of wealth meet with each other to discuss the questions in which working men are especially interested and to emphasize before the world that there is nothing dishonorable in the fact that one earns his bread in the sweat of his face. I am glad to stand in the presence of those to whom this nation is so largely indebted for all that it has been, for all that it is now, and for all that it can hope to be.

"I am not indulging in idle flattery when I say to you that no other people are so important to the welfare of society as those whose brain and muscle convert the natural resources of the world into material wealth.

"Let me now read to you the langauge used by one whose words have won for him the title of the wisest of men—Solomon. He said: 'Give me neither poverty nor riches; feed me with food convenient for me, lest I be full, and deny Thee and say, who is the Lord? Or lest I be poor, and steal and take the name of my God in vain.'

"Solomon desired neither poverty nor riches. He rightly estimated the dangers which lie at either extreme and preferred the —I was about to say, golden, but will call it the—golden and silver mean. Neither great wealth nor abject poverty furnishes the soil in which the best civilization grows. Those who are hard pressed by poverty lose the ambition, the inspiration and the high purpose which lead men to the greatest achievements; while those who possess too great riches lack the necessity for that labor which is absolutely essential to the development of all that is useful. Solomon was right, therefore, when he praised the intermediate condition, for the great middle classes are the bulwark of society, and from them has come almost all the good that has blessed the human race.

"The highest compliment ever paid to any class of people was paid to those who are called the common people. When we use that term there are some who say that we are appealing to the passions of the masses; there are some who apply the name demagogue to anybody who speaks of the common people. When the meek and lowly Nazarene came to preach 'peace on earth, good will toward men,' he was not welcomed by those who 'devour widow's houses and for a pretense make long prayers.' By whom was he welcomed? The Scriptures tell us that when he gave that great commandment, 'Thou shalt love thy neighbor as thyself,' the common people heard him gladly. This I repeat, is the highest compliment that has ever been paid to any class of people, and the common people are the only people who have ever received gladly the doctrines of humanity and equality.

"I am not here to tell you what opinions you should hold. I am not here to discuss the measures which, in my judgment, would relieve present conditions. But as an American citizen speaking to American citizens, I have a right to urge you to recognize the responsibilities which rest upon you, and to prepare yourselves for the intelligent discharge of every political duty imposed upon you. Government was not instituted among men to confer special privileges upon any one, but rather to protect all citizens alike in order that they may enjoy the fruits of their own toil. It is the duty of government to make the conditions surrounding the people as favorable as possible. You must have your opinions and, by expressing those opinions, must have your influence in determining what these conditions shall be. If you find a large number of men out of employment, you have a right to inquire whether such idleness is due to natural laws or whether it is due to vicious legislation. If it is due to legislation, then it is not only your right but your duty to change that legislation. The greatest menace to the employed laborer today is the increasing army of the unemployed. It menaces every man who holds a position and, if that army continues to increase, it is only a question of time when those who are, as you may say, on the ragged edge will leave the ranks of the employed to join those who are out of work.

"I am one of those who believe that if you increase the number of those who can not find work and yet must eat, you will drive men to desperation and increase the ranks of the criminals by the addition of many who would be earning bread under better conditions. If you find idleness and crime increasing, it is not your privilege only, it is a duty which you owe to yourselves and to your country, to consider whether the conditions can not be improved.

"There is one citizen in this country who can prove himself unworthy of the ballot which has been given to him, and he is the citizen who either sells it or permits it to be wrested from him under coercion. Whenever a man offers you pay for your vote he insults your manhood, and you ought to have no respect for him. And the man, who instead of insulting your manhood by an offer of purchase, attempts to intimidate you or coerce you, insults your citizenship as well as your manhood.

"My friends, in this world people have just about as much of good as they deserve. At least, the best way to secure anything that is desirable is to first deserve that thing. If the people of this country want good laws, they themselves must secure them. If the people want to repeal bad laws, they alone have the power to do it. In a government like ours every year offers the citizen an opportunity to prove his love of country. Every year offers him an opportunity to manifest his patriotism."

Bryan, remember, was making not one speech, but sometimes twenty speeches a day. They would not let him alone. At every station crowds were sure to be on the platform watching to see the Democratic candidate pass through. And if the train paused for so much as a minute they were certain to ask for a few words, meanwhile defeating their own request by crowding forward to get hold of the candidate's hand. It wasn't unusual for Bryan to get up at six o'clock in the morning, travel and speak all day, and not get to bed until after midnight. Not one day, but day after day. How he stood the strain was a marvel to those who accompanied him.

From Chicago he made a short jump to Milwaukee, and there he said in part:

"I learned early in life that a public officer was but a public servant, and I think that it is an idea which we ought always to bear in mind. It is well for the officer himself to remember it, and equally important for the people to remember it. A public officer is simply a hired man employed at a fixed salary for a certain time to do certain work. He is not in office merely because he wants to be; his only reason for being there ought to be that those whom he serves want him to be there. In other words, the officer is merely chosen by the people to do work which they must have done, and they have no reason for choosing him except that they believe that he can do that work for them. Officers are not elected to think for the people; people are supposed to think for themselves. They are elected to act for the people, simply because the people are so numerous that they cannot act for themselves. An officer, I might say, is a necessary evil. It would be better for the people if they could act for themselves, but that being impossible, they must do the next best thing and act through someone else; and the beauty of our form of government is that, instead of acting through somebody who rules by right divine, our people act through representatives whom they themselves choose and whom they can turn out of office whenever they so desire.

"Cicero, it is related, once said to his son: 'Do not go into the retail business; the retail business is a small and vulgar business. Go into the wholesale business; that is a respectable business.'

"My friends, this doctrine seems to be applied to those who would injure the government. If a man attempts to do the government a small injury, he is a contemptible man and ought to be punished, but if he attempts to do the government a great injury, he goes into the wholesale business and becomes respectable, and then the government must negotiate with him. When our Consti-

tution was based upon the theory that all men were created equal
and stood equal before the law, there was no provision in there
making an exception in behalf of financiers and asserting that they
are greater than anybody else.

"When will this policy end? There is but one end to it; there
is only one way to stop this constant issue of bonds, and that is to
return to the principle of bimetalism and allow the government to
exercise the option of redeeming its coin obligations in either gold
or silver. When I have seen how they go to the treasury and
draw out the gold and then demand bonds, and then draw out gold
to pay for the bonds, and so on without limit, I have been reminded
of a trick that a mother played upon her boy. He was taking some
medicine and the following dialogue took place between him and a
visitor: 'Do you like that medicine?' 'No, sir.' 'Well, you seem
to take it very nicely.' 'Mamma gives me five cents every time I
take a dose of it.' 'What do you do with the money?' 'I put it
in the bank.' 'And what do you do with the money in the bank?'
'Oh, mamma uses that to buy more medicine with.'

"Our opponents tell us that, if we will retire the greenbacks
and treasury notes, this drain on the treasury will stop. I ask
them how it will stop. Why, they say that the banks will issue paper
money and assume the obligation of furnishing whatever gold is
needed for export."

After returning to Chicago, the Commoner went home for an all
too brief rest. It was hardly rest either, for the home folks all
wanted to greet the fellow townsman who was bringing so much
honor to himself and to them. On this second trip—for the first was
the trip to New York—Bryan traveled 3,898 miles. He was getting
used to having people call him "Billy." It was the democracy of
politics that brought him the familiar title.

Also he was getting used to having people wake him up at night and demand that he shove up his sleeping car window and lean out to say a drowsy "hello" and reach out a hand to be shaken.

Just a few days later saw Bryan started on the third and by far the longest swing around the country. Mrs. Bryan remained at home for a time to see the children safely in school. She did not rejoin the tour until it reached St. Paul. Bryan regretted her absence, because she could do what he could not do—disappoint people by insisting that her husband take care of his health and get some rest.

The third trip began with a stop at St. Louis, then through Kentucky, into the Carolinas, Virginia, Washington, Delaware, Maryland, and back to Washington for a Sunday. Bryan never campaigned on Sunday. And this Sunday morning he spent attending a service at the New York Avenue Presbyterian church. He did not guess that twenty-nine years later his body was to lie in state in that same church and that representatives of the army and navy, come to do honor to his memory, would sit in the same famous Lincoln pew where he sat on that Sunday morning in '96.

Here are more examples of the words with which Bryan campaigned.

From the Lexington, Ky., Speech:

"In the olden times under the rule of those who wielded the scepter, as they said, by right divine, complaint was answered with the lash, but now the just complaint of the toiling millions of the United States is answered by the charge that they are anarchists.

"I protest against the use of that name for a purpose which deprives it of all its terrors. Those who are opposed to us can not afford to place the farmers and laborers of the country in the position of enemies of the government, because they are the only friends the government has ever had."

From the Raleigh, N. C., Speech:

"At last we have the line drawn so that a man can take his place on one side or the other, and the result is that a great many

Republicans who had hoped to secure bimetalism in the Republican party have now given up hope and joined with those who demand the immediate restoration of free coinage, and some in the Democratic party who had sought to further the gold standard by secret means have now joined with the Republican party, and a few, instead of going all the way, have stopped at the half way point to rest a moment before completing their journey. You may rest assured that the lines now drawn are drawn, not temporarily, but permanently. The man who leaves the Democratic party today, when the party is taking up its fight for the common people, must understand that if he comes back, he must come back in sack cloth and ashes. Not only that, but he must bring forth works meet for repentance. The men who are in the employ of trusts and syndicates and combinations are not leaving the party for their country's good; they are leaving their party for their party's good.

"There was a banker down in Oklahoma who told a depositor that money was not as important as it used to be. 'Why,' said the banker, 'if you deposit money in my bank you give a check for a given amount and it goes through various hands, and finally some one deposits it at the bank. No money changes hands. I merely transfer the amount on the books from one account to the other. Don't you see, money is not as important as it once was?' The depositor replied, 'I am glad to hear that. I have been keeping my money on deposit with the idea that it was just as important as ever; but now that you have shown me my mistake, I will draw out my money and go on checking as I did before.' 'Well, in your case that will not work,' said the banker. No, it won't work! The very people who tell you that money is not as important as it used to be are the ones who regard money as just as important as it ever was if you owe them and cannot pay."

From the Fredericksburg, Va., Speech:

"I am glad to visit this historic place. They say that here

George Washington once threw a silver dollar across the river; but remember, my friends, that when he threw that silver dollar across the river it fell and remained on American soil. They thought that it was a great feat then, but we have developed so rapidly in the last hundred years that we have financiers who can leave George Washington's achievement far behind. We have financiers who have been able to throw gold dollars all the way across the Atlantic, and then bring them back by an issue of bonds.

"Would you believe, my friends, that a silver dollar which was good enough to be handled by the father of his country is so mean a thing as to excite the contempt of many of our so-called financiers? Well, it is. It is so mean that they do not like it. Why, our opponents tell us that they want a dollar that will go all over the world. We have had dollars which have gone over the world so rapidly that we want a dollar that will stay at home without a curfew law.

"Our opponents tell us that they want a dollar which they can see anywhere in the world if they travel abroad. I am not so much worried about our dollars which travel abroad. I want a dollar that will not be ashamed to look a farmer in the face."

From the Baltimore, Md., Speech:

"We have commenced a warfare which will end now if it ends in success, but which will never end until it does end in success. No question is settled until it is settled right. Neither fraud nor intimidation nor corruption ever settled a question right. They tell us that our troubles come from agitation; that if we would stop agitating all would be well. We reply that when all is well agitation will stop of itself. They find fault because people complain; let them take away the cause of complaint and the complaint will cease. We complain because the conditions are hard for the producers of wealth, and then our opponents complain at our complaint, instead of complaining of the conditions which give rise to our complaint. They seem to have the idea which is said to have prevailed at one

The Wife—One of the last pictures taken of Mrs. Bryan before her husband's death. Posed for at the Florida home.

Great Grandfather—At their Florida home. From left to right: Bryan;
Mrs. Bryan; Mrs. William Meeker, granddaughter; Mrs. Reginald
Owen, daughter; in Mrs. Owen's lap, the great-granddaughter born dur-
ing the 1924 convention; and Miss Ruth Meeker.

time—namely, that it is not wrong to steal, but that it is a crime to be caught stealing. We denounce the gold standard as wrong; we denounce the dollar under a gold standard as a robber. Do you think that we have reached the end of the gold standard? There is no end. Do you think that we have drained the cup of sorrow to its dregs? No, my friends, you cannot set a limit to fianancial depression and hard times. If the influences which are at work are able to drive silver out of use as standard money here, those same influences will be turned toward other nations; if they succeed here, what reason have we to believe that they will fail when directed against weaker nations? Every nation which goes to the gold standard makes the dollar dearer still, and as the dollar rises in value, you must sacrifice more of all of the products of toil in order to secure it. As you sacrifice more and more, you will find that your debts virtually increase as your ability to pay your debts decreases, and, in the long run, the capitalistic classes will devour all the property.

"Our opponents say that this money question is a business question; they try to rid it of sentiment. But there is not much business which is devoid of sentiment. The man who toils all day is engaged in business, but why? Because he is working for those whom he loves better than his own life. He accumulates property; he lays aside something for a rainy day, but why? When a man accumulates, you call it a matter of business, and yet, my friends, his hopes and interests are entwined about his accumulations because he expects that after he is gone, his own flesh and blood will enjoy his property. Take sentiment from life and there is nothing left. When our opponents tell us that we are running a sentimental campaign and that they are running a business campaign, we reply to them that we are simply placing the heart of the masses against the pocketbooks of a few.

"Some one has said that no one can write a poem in favor of

the financial policy of the present administration, and why? Because there is nothing in it to appeal to the sentiment or to the heart. It would require a large reward to bring out a poem which would portray in beautiful language the advantage of having a syndicate run the Government of the United States."

From the Wilmington, Del., Speech:

"You will find in our cities preachers of the gospel, enjoying every luxury themselves, who are indifferent to the cries of distress which come up from the masses of the people. It was told of a princess in a foreign land that, when someone said to her, 'The people are crying for bread,' she replied, 'Why don't they eat cake?' Tell some of these ministers of the gospel that men out of work are driven into crime, and they cannot understand why everyone is not as well off as themselves. When I have seen preachers of the gospel using even more bitter speech than politicians against the clamorings of the people, I have wondered where they got the religion that they preach. My friends, the common people were never aided in their struggles by those who were so far beyond them that they could not feel their needs and sympathize with their interests."

From Washington it was New Jersey, then Philadelphia.

From the Philadelphia Speech:

"Your city is called Philadelphia, the City of Brotherly Love. I come to proclaim to you the gospel that is described by the name of your city, and yet it is said that you will give 100,000 majority against such a doctrine. I want to preach financial independence in the city which saw the Declaration of Independence signed. Do you say that this city, in which the forefathers gathered when they were willing to defy all foreign powers and declare their political independence, is afraid to favor financial independence? I shall not say that of the descendants of the forefathers of one hundred years ago unless you say so in the ballot which you cast next November.

"One of the papers said that I 'lacked dignity.' I have been looking into the matter, and have decided that I would rather have it said that I lacked dignity than to have it said that I lack backbone to meet the enemies of the government who work against its welfare in Wall street. What other presidential candidates did they ever charge with lack of dignity? (A voice: 'Lincoln'.) Yes, my friends, they said it of Lincoln. (A voice: 'Jackson'.) Yes, they said it of Jackson. (A voice: 'And Jefferson.') Yes, and of Jefferson; he was lacking in dignity, too. Now, I will tell you how dignified a man ought to be, because, you know, everybody has his idea of these things. I think a man ought to be just dignified enough—not too dignified—and not lacking in dignity. Now, it might be more dignified for me to stay at home and have people come to see me; but you know I said I was not going to promise to give anybody an office, and therefore, a great many people who might go to see a candidate under some circumstances would not come to see me at all. And then, too, our people do not have money to spare. Why, our people are the people who want more money, and if they could come all the way to Nebraska to see me, it might show that they have money enough now.

"I do not like to be lacking in any of the essentials, but I cannot see that there is any lack of dignity shown if I come before the people and talk to them and tell them what I stand for and what I am opposed to."

Then to Brooklyn, and on into New England. At New Haven, Conn., Bryan stopped to address some Yale students and there met a particularly violent brand of heckling. He did not hesitate to scourge the moneyed powers, though he knew that it was that same money which was sending some of his auditors to college. The students' conduct caused much comment, some favorable to them, some quite unfavorable.

Bryan quite took the staid old city of Boston by storm. When he appeared there to speak on the famous Common, tremendous mobs came to hear him. Dismayed statisticians recorded the crowd between 50,000 and 100,000. Down into New Jersey again the trip swung, then into New York, through Virginia, West Virginia, Ohio, and on to St. Louis for a promised attendance at the convention of the Democratic clubs of the United States. On to Chicago via Tennessee, with a stop at Indianapolis, where he was the guest of Mayor Taggart, who was later to become one of the great Democratic triumvirate of Murphy, Taggart, and Brennan.

In Chicago, Bryan achieved some measure of comfort when the private car, the "Idler," was provided for him. He didn't approve of the name, but he appreciated the unaccustomed luxury of not having to change cars any more. The trip led north into Minnesota.

From the Minneapolis, Minn., Speech:

"The money question is not too deep to be understood by the American people. The great questions of state are, after all, simple in their last analysis. Every great political question is first a great economic question, and every great economic question is in reality a great moral question. Questions are not settled until the right and wrong of the questions are determined. Questions are not settled by a discussion of the details; they are not settled until the people grasp the fundamental principles, and when these principles are fully comprehended, then the people settle the question and they settle it for a generation. The people are studying the money question, studying it as they have not studied it before; aye, studying it as they have been studying no economic question before in your lifetime or mine; and studying means understanding. To study we must commence at the foundation and reason upward."

After Minneapolis it was Michigan, Ohio, Indiana, Illinois, and once more Chicago.

From the Monmouth, Ill., Speech:

"Is it not strange that there can be anybody in this country so

far removed from the masses of the people as to think that the
masses of the people are being well cared for? No, it is not strange;
it is as old as history. In all times, in all countries and under all
conditions, those who are getting along well enough, as a rule, do
not feel for those who are suffering, and, therefore, the well-to-do
never reform an evil or bring relief from a bad condition."

One last speech at Chicago and the third great trip was almost
over. He went back to Lincoln. It was within a few days of election. One last hasty swing through the home state and the campaign was over. The record total was 18,009 miles. Bryan took to
his bed for a day, fagged out with the supreme effort.

It was election day.

The man whom millions had cheered, the man whom thousands
and tens of thousands had milled about, to shake his hand or tug
at his coat; the man who had moved men to tears and cheers all
up and down this land, sat in his home at Lincoln, awaiting the
returns.

Back of him was a phenomenal record of energy and oratory in
one of the most remarkable campaigns the world has ever witnessed.
In front of him were his hopes of the White House and an opportunity to translate into actuality those political tenets to which he
was dedicated and toward which his impassioned sincerity had
drawn thousands, millions.

Around and about the Commoner, as he waited, were, first of
all, his wife, who had made a large part of the campaign with him;
his family and friends. There were political friends there, and
humble folk from round about.

The room was literally packed with gifts. In a whimsy that had
an earnest significance, one admirer had sent Bryan a bouquet of
beautiful chrysanthemums. Sixteen white blossoms and one large
yellow bloom, in symbolism of the candidate's stand on free silver
and the sixteen-to-one ratio.

There were eagles, typifying Bryan's Americanism. Four live ones had been presented to him; one stuffed one. More than a score of canes. All manner of curios, mementoes and other gifts.

And the returns came in.

On the popular vote, McKinley received 7,107,822 votes as against Bryan's 6,511,073 votes. The balloting of the electoral college gave McKinley 271 votes, over against Bryan's 176.

William Jennings Bryan was beaten. He was not defeated.

As soon as the results of the election were definitely known Bryan issued a statement to the bimetalists of the United States. It concludes this chapter:

"Conscious that millions of loyal hearts are saddened by temporary defeat, I beg to offer a word of hope and encouragement. No cause ever had supporters more brave, earnest and devoted than those who have espoused the cause of bimetalism. They have fought from conviction, and have fought with all the zeal which conviction inspires. Events will prove whether they are right or wrong. Having done their duty as they saw it, they have nothing to regret.

"The friends of bimetalism have not been vanquished; they have simply been overcome. They believe that the gold standard is a conspiracy of the money-changers against the welfare of the human race, and they will continue the warfare against it.

"No personal or political friend need grieve because of my defeat. My ambition has been to secure remedial legislation, rather than enjoy the honors of office; and therefore defeat brings to me no feeling of personal loss. Speaking for the wife who has shared my labors, as well as for myself, I desire to say that we have been amply repaid for all that we have done. In the love of millions of our fellow citizens, so kindly expressed; in knowledge gained by personal contact with the people and in broadened sympathies, we find full compensation for whatever efforts we have put forth. Our hearts have been touched by the devotion of friends and our lives shall prove our appreciation of the affection of the plain people—an affection which we prize as the richest reward which this campaign has brought."

CHAPTER XI

Energy and Oratory

No Eight-Hour Day—Answers 60,000 Letters—Typical Campaign
Day—Drinks Water—Day's Time-Table—Health—Care of Voice—
Lost Syllables—Gestures—Style of Oratory—Anecdote—"Twi-
light Zone"—His Lesson to Spell-Binders.

There was never any eight hour day for William Jennings Bryan.
Nor ten, nor twelve. Often it was fourteen, during the stress of a
strenuous campaign it went up to sixteen, and more than once
climaxed itself in a full twenty-four hour schedule.

For the "Silver Tongued Orator" was also the great apostle of
energy.

The combination of the talent on the one hand, and the strength
on the other, proved so powerful a union that Bryan set up all
manner of records on his stumping trips. He wore out some of
the fastest shorthand reporters in the country giving them dictation
as he sat on the edge of his bed in his Pullman and phrased speeches
and letters and official replies.

His campaign tours left newspaper correspondents fatigued almost to the end of their endurance at a midnight that found Bryan
delivering a one hour speech from the rear of the train.

As a casual aftermath of the stupendous campaign of 1896, he
sat down in his study at Lincoln and, with the aid of his wife,
answered every one of the 60,000 letters which had accumulated
during his absence. It took them a year and a half to sandwich
the work in between a multiplicity of other duties; but Bryan took
the job as a matter of course and didn't chafe under it.

Another time, friends came upon him working zealously to auto-
graph several hundred photographs before he rushed off to a meet-

152

ing. At an adjacent desk, his brother, Charles W. Bryan, sat toying with his pen and making a signature that would have fooled even a handwriting expert into believing the Commoner had made it himself. Friends had the temerity to suggest that Charles Bryan sign the name William J. Bryan to some of the photographs. Mr. Bryan rebuked them for the suggestion, and continued his laborious task.

Strangely enough, this energy which projected him into the whirlwind campaign of 1896 did not taper off in the next, nor the next. In fact it gathered momentum. Of course, in point of statistics, he never quite equalled those records rolled up in the 1896 tour. But for individual days of amazing activity, his second trip beat the first, and the third beat the second.

First he set a record by making nineteen speeches in one day; then he increased that to twenty-one; and later capped the whole performance by delivering thirty-six speeches in twenty-four hours.

The significant thing about it all was that this ceaseless talking, this consistent alertness, did not mean that he had "set" speeches. Phrases, similes, quotations, pen pictures—the same ones occur again and again in his speeches. But those who campaigned with him, maintain that William Jennings Bryan never gave the same speech twice.

Here is a typical day, some five weeks before a presidential election, as described by a journalist who made the trip with him.

It is six o'clock in the morning, and Bryan's special is hurrying along through New York state. It was past midnight when Bryan got on the train the night before but he is having breakfast by six. He doesn't look fatigued as he comes to the table, and he doesn't act fatigued.

For his first words are ones of inquiry as to how the others have slept; Governor Jennings of Florida, Robert Rose, his secretary, and half a dozen newspaper men. He even remembers to ask about the condition of one of the reporter's hands, which had been slightly injured the day before.

He is just about reaching for the morning papers, with his breakfast but half eaten, when the train pulls into a little town. Only a hundred or so people at the station, but they are cheering. They want to see Bryan. Napkin in hand, he goes to the door. But they want to hear Bryan. So Bryan talks to them, until the train wheels begin to roll.

The correspondents crowd out to the platform. For they know that the two hundred or five hundred words which the candidate will speak to that tiny crowd may, very possibly, contain the text of his address for the day. Some identical phrases will be used over again and again during the day. But each speech will have a keynote of spontaneity. Each speech will be different.

The orator returns to his breakfast. The coffee is cold, but they bring him some fresh. By that time the train is again slowing down. It's a bigger town this time. Out on the platform again. After the speech the men and women crowd up on the step to shake hands with their candidate.

A third try at breakfast, and a third speech at a crossroads.

In the course of the morning, the journalist estimates, Bryan makes six or eight short speeches, and does a prodiguous amount of dictating. At noon he leaves the train, which has pulled in to a goodly sized town. A delegation of citizens escort him to the town square. For one hour he talks. Folks all about him jockey for position to see him, to be the first to get to him and shake his hand as he leaves the flag-draped platform.

Everywhere, small village, or lobby of a fashionable hotel, it is the same, they are tugging at his elbow, introducing themselves, their wives and all their friends, to him.

The noon meeting over, he talks to the farmer, to the business man, the president of the mother's club, the youngsters who have been dismissed from school in order to attend the meeting.

Then an afternoon that is much like the forenoon. And a series of long speeches that night. Bryan's doctor had ordered but one long speech a day. But it was more like one "longer" speech, with several long ones, and a host of small ones. His secretary, Mr. Rose, estimated that he spoke, on the average, between 60,000 and 100,000 words a day.

His voice, a powerful, wonderful thing, often got husky by night, but was ready for battle early the next morning. He was said to drink a glass of water every twenty-five minutes when speaking. He usually contrived to get the crowd laughing just before he paused to drink the water, and by the time their attention was again focused on him, he was beginning to talk.

For instance, in the campaign of 1908, he would say, with a twinkle in his eye, "When I first began running for President." The crowd would laugh, and he would drink his glass of water.

Here is yet another time table of an average day out campaigning:

7:30—Gets off train, after 300 mile journey, with a midnight "change cars" schedule.

8:30—Introductions and breakfast.

8:50—Stands on steps of fraternity building and addresses crowd.

9:30—Conference with a political committee.

10:15—Talks to more than 4,000 persons who have packed themselves into an auditorium with a seating capacity of 3,000.

12:15—Concludes talk in auditorium and goes outside to deliver another speech to the overflow meeting.

1:00—Lunch on the train. This train makes five stops in the next 100 miles. At each stop he makes a rear platform address.

3:45—Talks for two hours from an open-air stand, with a high wind trying to cut capers with his voice, but not succeeding.

5:50—On board train for 50 mile trip. Dinner en route.

7:30—Reception and 20 minutes of dictation to reporter.

8:15—Addresses 4,000 persons assembled in a badly lighted, poorly ventilated warehouse.

Midnight—So home and to bed. Only "home" is a Pullman, and "to bed" is a none too lengthy sleep, for he must be up early on the morrow as two formal addresses are scheduled; and there are six for the succeeding day.

A correspondent who made the 1908 tour with him presents the following as a record day.

According to this gentleman, Bryan made his first speech that day at four o'clock in the morning at St. Joseph, Missouri, and kept going all day long. By midnight the reporters were desperately tired. Only a few of them were up when he made his last speech, the thirty-second it was. Like most of the others, it was made in the open air. It was late, but a few hundred men had waited for his train to come by and Bryan did not want to disappoint them.

As an example of that persistent desire never to disappoint any assembly that expected him, there is the story of the October day, in 1922, when he was scheduled to address a large gathering of people at Newton, Kansas. On the way to Newton he suffered a painful injury to one of his feet. But he appeared on the program, and made his speech while seated.

To maintain a pace like the one we have just indicated, Bryan had to be careful of his health and careful of his voice.

While he taxed his strength to its utmost, he had quick recuperative powers and seemed able to "come back" with renewed force, after a night's rest. Then, too, he was a hearty eater. His eating, indeed, has been the subject of jest. Sweet corn was one of his favorite dishes, and he is said to have eaten it even for breakfast. He was regular in his meals; he ate simply but heartily, and he masticated his food well. He drank much milk. He never smoked. He often drank ginger ale at night.

Second only in importance to the care of his health came the care of his voice.

Beginning rather instinctively, Bryan, later in his career, quite consciously it would seem, saved his voice, even as he was using it, apparently to its fully capacity. While enunciating so clearly that the listener caught every syllable, he deliberately neglected, or as some analysts have said, "threw away" at least one-third of his syllables. That is, his stress and strain of voice technique was so worked out that he emphasized just the syllables that needed emphasis and conserved his energy on the others, almost to the point of tossing them aside.

The primary result may have been voice-saving, but the secondary result was a well poised voice accent that won new laurels for him as a speaker.

So it was that Bryan never strained his voice though he often wore it out.

In addition to the fundamental requisite of a powerful voice well trained, the "Silver Tongued Orator" knew how to handle himself on the platform. He did not gyrate about like a whirligig. Often he stood, straight, quiet, with his fingers at his sides or touching the edge of the table. He didn't throw away useless gestures. Some of his favorite ones were the right hand beating down on the left palm; both hands outstretched to the side; both hands upward obliquely; and the upraised right hand.

So much for the way he said things. An analysis of what he said, the recurrent oratorical characteristics, the use of Scripture, of the informal story, and of the simile, is best made in a laboratory method, with some of his speeches, or excerpts from them, before you. Such a laboratory, in a tabloid form, will be available in the next chapter.

Stylistically, his speeches have been criticised for their florid imagery. And many of the passages are a bit roccocco. There are even rhetorical inserts of "ginger-bread." But, in fairness to him, it must be remembered that in nearly every case, Bryan's words were meant to be spoken, rather than read. And the vigor of his voice, the personality of himself, the drama of the occasion, formed kindly yardsticks by which to judge anything that might have been too abundantly elaborate.

In speaking of the function of humor in a political speech, Bryan once said:

"I suppose I tell more stories in my speeches than any other public speaker. But as a rule I try to tell stories that will illustrate a serious point and people forget the funny part in remembering the point."

Just as Bryan employed anecdote in his speeches, so his speeches furnished anecdotes for him to tell about in other speeches.

For instance, there is that one about Governor Thayer of Nebraska, a political enemy of Bryan's. The governor was presiding at a non-partisan meeting, and when Bryan, one of the speakers, came up to the platform and sat down, Thayer, pretending not to recognize him, asked him his name.

"William Jennings Bryan. Oh! I see," the governor said. "I am glad to meet you, Mr. Bryan. Do you speak or sing?"

Years earlier, when an aspiring young orator back in Jacksonville, Bryan attended a meeting, as a listener, where the speakers were slow in arriving. Presently one of the townsmen tip-toed to the platform and whispered to the chairman that there was a "fine young fellow down there, quite a speaker, too," and suggested that he fill in the gap until the regular speakers came. The chairman agreed, and asked how to introduce the impromptu speaker.

"Oh, just say," the townsman replied, "that we will now hear from William J. Bryan, a rising attorney of this city."

The chairman motioned for silence. Then something must have flustered him. At any rate, this is what he announced:

"We will now have the pleasure of listening to William Rising Bryan, a jay attorney of this city."

One of Bryan's most famous phrases passed almost into a proverb.

The incident took place at a conference of governors and other officials at Washington about 1908. He was referring to the adroit way in which men representing what is called predatory wealth, escape punishment by going from the federal to the state courts, or from the state to the federal courts.

Bryan said:

"There is no twilight zone between the nation and the state in which exploiting interests can take refuge from both, and my observation is that most—not all, but most—of the contentions over the line between nation and state are traceable to predatory corporations which are trying to shield themselves from deserved punishment, or endeavoring to prevent needed restraining legislation."

Within twenty-four hours the President had adopted the phrase "no twilight zone," and it passed into both literature and politics.

An interesting revelation as to what Bryan considered the necessary attributes of a spell-binder was made by the orator in Chicago, March 1, 1918. He was in the city and learned that the Chicago Dry federation was holding a meeting at the Stevens' restaurant. The meeting had been called to instruct speakers in the dry campaign. Bryan dropped in and listened to the advice given by men sent out by the speakers' bureau.

At the conclusion of the meeting there was a call for Bryan. He protested that he had just dropped in for a few pointers, but they cheered until he addressed them. Here's his speech to spell-binders:

"The purpose of speaking is to convince. To convince you must make the people understand. Not only is certain truth self-evident, as we say in the Declaration of Independence, but all truth is self-evident and the most important element in speaking is to have yourself understood.

"A certain man is said to have sawed two holes in a door, one for the big cat and one for the kitten. It was unnecessary, for the hole big enough to let the big cat in would let in the kitten also. It is the same in speaking. If you speak in simple language both the learned and the unlearned will understand; the little words, like the kitten, can get through either the big or the little hole.

"I was glad to hear these 'trial sermons' tonight. It takes all kinds of speeches to reach all kinds of people. Some persons criticize me because, they say, I am too mild. They want to show me how to make my language stronger. There's Mr. Sunday. We are after the same thing, but we approach our subject from different angles.

"But you can't carry by spellbinding alone. You must organize every ward and precinct and get out the last voter. Iowa and Ohio were lost by over-confidence on the part of the drys. I know towns which were carried by a single vote.

"The temperance tide is rising and the vote in favor of ratification of the national amendment exceeds every time the estimate.

"The woman's vote is going to be a big factor in determining the vote in favor of the dry cause."

With the President—Bryan and Wilson in attendance at a state dinner
during the former's term as Secretary of State.

At Disarmament Parley—A center of interest at the international conference in Washington, which he attended as press correspondent.

Secretary of State—At his desk in Washington during his membership in President Wilson's cabinet.

CHAPTER XII

Syllables From the Silver Tongue

Estimate of Lincoln as Orator—Funeral Oration—Bible the Only
True Guide—To the Flag—Mystery of the Radish—Conversion—
The Dry Triumvirate—Woman Suffrage—Education—Money—
Illustration of the Hog—Democracy—Philosophy of Defeat.

Before going on to a consideration of some of the best
examples of Bryan's oratory, exclusive of the speeches or
excerpts from them which are printed elsewhere in this book, it is
profitable, as forming a basis for comparison, to read what
Bryan, the orator, thought of Lincoln, the orator.

The following extract from a speech Byran made at Springfield, Illinois, February 12, 1909, tells the story:

"In analyzing Lincoln's characteristics as a speaker, one is
impressed with the completeness of his equipment. He possessed the two things that are absolutely essential to effective
speaking—namely, information and earnestness. If one can be
called eloquent who knows what he is talking about and means
what he says—and I know of no better definition—Lincoln's
speeches were eloquent. He was thoroughly informed upon
the subject; he was prepared to meet his opponent upon the
general proposition discussed, and upon any deductions which could
be drawn from it. There was no unexplored field into which his
adversary could lead him; he had carefully examined every foot
of the ground, and was not afraid of pitfall or ambush; and,
what was equally important, he spoke from his own heart to
the hearts of those who listened. While the printed page can
not fully reproduce the impressions made by a voice trembling
with emotion or tender with pathos, one can not read the re-

ports of the debates without feeling that Lincoln regarded the subject as far transcending the ambitions or the personal interests of the debaters. It was of little moment, he said, whether they voted him or Judge Douglas up or down, but it was tremendously important that the question should be decided rightly.

"His reputation may have suffered, in the opinion of some, because he made them think so deeply upon what he said that they, for the moment, forgot him altogether, and yet, is this not the very perfection of speech? It is the purpose of the orator to persuade, and to do this he presents, not himself, but his subjects. Someone, in describing the difference between Demosthenes and Cicero, said that when Cicero spoke, people said, 'How well Cicero speaks'; but that when Demosthenes spoke, they said, 'Let us go against Philip.' In proportion as one can forget himself and become wholly absorbed in the cause which he is presenting does he measure up to the requirements of oratory.

"In addition to the two essentials, Lincoln possessed what may be called the secondary aids to oratory. He was a master of statement. Few have equalled him in the ability to strip a truth of surplus verbiage and present it in its naked strength. In the Declaration of Independence we read that there are certain self-evident truths, which are therein enumerated. If I were amending the proposition, I would say that all truth is self-evident. Not that any truth will be universally accepted, for not all are in a position or in an attitude to accept any given truth. In the interpretation of the parable of the sower we are told that 'the cares of this world and the deceitfulness of riches choke the truth,' and it must be acknowledged that every truth has these or other difficulties to contend with. But a truth may be so clearly stated that it will commend itself to anyone who has not some special reason for rejecting it.

" 'Brevity is the soul of wit,' and a part of Lincoln's reputation for wit lies in his ability to condense a great deal into a few words. He was epigrammatic. A molder of thought is not necessarily an originator of the thought molded. Just as lead molded in the form of bullets has its effectiveness increased, so thought may have its propagating power enormously enlarged by being molded into a form that the eye catches and the memory holds. Lincoln was the spokesman of his party—he gave felicitous expression to the thoughts of his followers.

"His Gettysburg speech is not surpassed, if equalled, in beauty, simplicity, force and appropriateness by any speech of the same length of any language. It is the world's model in eloquence, elegance, and condensation. He might safely rest his reputation as an orator on that speech alone.

"He was apt in illustration—no one more so. A simple story or simile drawn from every-day life flashed before his hearer the argument that he desired to present. He did not speak over the heads of his hearers, and yet his language was never commonplace. There is strength in simplicity, and Lincoln's style was simplicity itself.

"He understood the power of the interrogatory; some of his most powerful arguments were condensed into questions. No one who discussed the evils of separation and the advantage to be derived from the preservation of the Union ever put the matter more forcibly than Lincoln did when, referring to the possibility of war and the certainty of peace some time, even if the Union was divided, he called attention to the fact that the same questions would have to be dealt with, and then asked: 'Can enemies make treaties easier than friends can make laws?'

"He made frequent use of Bible language and of illustrations drawn from Holy Writ. It is said that when he was preparing his Springfield speech of 1858, he spent hours trying to find language that would express the idea that dominated his public career—namely, that a republic could not permanently endure half free and half slave, and that finally a Bible passage flashed through his mind, and he exclaimed: 'I have found it! "A house divided against itself can not stand."' And probably no other Bible passage ever exerted as much influence as this one in the settlement of a great controversy.

"I have enumerated some, not all—but the more important—of his characteristics as an orator, and on this day I venture for the moment to turn the thoughts of this audience away from the great work that he accomplished as a patriot, away from his achievements in the line of statecraft, to the means employed by him to bring before the public the ideas which attracted attention to him. His power as a public speaker was the foundation of his success, and while it is obscured by the superstructure that was reared upon it, it can not be entirely overlooked as the returning anniversary of his birth calls increasing attention to the widening influence of his work. With no military career to dazzle the eye or excite the imagination; with no public service to make his name familiar to the reading public, his elevation to the Presidency would have been impossible without his oratory. The eloquence of Demosthenes and Cicero were no more necessary to their work and Lincoln deserves to have his name written on the scroll with theirs."

That is what Bryan thought of Lincoln's oratorical qualities. Now, let us consider Bryan's own abilities in that line, as evidenced in the following gems from his most famous utterances:

A CHILD OF FORTUNE

I have been a child of fortune from my birth. God gave me

into the keeping of a Christian father and a Christian mother. They implanted in my heart the ideals that have guided my life. When I was in law school, I was fortunate enough, as I was in my college days, to fall under the influence of men of ideals who helped to shape my course; and when but a young man, not out of college yet, I was guided to the selection of one who, for twenty-four years, has been my faithful helpmate. No presidential victory could have brought her to me, and no defeat can take her from me. I have been blessed with a family. Our children are with us to make glad the declining years of their mother and myself. When you first knew me, they called me, in derision, "The Boy Orator of the Platte." I have outlived that title, and my grandchildren are now growing up about me. I repeat, that I have been fortunate, indeed. I have been abundantly rewarded for what little I have been able to do, and my ambition is not so much to hold any office, however great, as it is to know my duty and to do it, whether in public life or as a private citizen.

From concluding speech, campaign of 1908.

In the Minority

One can afford to be in a minority, but he can not afford to be wrong; if he is in a minority and right, he will some day be in the majority. If he is in the majority and wrong, he will some day be in the minority.

From "The Price of a Soul."

How Much Can You Earn?

Not only do I believe that a man can earn five hundred millions, but I believe that men have earned it. I believe that Thomas Jefferson earned more than five hundred millions. The service that he rendered to the world was of such great value that had he collected for it five hundred millions of dollars, he would not have been overpaid. I believe that Abraham Lincoln earned more than five hundred millions, and I could go back through history and give you the name of man after man who rendered a service so large as to entitle him to collect more than five hundred millions from society—inventors, discoverers, and those who have launched great economic, educational and ethical reforms. But if I presented a list containing the name of every man, who, since time began, earned such an enormous sum, one thing would be true of all of them, namely: That in not a single case did the man collect the full amount. The men who have earned five hundred million dollars have been so busy earning it that they have not had time to collect it; and the men who have collected five hundred millions have been so busy collecting it that they have not had time to earn it.

From "The Price of A Soul."

FUNERAL ORATION

If the Father deigns to touch with Divine power the cold and pulseless heart of the buried acorn, and make it burst forth from its prison walls, will He leave neglected the soul of man, who is made in the image of his Creator?

If He gives to the rose bush, whose withered blossom floats upon the breeze, the sweet assurance of another springtime, will He withhold the words of hope from the sons of man, when the frosts of winter come?

If matter, mute and inanimate, though changed by the force of nature into a multitude of forms, can never die, will the imperial spirit of man suffer annihilation after a brief sojourn, like a royal guest, in this tenement of clay?

Rather, let us believe that He, who in His apparent prodigality. wastes not the raindrop, the blade of grass or the evening's sighing zephyr, but makes them all to carry out His eternal plan, has given immortality to the mortal and gathered to Himself the generous spirit of our friend.   Then, let us look up to Him and say:

"Thy day has come, not gone;

Thy sun has risen, not set;

Thy life is now beyond the reach of change or death,

Oh, gentle soul, hail and farewell."

Funeral Oration delivered by Bryan over the body of a friend.

BY FAITH

Faith is the spiritual extension of the vision; it is the moral sense which reaches out toward the throne of God and takes hold upon those verities which the mind can not grasp.

The great things of the world have been accomplished by men and women who had faith enough to attempt the seemingly impossible and to trust to God to open the way.

Faith is a heart virtue; doubts of the mind will not disturb us if there is faith in the heart.

Faith in the triumph of truth, because it is truth, has ever been an unfailing source of courage and power. Faith leads us to trust the omnipotence of the Ruler of the Universe, and to put God's promises to the test.

Faith is as necessary to the heart of the individual as it is necessary to world-wide peace. What can equal the consolation that comes from reliance upon the care of Him who gives beauty to the lily, food to the fowls of the air, and direction to all?

From "The Fruits of the Tree."

BIBLE THE ONLY TRUE GUIDE

Next to the belief in God I would place the acceptance of the Bible as the word of God. I need not present arguments in its support: its claims have been established—the burden of proof is upon those who reject it. Those who regard it as a man-made

book should be challenged to put their theory to the test. If man
made the Bible, he is, unless he has degenerated, able to make as
good a book today.

Judged by human standards, man is far better prepared to write
a Bible now than he was when our Bible was written. The characters whose words and deeds are recorded in the Bible, were
members of a single race; they lived among the hills of Palestine
in a territory scarcely larger than one of our counties. They did
not have printing presses and they lacked the learning of the
schools; they had no great libraries to consult, no steamboats to
carry them around the world and make them acquainted with the
various centers of ancient civilization; they had no telegraph wires
to bring them the news from the ends of the earth and no newspapers to spread before them each morning the doings of the day
before. Science had not unlocked Nature's door and revealed the
secrets of rocks below and stars above. From what a scantily supplied storehouse of knowledge they had to draw, compared with
the unlimited wealth of information at man's command today! And
yet these Bible characters grappled with every problem that con-
fronts mankind, from the creation of the world to eternal life beyond
the tomb. They have given us a diagram of man's existence from
the cradle to the grave and they have set up warnings at every
dangerous point along the path.

Let the athiests and the materialists produce a better Bible than
ours, if they can. Let them collect the best of their school to be
found among the graduates of universities—as many as they please
and from every land. Let the members of this selected group travel
where they will, consult such libraries as they please, and employ
every modern means of swift communication. Let them glean in
the fields of geology, botany, astronomy, biology and zoology, and
then roam at will wherever science has opened the way; let them
take advantage of all the progress in art and in literature, in oratory

and in history—let them use to the full every instrumentality that is employed in modern civilization. And when they have exhausted every source, let them embody the results of their best intelligence in a book and offer it to the world as a substitute for this Bible of ours. Have they the confidence that the Prophets of Baal had in their God? Will they try? If not, what excuse will they give? Has man fallen from his high estate, so that we can not rightfully expect as much of him now as nineteen centuries ago? Or does the Bible come to us from a source that is higher than man—which?

But our case is even stronger. The opponents of the Bible can not take refuge in the plea that man is retrograding. They loudly proclaim that man has grown and that he is growing still. They boast of a world-wide advance and their claim is founded upon fact. In all matters, except in the science of life, man has made wonderful progress. The mastery of the mind over the forces of nature seems almost complete, so far do we surpass the ancients in harnessing the water, the wind and the lightning.

For ages, the rivers plunged down the mountain-sides and exhausted their energies without any appreciable contribution to man's service; now they are estimated as so many units of horse-power and we find that their fretting and foaming was merely a language which they employed to tell us of their strength and of their willingness to work for us. And, while falling water is becoming each day a larger factor in burden bearing, water, rising in the form of steam, is revolutionizing the transportation methods of the world.

The wind that first whispered its secret of strength to the flapping sail is now turning the wheel at the well.

Lightning, the red demon that, from the dawn of Creation, has been rushing down its zigzag path through the clouds, as if intent only upon spreading death, having been metamorphosed into an errand boy, brings us illumination from the sun and carries our messages around the globe.

Inventive genius has multiplied the power of the human arm and supplied the masses with comforts of which the rich did not dare to dream a few centuries ago. Science is ferreting out the hidden causes of disease and teaching us how to prolong life. In every line, except in the line of character-building, the world seems to have been made over, but the marvelous changes by which old things have become new only emphasize the fact that man, too, must be born again, while they show how impotent are material things to touch the soul of man and transform him into a spiritual being. Wherever the moral standard is being lifted up—wherever life is becoming larger in the vision that directs it and richer in its fruitage, the improvement is traceable to the Bible and to the influence of the God and Christ of whom the Bible tells.

The atheist and the materialist must confess that man ought to be able to produce a better book today than man, unaided, could have produced in any previous age. The fact that they have tried, time and time again, only to fail each time more hopelessly, explains why they will not—why they can not—accept the challenge thrown down by the Christian world to produce a book worthy to take the Bible's place.

They have prayed to their God to answer with fire—prayed to inanimate matter with an earnestness that is pathetic—and they have employed in the worship of blind force a faith greater than religion requires, but their almighty is asleep. How long will they allow the search for the strata of stone and fragments of fossil and decaying skeletons that are strewn around the house to absorb their thoughts to the exclusion of the Architect who planned it all? How long will the agnostic, closing his eyes to the plainest truths, cry "night, night," when the sun in his meridian's splendor announces that the noon is here?

To the young man who is building character I present the Bible as a book that is useful always and everywhere. It guides the footsteps of the young; it throws a light upon the pathway during the mature years, and it is the only book that one cares to have beside him when the darkness gathers and he knows that the end is near. Then he finds consolation in the promises of the Book of Books and his lips repeat, even when his words are inaudible, "Yea, though I walk through the valley of the shadow of death, I shall fear no evil, for Thou art with me, Thy rod and Thy staff, they comfort me," or "I go to prepare a place for you," that "where I am, there ye may be also."

From "The Making of a Man."

They Make It Hard For Others

The immoral church member who borrows his habits from the outside world, and the moral man outside the church who borrows his virtues from the church, are stumbling blocks only because their inconsistencies are not clearly understood by the unconverted.

From "The Fruits of the Tree."

To the Flag

That is the most beautiful flag that kisses the breezes today. If you have ever had a chance to compare that flag with other flags, you will agree with me that no flag that floats is so pleasing to the eye. Not only does it gratify the artistic sense, not only is it beautiful in its combinations and arrangements of colors, but it possesses a significance that adds to its charms.

The white indicates the purity of the nation's purpose, the red the blood that has been shed in the nation's defense, and that will be shed if the principles for which the flag stands are ever assailed; the stars represent each one a state, and the last Fourth of July an additional star was added to the sky of blue—forty-six now. It represents an indissoluble union of indestructible states, and in that flag there is presented that idea of government which combines national sovereignty with the preservation of local self-government, the greatest idea of government that has been presented since the original idea of self-government was enunciated; that idea of separate communities, independent in their local affairs and yet united in matters of national importance, that idea is the safety of our republic.

There is no area of territory too large for a republic like that. Preserve the idea of the state taking care of its domestic affairs, and the united representation of the states acting together, and you can spread the idea indefinitely; but without these two ideas both preserved, a great republic is impossible. Our flag, therefore, is not only beautiful, but it contains a thought that will never die.

Flag-raising at Omaha, July 26, 1908.

Beware Imperialism

The fruits of imperialism, be they bitter or sweet, must be left to the subjects of monarchy. This is the one tree of which citizens of a republic may not partake. It is the voice of the serpent, not the voice of God, that bids us eat.

From "Naboth's Vineyard."

We Need Moses

Shame upon a logic which locks up the petty offender and enthrones grand larceny. Have the people returned to the worship of the Golden Calf? Have they made unto themselves a new commandment consistent with the spirit of conquest and lust for empire? Is "thou shalt not steal upon a small scale" to be substituted for the law of Moses?

Awake, O ancient law-giver, awake! Break forth from thine unmarked sepulchre and speed thee back to cloud-crowned Sinai; commune once more with the God of our fathers and proclaim again the words engraven upon the tables of stone—the law that was, the law that is today—the law that neither individual nor nation can violate with impunity!

From Speech on Imperialism.

DOWN WITH PLUTOCRACY

Plutocracy is abhorrent to a republic; it is more despotic than monarchy, more heartless than aristocracy, more selfish than bureaucracy. It preys upon the nation in time of peace and conspires against it in the hour of its calamity. Conscienceless, compassionless and devoid of wisdom, it enervates its votaries while it impoverishes its victims.

From Speech on Imperialism.

THE MYSTERY OF THE RADISH

Did you ever raise a radish? You put a small black seed into the black soil and in a little while you return to the garden and find the full-grown radish. The top is green, the body white and almost transparent, and the skin a delicate red or pink. What mysterious power reaches out and gathers from the ground the particles which give it form and size and flavor? Whose is the invisible brush that transfers to the root, growing in darkness, the hues of the summer sunset? If we were to refuse to eat anything until we could understand the mystery of its creation we would die of starvation—but mystery, it seems, never bothers us in the dining room; it is only in the church that it causes us to hesitate.

From "The Value of an Ideal."

CONVERSION DOESN'T TAKE LONG

Conversion, as I understand it, is surrender of one's self to God—obedience to the first commandment. It is putting the kingdom of God and His righteousness first. And how long does it take to be converted? Not longer, I rejoice to believe, than it does to reject God. It does not take longer to be converted to righteousness than to be converted to sin. It takes but an instant for an honest man to be converted into a thief—just the instant in which he decides to steal. It takes just an instant for a law-abiding man to become a murderer. And so it takes but an instant for the heart to surrender itself to its Maker and pledge obedience to God. A man may spend weeks weighing the question before deciding to steal, but the decision to steal is made in a moment; a man may harbor revenge for months and brood over a real or imagined wrong, but the decision is made in a moment. And so a man may consider for years whether he will change his course, but it takes but a moment to resolve "I will arise and go to my Father."

From "The First Commandment."

INDIVIDUAL IS LIKE JAPANESE VASE

Of all the artistic work done in Japan, the cloisonné ware pleases me most—possibly because it so perfectly illustrates the process of development through which we all pass.

There is first the vase, then the tracing of the design upon it, then the filling in of the colors, and, finally, the polishing that brings out the beauty.

And so with the individual. There is first the basic material of body and mind, then comes the selection of the ideals that control the life. Then follows the filling in of the moral qualities that give tone and color, and, finally, the polish that comes with education and experience. All these are necessary to the finished product.

Speech at Keio College, Tokio, in 1905.

FRIENDLY NEIGHBORS

The Lord has made us neighbors; let justice make us friends.

Motto suggested for Pan-American Union.

INTERNATIONAL BANYAN TREE

In the procession which escorted President-elect Palma to his home when he returned from exile, a number of Cuban ladies represented the republics of the western hemisphere, the United States being the eldest, Cuba the youngest of the group. It reminded me of the great banyan tree under which our party rested for a moment as we passed through Key West; for are not these republics much like the banyan tree? Free government was planted upon American soil a century and a quarter ago; it grew and sent forth its influence like branches in every direction, and these branches taking root now support the parent tree; beneath the influence of these republics, separate in their government and yet united in their aspirations, an ever-increasing multitude finds shelter and protection. Long live the international banyan tree—the American Republics!

From "Birth of the Cuban Republic."

DRY TRIUMVIRATE

The Christian has three reasons for abstaining from the use of intoxicating liquors as a beverage, and the reasons ought to appeal to those outside of the church.

First: Having given himself in service to his Maker and his Saviour, the Christian can not afford to impair the value of that service by the use of alcohol. Neither can be afford to contract a habit which may in his case, as it has in the case of millions of others, destroy both the capacity and the disposition to serve.

Second: He can not afford to spend any money on intoxicating liquor when there are so many worthy causes in need of funds. How can a Christian pray "Thy will be done," and rise up and spend on alcohol money that might then be used to advance God's kingdom on earth?

Third: The Christian can not afford to put his example on the side of the use of intoxicating liquor. He will have enough to answer for before the judgment day without having a soul, ruined by drink, lay the blame upon his example. If Paul could say, "If eating meat maketh my brother to offend I shall eat no meat," surely the Christian can say: "If drinking maketh my brother to offend, I shall not drink."

From Total Abstinence Speech, New York, 1915.

FOR NEW YEAR'S EVE

Conscious of my responsibility to God for every thought and word and deed, and in duty bound to render to my fellowmen the largest possible service as the best evidence of my love for my Heavenly Father, I resolve to strive during the remainder of my life to increase my capacity for usefulness. To this end I will give up any practice or habit that tends to weaken my body, impair the strength of my mind or lower my moral purpose, and I will not only endeavor to cultivate habits of industry in both body and mind but will seek and follow worthy ideals.

From Total Abstinence Speech, New York, 1915.

ON WATER, IN WATER

At the Togo reception at Tokio, 1905, Mr. Bryan declined an admiral's suggestion that he drink champagne, by drinking the admiral's health in water in these words:

"You won your victories on water and I drink to your health in water; whenever you win any victories on champagne I shall drink to your health in champagne."

TO LABOR

Can the rosebud, blooming in beauty, despise the roots of the bush through which it draws its lifeblood from the soil? As little can those in the parlor and the drawing-room afford to forget the

After Resignation—Taken following disagreement over Lusitania note which caused Bryan's withdrawal from Wilson's cabinet.

Dry Leader—Bryan holding cup presented by the National Dry Federation of which he was president in 1919. Insert—A cartoon, "A moon of oratorical silver over a dry, dry desert," by the Rev. Branford Clark artist-evangelist.

men and women who toil in the kitchen, field and factory that the world may have food and clothing.

Said in New York in late '90's.

WAR ON ALCOHOL

I do not agree with those who fear attack from abroad, but there is one kind of preparation in which I am willing to join. If this nation ever goes to war, its supreme need will be men—men whose brains are clear, men whose nerves are steady, men who have no appetite to rob them of their love of country in their nation's crucial hour. Let us unite and drive alcohol out of the United States; then, if war comes, every American can render the maximum of service to his country. And, if war does not come, this kind of preparation can be used in the arts of peace.

From 1916 Prohibition Speech.

WOMAN SUFFRAGE

The strongest argument in favor of woman suffrage is the mother argument. I love my children—as much, I think, as a father can; but I am not in the same class with my wife. I do not put any father in the same class with the mother in love for the child. If you would know why the mother's love for a child is the sweetest, tenderest, most lasting thing in the world, you will find the explanation in the Bible: "Where your treasures are there will your heart be also."

The child is the treasure of the mother; she invests her life in her child. When the mother of the Gracchi was asked: "Where are your jewels?" she pointed to her sons. The mother's life trembles in the balance at the child's birth, and for years it is the object of her constant care. She expends upon it her nervous force and energy; she endows it with the wealth of her love. She dreams of what it is to do and be—and, O, if a mother's dreams only came true, what a different world this world would be! The most pathetic struggle that this earth knows is not the struggle between armed men upon the battlefield; it is the struggle of a mother to save her child when wicked men set traps for it and lay snares for it. And as long as the ballot is given to those who conspire to rob the home of a child it is not fair—no one can believe it fair to tie a mother's hands while she is trying to protect her home and save her child. If there is such a thing as justice, surely a mother has a just claim to a voice in shaping the environment that may determine whether her child will realize her hopes or bring her gray hairs in sorrow to the grave.

Because God has planted in every human heart a sense of justice, and because the mother argument makes an irresistible appeal to this universal sense, it will finally batter down all opposition and open woman's pathway to the polls.

From Washington Banquet Speech, 1916.

WIFE SHOULD VOTE

The wife is the husband's partner in the finances of the family—she helps him to lay away money for a rainy day.

The wife is the husband's partner in the raising of the family—she has the care of the body, the mind and the soul of the child.

The wife is the husband's partner in all his plans and aspirations —no one so loyal and faithful as she. Why should she not be his partner at the polls?

From a 1916 Campaign Speech.

EDUCATION

In this day of increasing education the father who denies to his son the advantages of the schools, and sends him out half educated to compete with the boys well educated, is more cruel than the father who would cut off a son's arm. Loss of an arm is not nearly so great a handicap as lack of education.

From Speech on "Education."

Yes and No

We have found many curious things in this country, but Mrs. Bryan and I have been especially interested in what they call the "Korean Lions." I do not know whether other Americans have been impressed by these, but we shall take two Korean lions home with us (if we can secure a pair) and put them as a guard in front of our house. The Korean lions are interesting for several reasons, and one of the most important is that they represent the affirmative and the negative. I noticed today that one of them had his mouth open as though he were saying "yes," and the other had his mouth tightly closed as if he had just said "no." Both the affirmative and the negative are necessary. You find everywhere the radical and the conservative. Both are essential in a progressive state. The conservative is necessary to keep the radical from going too fast, and the radical is necessary to make the conservative go at all. One is as necessary to the welfare of the nation as the other. There must be a party in power, and there must be a party out of power, although I think that, for convenience sake, they ought to change places occasionally. When a party goes into power it is apt to be more conservative than when out of power, and when a party goes out of power it is likely to become more radical. I might give a number of reasons for it. In the first place, responsibility tends to make a party more deliberate—it sobers it. Then, too, a party that is defeated often learns from the victor how to win, and sometimes the successful party learns from the defeated one.

From speech at Ambassador's dinner in Tokio.

Need Elijah

We need more Elijahs in the pulpit today—more men who will dare to upbraid an Ahab and defy a Jezebel. It is possible, aye, probable, that even now, as of old, persecution would follow such boldness of speech, but he who consecrates himself to religion must smite evil where he finds it, although in smiting it he may risk his salary and his social position. It is easy enough to denounce the petty thief and the back-alley gambler; it is easy enough to condemn the friendless rogue and the penniless wrong-doer, but what about the rich tax-dodger, the big law-breaker and the corrupter of government? The soul that is warmed by Divine fire will be satisfied with nothing less than the complete performance of duty; it must cry aloud and spare not, to the end that the creed of the Christ may be exemplified in the life of the nation.

From "The Price of a Soul."

How Much?

How much can a man rightfully collect from society?

Not more than he honestly earns. If he collects more than he earns he collects what some one else has earned—something to which he is not entitled.

And how much can a man honestly earn? Not more than fairly measures the value of the service that he renders to society. One cannot earn money without giving an equivalent service in return. That each individual member of society is entitled to draw from the common store in proportion as he contributes to the common welfare is the most fundamental of economic laws. He suffers injustice if he is denied this; he does injustice if he secures more.

From "A Conquering Nation."

Destiny

Destiny is not a matter of chance; it is a matter of choice. It is not a thing to be waited for, it is a thing to be achieved.

Man's opinion of what is to be is half wish and half environment. Avarice paints destiny with a dollar mark before it; militarism equips it with a sword.

From "America's Mission."

RICH AND DEPENDENT

We speak of people being independently rich. That is a mistake; they are dependently rich. The richer a man is the more dependent he is—the more people he depends upon to help him collect his income, and the more people he depends upon to help him spend his income.

From "The Price of a Soul."

CONSIDER THE HOG

I am indebted to some hogs for one illustration. I was riding through Iowa, back in the nineties, and saw some hogs rooting in a meadow near the railway track. The first thought that came to me was that the hogs were doing a great deal of damage and this recalled our practice, when I lived on the farm, of putting a ring in the hog's nose. The purpose was not to keep the hog from getting fat; we were more interested in its getting fat than it was. The more quickly it fattened, the sooner it died; the longer it was getting fat, the longer it lived.

Why was the ring put in the hog's nose? For the simple purpose of keeping it from destroying more than it was worth, while it was getting fat. This practice suggested to me that one of the purposes of government is to put a ring in the nose of the human hog. I do not mean to use the language in an offensive sense, but we are all more or less hoggish. In the hours of temptation we are likely to trespass on the rights of others. Society is interested in each individual's success, but a man must not be allowed to destroy more than he is worth while he is getting rich. Civilization is possible, because man, in his sober moments, is willing to put restraints upon all, including himself, to protect society from human selfishness.

Said at Anti-Trust Conference in Chicago in 1899.

BRICKS AND EDUCATION

A single brick is a useless thing, but many bricks joined together by mortar make a wall, and a wall is of great value. So one lesson seems of little importance, but many lessons, joined together, make an education, and an education is priceless. And, as one brick taken out of a wall leaves an ugly hole, so one lesson missed mars the beauty and strength of the education.

From Speech on "Education."

HE KEPT THE FAITH

Eight years ago a Democratic national convention placed in my hand the standard of the party and commissioned me as its candidate. Four years later that commission was renewed. I come to-night to this Democratic national convention to return the commission. You may dispute whether I have fought a good fight, you may dispute whether I have finished my course, but you can not deny that I have kept the faith.

From St. Louis Convention Speech, 1904.

HIS APPEAL

And I close with an appeal from my heart to the hearts of those who hear me: Give us a pilot who will guide the Democratic ship away from the Scylla of militarism without wrecking her upon the Charybdis of commercialism.

From St. Louis Convention Speech, 1904.

DEMOCRACY

The Democratic party has led this fight until it has stimulated a host of Republicans to action. I will not say they have acted as they have because we acted first; I will say that at a later hour than we, they caught the spirit of the times and are now willing to trust the people with the control of their own government.

We have been traveling in the wilderness; we now come in sight of the promised land. During all the weary hours of darkness progressive Democracy has been the people's pillar of fire by night; I pray you, delegates, now that the dawn has come, do not rob it of its well-earned right to be the people's pillar of cloud by day.

From a Speech at the Baltimore Convention, 1912.

SIN BLACKMAILS SILENTLY

Sin is a silent blackmailer; it hushes the lips that would otherwise speak out against wrongdoing. Even after reformation the fear of exposure haunts the victim and often paralyzes his usefulness.

From a Billy Sunday Meeting.

PHILOSOPHY OF DEFEAT

If we can fight our political battles upon this plane, there is no humiliation in defeat. I have passed through three presidential campaigns, and many have rejoiced over my defeats, but if events prove that my defeats have been good for my country, I shall rejoice over them myself, more than any opponent has rejoiced. And when I say this I am not unselfish, for it is better for me that my political opponents should bring good to my country than that I should, by any mistake of mine, bring evil.

From "The Value of An Ideal."

CHAPTER XIII

Anti-Imperialism

Imperialism the Issue of 1900—War with Spain—Offers Services to McKinley—Colonel of 3d Nebraska Volunteers—Resigns Commission After Five Months Service—Declares Position on Imperialism—Bryan and Stevenson Nominated—Whirlwind Campaign—Utterances on the Paramount Issue—Political Defeat—"Imperialism Like Heart Disease; Tariff Just a Stomach Ache."

In the career of William Jennings Bryan, the year 1900 and the slogan of anti-imperialism are inseparably joined together. On the question of whether the United States should or should not retain the dominion of the Philippines, which she had won in the war with Spain, turned the fortunes of the next presidential campaign after that of 1896. Bryan declared against the government of foreign colonies by the United States. He lost on this issue in 1900; but again, he was only beaten, not defeated. The policy that he set forth even before the Spanish-American war was justified in the end by his nation.

Though beaten in 1896, Bryan determined to stay in politics. He loved the game; he felt that he must continue in the leadership which his party had bestowed upon him and which it now looked to him to carry on. So instead of re-entering law practice in Lincoln, he turned to lecturing and writing as a means of livelihood. This kept his name and opinions before the voters but he could easily turn aside when the demands of politics required.

On the day that war was declared against Spain, political differences were set aside and Bryan sent a telegram to President McKinley offering his services. He wired:

"Hon. William McKinley, President,

"My Dear Sir: I hereby place my services at your command

188

during the war with Spain and assure you of my willingness to perform, to the best of my ability, any duty which you, as the Commander-in-Chief of the army and navy, may see fit to assign me.

"Respectfully yours,

"W. J. BRYAN."

A short time later Governor Holcomb of Nebraska requested Bryan to raise a regiment; Bryan accepted, and became colonel of the 3d Nebraska volunteer infantry. Like other notable men with war-won titles, Bryan retained the title of "Colonel" throughout his life. It was his service in the war with Spain which gave him the right on his death to be buried in Arlington National cemetery. The 3d Nebraska under Bryan saw no active fighting; like many other regiments, they found that their battle was one against disease in a Florida training camp. They were encamped at Jacksonville, Fla., at Pablo Beach, Fla., and at Savannah, Ga. During his five months of military life Bryan himself suffered from malaria and passed safely through a mild attack of typhoid. In December, after the cessation of hostilities, and when the terms of the treaty had been agreed upon, Bryan forwarded the resignation of his commission, declaring that he believed that "under present conditions, I can be more useful to my country as a civilian than as a soldier." With expressions of praise and regret from his superior officers, Bryan was allowed to leave the army.

The usefulness to his country to which Bryan referred, turned out to be the leadership of the fight against imperialism. It was a fight against the national spirit of conquest and subjugation stirred up by the war. Bryan was the first great political leader to take a definite stand against this war-born tide.

He had marked out his position definitely from the very first. Even while raising his regiment, he spoke against the policy of annexing the Philippines. The political map of the country underwent some changes on the imperialism issue. In the east Bryan made gains, for many of the political leaders who were against him there on the question of free silver now found themselves beside him on anti-imperialism. The central states and the west, the west especially, were in favor of annexation, and many of the western states returned to the Republican fold which they had left through the split over bimetalism. His own party was hardly with Bryan on the question of imperialism. Yet with characteristic courage he openly stated his position, refusing to trim his sails to the popular post-war sentiment. How well he succeeded in turning the Democratic party toward his way of thinking may be shown by an inspection of the Democratic platforms of 1900, 1904, 1908 and 1912. Every one of them contains an anti-imperialism plank written in through Bryan's influence. How well he prophesied the trend of national thought was proved later when Congress declared the right of the Philippines to self-government and eventual independence.

"Our nation is in greater danger now than is Cuba," said Bryan after the resignation of his military command. "The imperialistic idea is directly antagonistic to the ideas and ideals which have been cherished by the American people since the signing of the Declaration of Independence. A nation can not endure half republic and half colony. It would be easier to ratify the treaty and deal with the question in our own way. The issue can be presented directly by a resolution of Congress declaring the policy of the nation upon this subject. Such a resolution would make a clear-cut issue between the doctrine of self-government and the doctrine of imperialism."

With the paramount issue defined, Bryan was nominated unanimously at the Kansas City convention. His running mate on the ticket was Adlai E. Stevenson of Illinois, Vice-President during Cleveland's second administration. Then followed another whirlwind speaking trip covering the country from one end to the other.

It was not as sensational as the first tour, but it was a spectacular trip, well enough.

With McKinley and Roosevelt the Republican candidates, the Republican party was almost solidly in favor of keeping the Philippines.

Bryan declared: "I want to know whether the mothers of this land have no higher ambition for their sons than to raise them up and send them across the seas to fight the ideas of freedom in a foreign land, in order that somebody may get railroad franchises?"

There was much criticism directed at Bryan for the seeming inconsistency between his stand against imperialism and the fact that he had approved ratification of the treaty with Spain, giving the United States the Philippines. He made answer to these attacks in his speech accepting the 1900 nomination:

"In view of the criticism which my action aroused in some quarters, I take this occasion to re-state the reasons given at that time. I thought it safer to trust the American people to give independence to the Filipinos than to trust the accomplishment of that purpose to diplomacy with an unfriendly nation.

"Lincoln embodied an argument in the question when he asked, 'Can aliens make treaties easier than friends can make laws?' I believe that we are now in a better position to wage a successful contest against imperialism than we would have been had the treaty been rejected. With the treaty ratified a clean-cut issue is presented between a government by consent and a government by force, and imperialists must bear the responsibility for all that happens until the question is settled.

"If the treaty had been rejected the opponents of imperialism would have been held responsible for any international complications which might have arisen before the ratification of another treaty. But whatever difference of opinion may have existed as to the best method of opposing a colonial policy, there never was any difference as to the great importance of the question and there is no difference now as to the course to be pursued.

"The title of Spain being extinguished, we were at liberty to deal with the Filipinos according to American principles. The Bacon resolution, introduced a month before hostilities broke out at Manila, promised independence to the Filipinos on the same terms that it was promised to the Cubans. I supported this resolution and believed that its adoption prior to the breaking out of hostilities would have prevented bloodshed, and that its adoption at any subsequent time would have ended hostilities.

"If the treaty had been rejected considerable time would have necessarily elapsed before a new treaty could have been agreed upon and ratified, and during that time the question would have been agitating the public mind. If the Bacon resolution had been adopted by the Senate and carried out by the President, either at the time of ratification of the treaty or at any time afterwards, it would have taken the question of imperialism out of politics and left the American people free to deal with their domestic problems. But the resolution was defeated by the vote of the Republican Vice-President, and from that time to this a Republican Congress has refused to take any action whatever in the matter."

In other utterances he repeated his axiom that no nation could exist, part republic and part colonial empire:

"Behold a republic in which civil and religious liberty stimulate all to earnest endeavor, and in which the law restrains every hand uplifted for a neighbor's injury—a republic in which every citizen is sovereign, but in which no one cares to wear a crown.

"Behold a republic standing erect, while empires all around are bowed beneath the weight of their own armaments—a republic whose flag is loved, while other flags are only feared.

"Behold a republic increasing in population, in wealth, in strength and in influence, solving the problems of civilization and hastening the coming of a universal brotherhood—a republic which shakes thrones and dissolves aristocracies by its silent example, and gives light and inspiration to those who sit in darkness.

"Behold a republic. gradually but surely becoming the supreme moral factor in the world's progress and the accepted arbiter of the world's disputes—a republic whose history, like the path of the just, 'is as the shining light that shineth more and more unto the perfect day.' "

And: "History is replete with predictions which once wore the hue of destiny, but which failed of fulfilment because those who uttered them saw too small an arc of the circle of events. When Pharaoh pursued the fleeing Israelites to the edge of the Red sea he was confident that their bondage would be renewed, and that they would again make bricks without straw, but destiny was not revealed until Moses and his followers reached the farther shore dry shod and the waves rolled over the horses and chariots of the Egyptians. When Belshazzar, on the last night of his reign, led his thousand lords into the Babylonian banquet hall and sat down to a table glittering with vessels of silver and gold, he felt sure of his kingdom for many years to come, but destiny was not revealed until the hand wrote upon the wall those awe-inspiring words, 'Mene Mene, Tekel Upharsin.' When Abderrahman swept northward with his conquering hosts his imagination saw the Crescent triumphant throughout the world, but destiny was not revealed until Charles Martel raised the Cross above the battlefield of Tours and saved Europe from the sword of Mohammedanism. When Napoleon emerged victorious from Marengo, from Ulm and from Austerlitz, he thought himself the child of destiny, but destiny was not revealed until Blücher's forces joined the army of Wellington and the vanquished Corsican began his melancholy march toward St. Helena. When the red-coats of George the Third routed the New Englanders at Lexington and Bunker Hill there arose before the British sov-

ereign visions of colonies taxed without representation and drained
of their wealth by foreign-made laws, but destiny was not revealed
until the surrrender of Cornwallis completed the work begun at
Independence Hall, and ushered into existence a government deriving its just powers from the consent of the governed."

He told, too, how Christianity and imperialism conflicted one
with the other:

"If true Christianity consists in carrying out in our daily lives
the teachings of Christ, who will say that we are commanded to
civilize with dynamite and proselyte with the sword? He who
would declare the Divine will must prove his authority either by
Holy Writ or by evidence of a special dispensation.

"Imperialism finds no warrant in the Bible. The command, 'Go
ye into all the world and preach the gospel to every creature,' has
no Gatling gun attachment. When Jesus visited a village of Samaria
and the people refused to receive him, some of the disciples suggested that fire should be called down from Heaven to avenge the
insult; but the Master rebuked them and said: 'Ye know not what
manner of spirit ye are of; for the Son of Man is not come to
destroy men's lives, but to save them.' Suppose he had said: 'We
will thrash them until they understand who we are,' how different
would have been the history of Christianity! Compare, if you will,
the swaggering, bullying, brutal doctrine of imperialism with the
golden rule and the commandment, 'Thou shalt love thy neighbor
as thyself.'

"Love, not force, was the weapon of the Nazarene; sacrifice for
others, not the exploitation of them, was His method of reaching
the human heart. A missionary recently told me that the Stars
and Stripes once saved his life because his assailant recognized our
flag as a flag that had no blood upon it.

"Let it be known that our missionaries are seeking souls instead
of sovereignty; let it be known that instead of being the advance

guard of conquering armies, they are going forth to help and uplift, having their loins girt about with truth and their feet shod with the preparation of the gospel peace, wearing the breastplate of righteousness and carrying the sword of the spirit; let it be known that they are citizens of a nation which respects the rights of the citizens of other nations as carefully as it protects the rights of its own citizens, and the welcome given to our missionaries will be more cordial than the welcome extended to the missionaries of any other nation."

But Bryan's stand on imperialism was not to bring him political victory. The campaign of 1900 ended in defeat. McKinley polled 7,207,923 popular votes against Bryan's 6,358,133—very little change from the popular vote of four years before. The electoral vote was 292 for McKinley against 155 for Bryan.

But again, in defeat, Bryan, the fighter, kept his courage. Not in the loftier vein of his formal speeches, but in an interview with a newspaper correspondent and in whimsical, every day language, he declared:

"Imperialism is still the most important question before the people. It is like an attack of heart disease, while the tariff question can be compared to the stomach ache, which is uncomfortable, but not vital."

CHAPTER XIV

The Commoner

At the turn of the century, in the month of January, 1901, William Jennings Bryan established a weekly publication, The Commoner, in Lincoln.   He had been chief of the editorial staff of
the Omaha World-Herald; he had reported the Republican convention of 1896 in St. Louis for the paper; he had been a special
writer for newspaper syndicates.   And now he became a publisher.

The paper grew and was circulated all over the United States.
Daily journals watched its editorial comment.   Frequently, in the
midst of some vivid issue in which Bryan was interested, the newspapers of the country would carry, in their news columns, a story
to the effect that "tomorrow The Commoner will say" thus or so.

For releases of Bryan's editorials were given to the press the
night preceding their actual appearance.

For twenty-two years The Commoner was a significant figure
in both the publication and the political world.   It was founded
by Bryan, and he was virtually always its editorial writer.   But
his brother, ex-Governor Charles Bryan of Nebraska, was for
many years its managing director.   Outside duties grew so mani-
fold and pressed down so heavily on the brothers that Charles
Bryan, on the 20th of April, 1923, announced that the monthly
paper would cease publication with the April issue.

Commoner and Evangelist—Bryan meets and chats with Billy Sunday.
The two were always warm friends and mutual admirers.

Onward, Christian Soldiers—Bryan addressing some 15,000 delegates to the Sixth World Christian Endeavor Convention, July 9 1921. The picture was taken in Central park, New York, following the delegates' giant parade up Fifth avenue.

But The Commoner was more than a journal issued so many times a year and read by many. It was a concrete evidence of those attributes in William Jennings Bryan which won for him the name, the "Great Commoner." Its very name reflected one of the big, motivating forces in the life of its founder.

Even in the administration of the paper, the attributes of the Commoner were manifest. The western advertising manager for the publication was wont to mourn over the beggarly two or three columns of advertising carried by an influential paper with a large circulation.

The answer was that Bryan refused to divorce editorial responsibility from advertising income. He felt, nay he insisted, that no advertisement should appear in the paper, for which the editors could not vouch, morally, as well as every other way.

In another way, too, the administration of the affairs of the paper exemplified the characteristics of its editor and founder.

Though Bryan seldom went to the newspaper office and did most of his writing in his study at home, he had a strict office rule, and that was that there must be an eight hour day for everyone. Paradoxically enough, some rebelled at this. Once, the assistant editor, a former daily newspaper man, growled and fussed, at a great rate, all because "the boss" wouldn't let him follow his accustomed schedule of many more hours than eight.

Once a year the entire force was taken out on an all-day picnic. And it wasn't "Mr. Bryan, the editor," it was "Will" Bryan, the good fellow. He ran in the races; he climbed the greased pole. Or, as a faithful reporter records, "he tried to." And, with still something of that college boy agility which used to distinguish him in the broad jump, Bryan would play baseball and play it well.

Of course he knew every man and woman connected with the publication of the paper. He knew pretty nearly everybody in Lincoln, they say.

Bryan had a wonderful memory for names and for faces. Nor did he neglect that talent as soon as a campaign was over. He was the commoner, not the politician, in his pursuit of friends.

One day about this time he was watching a crowd of workingmen busy on the construction of a house which was being built by his old friend, Judge Tibbetts. Bryan called each man by name. Presently he noticed a man digging for the cellar foundation.

"There's a man I don't know," the Commoner remarked to Judge Tibbetts, "Who is he?"

The judge told him.

"I'd like to meet him," Bryan continued. And the judge brought about an immediate introduction.

A few years later, in his Labor Day speech of 1908, which he delivered in Chicago, he explained his reasons for naming his paper as he did, and his belief that "we're all, or nearly all, in the same class."

"The effort of the Democratic party, my friends," he said, "is to protect the rights and guard the interests of the average man. I want to remind you that we're all, or nearly all, in the same class. When I gave my paper the name 'Commoner,' the Republicans made fun of it and said it was reflecting on the people to call them the common people. Yet the fact is that the highest compliment ever paid to any one was to the common people. When Christ was on earth preaching to men the Bible says the 'common people heard Him gladly.'

"Just a few can claim to be out of the ranks of the common people. The uncommon people are not so numerous as they think they are and not nearly so important. Lincoln said God must have loved the common people because He made so many of them.

"I have no fear of the future because the kindness of my countrymen has given me an advantage that places me above want. But why should I be less interested in the welfare of others just because

I happen to be beyond the fear of want. It was not my fault that my father was able to send me to school where he had to school himself. And when I was in college I used to envy those who worked their way through. I wondered if I could do as well as that. My father worked hard for the little he got in this life, yet I would rather have the blood of that father in my veins than the blood of the proudest nobleman of Europe."

And in another speech in which he outlined his ideas of the ethics of accumulation in this world, he had this to say:

"In this country, more than anywhere else in the world, we appreciate the dignity of labor and understand that it is honorable to serve. And yet there is room for improvement, for all over our land there are, scattered here and there, young men and young women—and even parents—who still think that it is more respectable for a young man to spend in idleness the money someone else has earned than to be himself a producer of wealth. And as long as this sentiment is to be found anywhere, there is educational work to be done, for public opinion will never be what it ought to be until it puts the badge of disgrace upon the idler, no matter how rich he may be, rather than upon the man who with brain or muscle contributes to the nation's wealth, the nation's strength and the nation's progress. But, as I said, the inheritance is an apparent, not an actual, exception, and we will return to the original proposition—that one's earnings must be measured by the service rendered."

Bryan did more than talk about being a commoner; more even than acting the part of one. He looked like one. Why, they are still telling the story, in Chicago, of the day he got into town, a delegate to the Democratic convention of 1896. He went to one of the downtown hotels and he was so plainly dressed that the clerk, after taking one look at him, requested him to pay in advance.

And then, the yarn goes, they put him in a room with seven Republicans.

Bryan had a democratic mind. He didn't care for what he called "intellectual snobbishness." The newest things in the drama, in poetry, in the opera or any of the other arts, didn't appeal to him.

What was good enough for the common man was good enough for him. He read Emerson and Longfellow where he left uncut, perhaps, the pages of Nietzsche, Schopenhauer and Ibsen.

It was the same with clubs. Bryan knew everybody; Bryan liked to make new friends. Meeting people was never a task for him. And yet, back in Lincoln, he preferred the Farmers' club to the Country club. The Country club, he argued, was of no interest to him. He'd rather raise potatoes than drive a golf ball over the fairway. Besides, the Country club had a bar, and he didn't approve of that.

So the Farmers' club it was. It was an old-fashioned organization, holding monthly meetings during the winter at the homes of its members. They'd come in the morning, mother, father, all the children, and maybe an aunt or two. And they'd stay all day. Each family brought its own lunch basket, filled with the best things the best cooks could make. After dinner the women would retire to the kitchen and do the dishes. The men would sit in the "front room," smoke and talk.

Dishes over with, the women came in, took out their sewing and discussed household problems.

The Bryans went to these meetings and every once in so often the Farmers' club held its meeting at the home of Mr. and Mrs. Bryan.

One of the favorite stories told in Lincoln, illustrating the characteristics of the Commoner, is the one about Johnny Cole, a trolley car conductor, and his plum pudding.

Johnny Cole, it seems, was a native of Oxfordshire, England, and as he took in the fares and rang the bell up and down the Lincoln streets he thought often of his mother, still over in England.

Just before Bryan started for his trip around the world, Johnny Cole had him as a passenger on the way from Lincoln to his Fairview farm. As Bryan handed him his fare, the conductor, very embarrassed, leaned over and whispered into the Commoner's ear:

"Say, Mr. Bryan, when you get to England would you please look my mother up?"

"Certainly, Johnny," and Bryan already had his pencil and paper waiting to take down her address.

Months later, Bryan slipped away from his London engagements and went out to Oxfordshire. He spent an entire day with Mrs. Cole. When he was going she hesitatingly produced a fat bundle, saying, as she handed it over:

"God bless you, Mr. Bryan, for this visit. My boy writes me you are the greatest man in the world, and I believe him. Would you do a mother a favor, just as you did her son a favor? Would you please take this to Johnny?"

The package contained a plum pudding, a big one.

Mr. Bryan kept the faith with that pudding. He stowed it away in his luggage and, in the course of time, delivered it to the ecstatic trolley car conductor.

Johnny Cole's plum pudding was long preserved under a glass case. Perhaps it still is. At least the story is.

And one more story of the Commoner. This time it took place when he was secretary of state. In Washington he had the same coachman who had been in the employ of many former Secretaries of State. Bryan took an interest in him. A few days before the St. Patrick's Day dinner which the Irish societies of the city were giving, he asked his driver if he were going to attend. He said no.

Bryan, who was going to deliver an address at the banquet, promptly promised to see that the coachman was sent an invitation.

The night of March 17 came around. Bryan went up to the table. The driver was there. More than that, he was on the program. For being a guest of honor, and bearing the name "Barry," which chanced to take alphabetical precedence over every other name that night, the delighted but bewildered coachman found that his name, like Abou Ben Adam's, led all the rest.

CHAPTER XV

Around the World

Bryan may have been in the political background in those years between 1904 and 1908; but he was certainly in the public foreground. He was writing articles; he was making speeches; and he was traveling about the world, dining with potentates, supping with cottagers, and meeting new people every day.

In 1904 Bryan retired temporarily and Alton B. Parker, then Chief Judge of the Court of Appeals of New York State was made the Democratic nominee for President. At the party's convention that year Bryan definitely opposed what he charged was the assembly's conservative attitude in naming Judge Parker.

Out of the main whirl of politics, and with his new farm at Fairview well in order, Bryan, after a year of writing and speech-making, determined to go abroad. Back in 1903 he and his son, William Jennings Bryan, Jr., had gone to Europe and toured something like ten of the countries. This time it was to be a round-the-world jaunt, and he took with him his wife, their son, and their younger daughter, Grace.

With many a cheer sounding, the Bryan party left Fairview on the 21st day of September, 1905, and sailed out of San Francisco the 27th of that month. The fifth of the following September, with many a flag waving and the band playing, they returned to their home town, having circled the globe in just sixteen days less than a year.

The trip couldn't have brought much rest to Bryan; but it gave him many new contacts, many new experiences. As the world traveler, he exemplified three of the titles which his own country had already given him.

As the "Peerless Leader" he enunciated several of his policies: international peace, disarmament, to mention just two, before great bodies in the nation's capitals.

As the "Boy Orator of the Platte" he literally talked his way around the world.

And as the "Great Commoner" he slipped away from important gatherings to chat with a cabby; he ran off to call on the mother of a trolley car conductor; he was never too busy to stop and become acquainted with some humble soul.

The Bryans went first to Japan and China. In Japan it was one long triumph for the man from Nebraska. His speech entitled, "The White Man's Burden," especially delighted the Nipponese, and was highly commended by the Japanese-American society. He and his wife were presented to the Emperor.

In his speech acknowledging the hospitality of the ruler, Bryan, in a rhetorical image that was fanciful, humorous, but still mindful of the 1896 campaign for free silver and the 16 to 1 ratio, said:

"I have been tenderly drawn toward the Emperor of Japan because when His Majesty established the chrysanthemum as the imperial emblem, he drew the flower with sixteen petals, thus giving the highest Oriental sanction to the doctrine of sixteen to one."

It was in Japan that he chose the cloisonné ware as the country's most artistic offering. His reason, he said, might have been tied up with the fact that a cloisonné vase always seemed to him to illustrate the development of man.

"There is first the vase, then the tracing of the design upon it, then the filling in of the colorings, and, finally, the polishing that brings out the beauty."

At a reception in Tokio, when an admiral suggested that he use champagne instead of water to drink a toast, Bryan made his famous reply:

"You won your victories on water and I drink to your health in water; whenever you win any victories in champagne I shall drink your health in champagne."

The incident was told of all over Japan and the National Temperance society presented Bryan with a badge in recognition of his service to the cause.

At the ambassador's dinner in Tokio, Bryan praised the "Korean Lions" for "several reasons and one of the most important is that they represent the affirmative and negative. I noticed today that one of them had his mouth open as though he were saying 'Yes,' and the other had his mouth tightly closed as if he had just said 'No.' Both the affirmative and the negative are necessary. The conservative is necessary to keep the radical from going too fast, and the radical is necessary to make the conservative go at all."

A few days later the Bryans were presented with a pair of the "Korean Lions," which they took home and placed as guards at the portal of their Fairview home.

In China, Bryan collected material for a monograph which he was soon to write, entitled "Letters to a Chinese Official." It was a defense of a Christian civilization, and was an answer to a book, "Letters of a Chinese Official," which he had read several years before and which had aroused his indignation.

Bryan's liberal views on Filipino independence endeared him to the natives in the Philippine Islands. The Moros of Mindanao Island made him a "datto," or chief.

Then on to India, Palestine, all through the Holy Land. The Bryans gathered up pebbles from the Sea of Galilee and carried back a pebble as a remembrance for each member of the congregation of their church at Normal, Nebraska, the town near Lincoln in which Fairview was located.

A sunrise in the Himalayas moved him to this symbolic description:

"But to return to the mountains themselves; the view from Darjeeling is unsurpassed. The Kinchinjunga Peaks rise to a height of 28,156 feet above the sea, or nearly twice as high as Pike's Peak, and although forty-five miles distant, are clear and distinct. The summits, seen above the clouds, seem to have no terrestrial base, but hang as if suspended in mid air. The best view is obtained from Tiger Hill, six miles from Darjeeling at an altitude of 9,000 feet. We made this trip one morning, rising at three o'clock and reaching the observation point a little before sunrise. I wish I were able to convey to the reader the impression made upon us.

"While all about us was yet in darkness, the snowy robe which clothes the upper 12,000 feet of the range, caught a tint of pearl from the first rays of the sun, and, as we watched, the orb of day, rising like a ruby globe from a lake of dark blue mist, gilded peak after peak until at last we saw Mount Everest, earth's loftiest point, one hundred and twenty miles away and nearly a thousand feet higher than Kinchinjunga. We saw the shadows fleeing from the light like hunted culprits and hiding in the deep ravines, and we marked the triumph of the dawn as it swept down the valleys.

"How puny seem the works of man when brought into comparison with majestic nature! His groves, what pigmies when measured against the virgin forest! His noblest temples, how insignificant when contrasted with the masonry of the hills! What canvas can imitate the dawn and sunset! What inlaid work can match the mosaics of the mountains!

"Is it blind chance that gives these glimpses of the sublime? And was it blind chance that clustered vast reservoirs about inaccessible summits and stored water to refresh the thirsty plains through hidden veins and surface streams?

"No wonder man from the beginning of history has turned to the heights for inspiration, for here is the spirit awed by the infinite and here one sees both the mystery of creation and the manifestations of the Father's loving kindness. Here man finds a witness, unimpeachable though silent, to the omnipotence, the omniscience and the goodness of God."

Turkey, Austria-Hungary, Germany, and into all the principal countries of Europe. In Italy, in the Catholic capital, Bryan found much to please him.

"The dominant feature of Rome," he wrote, "is the religious feature, and it is fitting that it should be so, for here the soil was stained with the blood of those who first harkened to the voice of the Nazarene—here a cruel Nero lighted his garden with human torches, little thinking that the religion of those whom he burned would in time illumine the earth."

In Germany a Reichstag custom, which he recommends to the consideration of our own Congress, won his interest.

"In the Reichstag they have resorted to a device for saving time in roll call. Each member is supplied with a quantity of tickets, some pink and some white. Each ticket bears on both sides the name of the member. On the white tickets the word 'Ja' (yes) appears under the name; on the pink ones 'Nein' (no). These ballots are gathered up in vases containing two receptacles, one white and the other pink. The vases are carried through the hall and votes deposited according to color. As they are deposited in the different receptacles and are distinguished by color, the ballot is quickly taken and counted—in about one-fourth the time, I think, formerly required for roll call. This is a method which our Congress might find it convenient to adopt."

Of Switzerland he said, "No wonder it is free. The beauty of the country inspires a love of native land and the mountains form a natural fortress behind which the Swiss people could withstand armies many times the size of their own."

In France, Bryan was impressed with the beauty and the solemn dignity of Napoleon's tomb on the banks of the Seine, adjoining Les Invalides. The scene moved him to an utterance on peace and the Prince of Peace as contrasted with this mighty soldier.

"Looking down upon the sarcophagus," Bryan said, "and the stands of tattered battle flags that surround it, I reviewed the tragic career of this grand master of the art of slaughter, and weighed, as best I could, the claims made for him by his friends. And then I found myself wondering what the harvest might have been had Napoleon's genius led him along peaceful paths, had the soil of Europe been stirred by the ploughshare rather than the trenchant blade, and the reaping done by implements less destructive than his shot and shell.

"Just beyond and above the entombed emperor stands a cross upon which hangs a life-sized figure of the Christ, flooded by a mellow lemon-colored light, which pours through the stained glass windows of the chapel.

"I know not whether it was by accident or design that this god of war thus sleeps, as it were, at the very feet of the Prince of Peace.

"Whether so intended or not, it will to those who accept the teachings of the sermon on the Mount, symbolize love's final victory over force and the triumph of that philosophy which finds happiness in helpful service and in doing good."

Bryan arrived in London on the third of July, 1906. The following day he delivered a Fourth of July speech which was widely quoted in European and American newspapers.

Its concluding paragraph follows:

"On the walls of the temple at Karnak an ancient artist carved the likeness of an Egyptian king; the monarch is represented as holding a group of captives by the hair, the other hand raising a club as if to strike a blow. What king would be willing to confess himself so cruel today? In some of the capitals of Europe there are monuments built of, or ornamented with, cannon taken in war; this form of boasting, once popular, is still tolerated, though it must in time give way to some emblem of victory less suggestive of slaughter. As we are gathered tonight in England's capital, permit me to conclude with a sentiment suggested by a piece of statuary which stands in Windsor Castle. It represents the late lamented Queen Victoria leaning upon her royal consort; he has one arm about her, and with the other hand is pointing upward. The sculptor has told in marble an eloquent story of strength coupled with tenderness, of love rewarded with trust, of sorrow brightened by hope, and he has told the story so plainly that it was scarcely necessary to chisel the words: 'Allured to brighter worlds, and led the way.' It was a beautiful conception—more beautiful than that which gave to the world the Greek Slave, the Dying Gladiator, or the Goddess Athena, and it embodies an idea which, with the expanding feeling of comradeship, can be applied to the association of nations, as well as to the relations that exist between husband and wife. Let us indulge the hope that our nation may so measure up to its great opportunities, and so bear its share of the White Man's Burden, as to earn the right to symbolize its progress by a similar figure. If it has been allured by Providence to higher ground, may it lead the way, winning the confidence of those who follow it, and exhibiting the spirit of Him who said, 'I, if I be lifted up, will draw all men unto Me.' "

While in London he attended the English session of the Interparliamentary Union and made several internationally important speeches.

On this trip, Bryan met King Edward VII, the Emperor of

Russia and scores of officials through Europe. On his earlier visit, in 1903, the Commoner had spent a day with Count Leo Tolstoi, whom he greatly respected, and to whom he made frequent reference in his writing and talking.

In his article, "The Value of An Ideal," he has this to say of the Russian philosopher:

"A few months ago it was my good fortune to spend a day in the country home of the great philosopher of Russia. You know something of the history of Tolstoi, how he was born in the ranks of nobility and how with such a birth he enjoyed every possible social distinction. At an early age he became a writer of fiction and his books have given him a fixed place among the novelists of the century. 'He sounded all the depths and shoals of honor' in so far as honor could be derived from society or from literature, and yet at the age of forty-eight life seemed so vain and empty to him that he wanted to die. They showed me a ring in the ceiling of a room in his house from which he had planned to hang himself. And what deterred him? A change came in his ideal. He was born again; he became a new creature, and for more than twenty-eight years, clad in the garb of a peasant and living the simple life of a peasant, he has been preaching unto all the world a philosophy that rests upon the doctrine, 'Thou shalt love the Lord thy God with all thy heart and thy neighbor as thyself.' There is scarcely a civilized community in all the world where the name of Tolstoi is not known and where his influence has not been felt. He has made such an impression upon the heart of Russia and the world that while some of his books are refused publication in Russia and denied importation from abroad, and while people are prohibited from circulating some of the things that he writes, yet with a million men under arms the government does not lay its hands upon Tolstoi."

In connection with that first visit to Count Tolstoi, one recalls the story which Bryan loved to tell. It relates to the day he spent with the Russian, of their long walk and their horseback ride. Upon their return to Tolstoi's home, Bryan confided to the philosopher's physician that he feared he had tired the old gentleman by the strenuous exercise.

Whereupon the physician countered, laconically. "On the contrary, Mr. Tolstoi was fearful lest he should fatigue you. Consequently he curtailed both his walk and his ride this morning."

His world tour completed, Bryan, after receiving as much recognition as if he had been the chief executive of a nation, prepared to return to America. Then his homeland began to bid for first opportunity to welcome him. Cablegrams arrived from New York, from Lincoln, from the small town of Normal, from scores of places on the route between New York and Lincoln.

Just as he stepped aboard the liner which was to bring him to America he was handed a cablegram, which read: "Do nothing until you hear from Normal." In spite of this zeal on the part of the people in Normal, Bryan and his party were feted all across the continent.

While in Egypt, some months before, the Traveling Men's Bryan club of New York had written to invite the Commoner to attend a welcoming reception in New York City to be held under their auspices. Bryan accepted.

Begun as a small enough affair, it went along like a snowball, gathered up groups here, delegations there. Virtually every state in the union sent representatives; the leading Democrats they were. The homecoming took on national, rather than local proportions. The original plan to hold it in a hotel had to be abandoned.

The reception was held in Madison Square garden. Bryan's speech on that occasion charted out the questions which seemed an inevitable part of the next presidential campaign. Bryan was proclaimed as the next nominee of the party for President and a substantial boom was launched and continued, unopposed, for some months until some of the eastern Democrats started the Johnson boom.

Leaving New York, Bryan, with his family and a delegation of "boomers," traveled across the country in a five-coach special train which made stops along the way to enable the "Peerless Leader," as he was called on many a lip, to fill speaking engagements.

On the day of his arrival in Lincoln the leading Republican paper printed his picture on the front page, and beneath it a double column of verse beginning:

"Praise the Lord for times when people, bidding politics to be still, Meet and greet the common hero with expressions of good will."

Each stanza concluded with the phrase, "You are welcome, Mr. Bryan, we are glad to see you back."

At the grounds of the state capitol a Republican mayor presided, while 60,000 persons from the city and country shook hands with their neighbor who had returned to them.

Then on to Normal, out about four miles from Lincoln, where his farm estate, "Fairview," was located. The little church had been turned into a festive bower of goldenrod and American flags. As Mr. and Mrs. Bryan entered the church the congregation rose and sang, "My Country, 'Tis of Thee." Speeches of welcome were made by the minister, the superintendent of the Sunday school, the village grocer, and "Uncle" Jack Wolfe.

In his response, Bryan, his voice choked with feeling, said:

"We have visited the temples of the Orient. We have stood in the most magnificent cathedrals of Europe, my wife and I, but after all, we'd rather be here in this little white church at Normal."

Then he distributed to each member of the congregation the pebbles which he and Mrs. Bryan had gathered up from the Sea of Galilee.

Candidate of 1920—Bryan with James M. Cox, former governor of Ohio. and presidential candidate in 1920.

Candidate of 1924—Bryan, with his brother, Charles W. Bryan, former governor of Nebraska, and vice-presidential candidate in 1924.

Four Famous Men Now Dead—This group, taken at the White House, Washington, shows, left to right: Andrew Carnegie. steel magnate; William Jennings Bryan; J. J. Hill, railroad president; and John Mitchell president of the United Mine Workers of America.

CHAPTER XVI

The Fairview Farmer

That September day when Bryan returned from his famous trip
around the world, he went, you will recall, out to Normal, Nebraska,
a village some four miles to the south and east of Lincoln. This
had been the Bryan home ever since October, 1902, when they had
moved into "Fairview," their farm estate.

Quite appropriately, it was on October 1, 1901, the seventeenth
anniversary of their marriage, which was also the fourteenth anniversary of the arrival in Nebraska of the young Jacksonville lawyer,
that Mr. and Mrs. Bryan saw the first spadeful of earth removed
from the plot of ground on which their new home was to stand.

Exactly one year later, October 1, 1902, the home was ready
for occupancy and the Bryans, with their three children, moved
into it.

Mrs. Bryan, in the closing paragraphs of her sketch of her husband's earlier life, says:

"The house stands upon a knoll and the place is called 'Fairview,' because of the beauty of the valley which the house overlooks.
Here Mr. Bryan spends the time not occupied in traveling and the
family enjoys the advantages of both the country and the city."

This estate, in its full glory, comprised 153 acres. But it had a
modest beginning, not inconsistent with the Commoner's way of
doing things.

217

Just a few years after the "boy orator" had removed to Lincoln he saved up enough money to purchase five acres of farm land in Normal. The land sold for $250 an acre, or, as he phrased it:

"I paid $100 for scenery on each acre, $100 for climate, and $50 for soil."

Gradually he accumulated more and more land until the entire 153 acres were his. The house was large, rambling, with an attractive veranda. Flanking the broad stone steps leading to the porch were reproductions of the two Korean lions which Bryan had so much admired when in Korea; Radicalism, with his lips seeming to say "Yes"; and Conservatism, with his lips tightly compressed, as if scrunching down on an emphatic "No."

On the first floor of the home, the most interesting room, undoubtedly, was the library. From the windows looked down portraits of Lincoln, of Webster, and one of the Great Commoner himself, done in oil; and of course there was a picture of his friend, Count Tolstoi. Thomas Jefferson, another one of his revered heroes, looked down from over a bookcase. And Mrs. Bryan smiled her serene smile out across the room.

More fancifully, near the door, hung a picture of our national capitol in Washington, cunningly contrived in straw, the work of an Italian admirer.

Book shelves lined the walls. There were books on history, on politics, many on religion, some on poetry. George Ade was there. And Shakespeare and Longfellow.

All about were curios, sent in from all parts of the world. Hundreds of bits of bric-a-brac, the gifts of hundreds of Bryan's hosts on his international trip, stood on tables and shelves, rested in cases, or edged themselves into stray corners. It was like studying a geography lesson to step inside the room.

Up one floor, in the billiard room, was another cross section of the world. For this room was literally laden down with mementoes sent to Bryan from some of his missionary friends. There was a coy Buddhist god, marvelously wrought in gold. There were other gods, fashioned in other materials.

One of Bryan's favorite collections was a group of hats, sent in from the Philippines, from Samoa, from Korea and Borneo; a jaunty hat from Paris; a staid one from London; a richly made one from Persia. Hats denoting caste and hats signifying the lack of it. Hats for priests and poets; for maidens and chieftains. Bryan loved to play with these quaint bits of headgear.

A pleasant way he had of delighting a guest and entertaining himself, was to take the visitor to the billiard room and stage a merry pantomime. With hat number one went a certain grimace. Hat number two called for an entirely different set of facial expressions and gestures.

But Bryan loved to don them all, even including the fantastic and grotesque bonnet for the Parsee widow.

The desk in the library was usually swept almost clean of papers and working materials. This was because Bryan did most of this work in his study, located in the basement. Here he dictated to secretaries. Here he saw to the answering of every one of the thousands of letters which came in to him. Here he and Mrs. Bryan once sent replies to every one of the 60,000 letters which had accumulated during a campaign. Here he wrote his editorials for The Commoner.

Out at Fairview Bryan was not only the politician and the writer and orator. He was also the farmer. Like his newspaper office, the farm was run after the Commoner's own ideas. For instance, there were the conferences which he held with his hired men.

No formal meetings, with an order preceding them, and a meeting place around a table. Rather, these conferences were chance affairs, likely to occur at almost any time, and in almost any place.

One time it would be the pig-sty; another time the barn. Again, it might be the garden or the wheat field.

Bryan found the advantages of farming many and satisfying. He argued that the farm environment gave a child a good mental background. The enforced leisure of the long winter evenings furnished a splendid opportunity, in his judgment, for extensive reading on the part of the younger as well as of the older folks.

More deeply, knowledge of the minutiae of the farm detail gave a young girl or boy a moral preoccupation that would carry over into mature life, he thought. The miracles of the Bible, according to this theory of his, were more readily understandable to the young person who had grown up filled with first hand information about the miracles of plant and animal life on the farm.

As a rhetorical by-product of Bryan's life on the farm, we find his extensive use of the farm simile. The hog, with the ring in his nose to restrain his hoggish tendencies of over-eating, was used in one of his famous speeches. Scores of other passages bring in farm animals. There is the simile of the radish, another of the watermelon, and so on, through a number of different subjects.

On the farm at Fairview, as well as in European capitals or on nationally known rostrums, Bryan looked, as well as acted, the role of Commoner. Plain clothes, usually dark in color and frequently black. He turned from the Prince Albert of earlier days to the more modern seersucker suit. His most characteristic accessories to the plain, easy-fitting suit were a low-cut collar and the string-bow tie which once became so identified with him that it was called the "Bryan" tie.

As the Fairview farmer, Bryan was out in the open air much of the time, and had a husky appetite. "Chicken with plenty of gravy" was an epicurean dainty to him. So also was sweet corn.

At the time of campaigns when he was so much the pivot figure that his breakfast menu and the size of his collar were journalistic bulletins, many stories used to be printed about his eating habits. For everybody knew that he liked to eat; the lines of his figure helped along that story.

And so it was that the news-gatherers then wrote paragraphs on the fact that he drank no liquid of any kind with his meals.

"It's not because I don't enjoy washing down my food," Bryan's chroniclers would quote him as saying, "but experience has taught me that if I do, I'll get too fat. I'm fat enough as it is."

Banquets, however, held no lure for Bryan. During the latter years of his life, he turned rather away from meats and preferred an almost vegetarian diet. There are stories, some of them a bit vague, extant in Lincoln telling of banquets to which the Fairview farmer had been invited, and at which he rather astonished the guests by appearing with a supply of carrots, radishes, turnips and other produce from his own garden.

The ancestor of this anecdote, like so many that were circulated about the Democratic leader, may easily have had its source in the whimsy of an alert imagination of the teller, and may have gathered momentum as it went. But jokes on himself didn't disturb Bryan. He liked cartoons and often made merry over the many caricatures of himself which appeared in newspapers throughout this and other countries, almost unintermittently, for the twenty-nine years beginning with 1896 and ending with his death.

"I like, as much as anybody," he would say, "to see these cartoons of myself. I enjoy them immensely. And, besides, the cartoonist must live."

It was during the more or less quiet interludes at Fairview, between campaigns and speaking tours, that anecdotes not so directly connected with his public life were circulated.

For instance, the episode, and it is a true one, of the Japanese boy who insisted upon being Bryan's foster-son.

It seems that in Japan it is not unusual for a youth who respects and admires some famous man to adopt that man as a father, and a hard and fast custom obligates the foster-father thus chosen to care for the young man, at least until he becomes of age. So it was that, back in 1896, when Bryan's fame was penetrating every village and hamlet in the United States, word of him reached over into Japan and stirred the heart of a young Nipponese student.

Presently came a letter to Bryan, making the somewhat startling revelation that the boy had "chosen you to be my father," and would sail at once for the United States. The news was disconcerting, to say the least, to the Bryan household. The collector of the port at San Francisco couldn't suggest a way out of the dilemma. And so one morning, with no further ado, there was a ring at the door.

Bryan was the Commoner; Bryan answered his own door bell. That morning he flung wide the door in an hospitable gesture that revealed to his gaze a personable looking Japanese boy who wasted no preliminary words when he announced:

"I have come."

And he had.

He was taken into the Bryan household. He was given an education not unlike the one William Jennings Bryan, Jr., received. And not so many months after the family removed to Fairview, the Japanese foster-son left their hearth to make his way in the world. For many months one Yamachita Y. Bryan was traveling about the United States as private secretary to a member of the Japanese parliament who was in this country studying American industries.

It was in the Fairview study that Bryan first enunciated his idea of the qualities necessary in a President of the United States, a theme which was later to be expanded into magazine articles.

The prime requisite, as Bryan saw it, was a sympathy with the entire people rather than with any faction of this country. Second, he placed a thorough knowledge of public questions and an intuitive sense which should enable the executive to distinguish between the true and the false.

Equally important with this point, Bryan believed, was the fact that the President ought not to have any personal ambition, but should concentrate everything on his ambitions for his country. Consequently, he thought it bad for a President to take office, cherishing, even in the back of his head, a hope of a second term.

It was at Fairview, too, that Bryan's philanthropic enterprises flourished. Upon his return from his round-the-world trip, in the course of an address to members of the Presbyterian Board of Foreign Missions, he announced that he was maintaining eight scholarships in American colleges in Japan, China and India.

"I created them during my recent tour in the East," he said, "and I expect to continue them as long as I am able, which I rather believe will be for some time.

"As I told an Englishman whom I met in the East," he continued, "America can not boast that the sun never sets on her possessions; but we can make the prouder boast that the sun never sets on American philanthropy. What America has done for Christianity in the eastern parts of Asia has been equalled by no other country. Wherever one goes he finds the American workers and sees the beneficent results of American influence."

Even while he was staying home at Fairview, holding farm conferences, attending meetings of the Farmers' club, writing articles, riding horseback and chatting with neighbors, Bryan's popularity was not tapering off by any manner of means.

For, on a trip to Chicago during this period, Bryan was buying some newspapers at a stand in a big hotel. He gave the girl at the counter half a dollar. While she was making change a young man, standing back of the Commoner, began to signal to her frantically.

She started to turn away haughtily, but tarried a bit when the young man stepped up as Bryan turned away, and offered her a dollar for the coin which was just about to loose its identity in the cash register. The Bryan fan pocketed the half dollar, handed over his dollar and walked away exultant.

CHAPTER XVII

Mary Baird Bryan

"There is an American ideal of marriage," wrote William Jennings Bryan in "The Value of an Ideal."

Then followed this:

"When two persons, drawn together by the indissoluble ties of
love, enter marriage, each one contributing a full part and both
ready to share life's struggles and trials as well as its victories and
its joys—when these, mutually helpful and mutually forebearing,
start out to build an American home it ought to be the fittest earthly
type of heaven."

And the passage might have been autobiographical.

For it wasn't a mere flight of rhetoric that prompted him to
make that now famous bit of repartee at the railroad station at
Lincoln, Nebraska, during one of the home-comings of the 1896
campaign.

Bryan and his wife, who made a large part of the strenuous
campaign with him, got off their train and were met by a tremendous
crowd of shouting, screaming, jubilant home-folks, who loved Bryan,
the neighbor, even though they may have disagreed with Bryan,
the politician.

One man from the crowd, climbing up to the vantage point of
a baggage truck, waved his arms as if to lead the men and women
in a cheer, as he shouted:

"Three cheers for the next First Lady of the Land."

"My friends and neighbors," replied Bryan, when the noise had died down a bit, "I am much obliged to you for your implied compliment. But to me she has always been the First Lady of the Land."

And she had.

Ever since those early days, back in Jacksonville, when the girl from the Jacksonville Female seminary became the bride of the prize orator at Illinois college, Mary Baird Bryan had been a comrade and a companion to her husband.

When she married him, Bryan was a young lawyer. Mrs. Bryan proceeded to take a full course in law, and a few years later when she removed to Nebraska with him, she was admitted to the Nebraska state bar. She did not become a lawyer with the idea of actively practicing, but rather of better understanding her husband's work, of more adequately helping him, and of more deeply coinciding with his interests.

"I studied law under my husband's direction," she once told a friend, "because I wanted to know as nearly as possible all that he knew in order that our camaraderie might be more perfect."

Then she added a whimsical postscript:

"My father used to say the reason I studied law and was admitted to the bar was that I didn't want Mr. Bryan to know anything that I didn't know."

As a matter of fact, however, she did do no small part of the work of looking up records and the like in the cases which came to the young lawyer's attention in the earlier days of his career.

"I knew nothing, absolutely nothing, of politics or public affairs when I was married," Mrs. Bryan admitted during the 1896 campaign.

"But my idea of marriage was then and still is that the wife, to be the husband's companion, must be his intellectual as well as moral complement. Had Mr. Bryan been a horseman instead of a lawyer and politician, I would have acquainted myself as cheerfully and thoroughly with the details of that business as I have with his present occupation."

How adequately Bryan's wife lived up to her definition of a wife and companion the world will never fully appreciate. But outsiders marveled at the fullness of her comradeship, even as they glimpsed it.

Besides serving as a law clerk, looking up authorities for her husband, Mrs. Bryan often acted as his secretary. When, about the time they moved to Fairview, Bryan spent a large part of his time writing articles for The Commoner, preparing drafts of speeches, and outlining Chautauqua addresses, Mrs. Bryan learned how to use a typewriter. Next to his big desk in the basement study of the Fairview home was a small typewriter stand. Here Mrs. Bryan sat, took dictation on her machine, and answered the thousands of letters that had to be given attention.

At that time all of his mail was delivered to the newspaper office, and supervised by his brother Charles before it was passed on to him. An annual post-bag containing 300,000 letters was not anything unusual.

Nor did the wife stop there. As a bride she had coached her husband, the story goes, in best methods of delivery, until the "boy orator," following many directions which she had given him, finally won his spurs so signally the day he delivered the "Cross of Gold" speech at the Chicago convention.

But she did more than help her husband in his creative work. She was anxious that he be en rapport, as much as possible, with the opinions of those at home and abroad, who were commenting on him, who were criticizing him.

And so it developed that, along about 1900, Mrs. Bryan, from the midst of a day packed full with household duties, political cares, social obligations and domestic demands, found time to steal away each morning for a few hours, to take a university course in German.

A visitor, spending the night at Fairview, came to the breakfast table the next morning, marked Mrs. Bryan's absence and was told by his host:

"Oh, three times a week she goes to the university before breakfast for an early class in German."

"You see," he continued, "I can't read German and Mrs. Bryan thought it might be a good thing to have someone in the family who could get at first hand the sentiment of the German press."

That first amazingly energetic campaign of 1896 saw Mrs. Bryan accompanying her husband on a goodly arc of the swing he made around the country. Toward the last part of that trip, in the late summer, she was obliged to leave him to return home and see that their children were properly established in their respective schools.

During the early part of the trip, newspaper correspondents aboard the campaign train indulged in almost daily pessimistic predictions as to how the candidate's wife would stand the terrible strain. Tomorrow, they wrote, her nerves must surely break. Or next day, she must give way under the strain. It seemed inevitable. But her nerves didn't break. And she didn't give way under the strain. The girlish figure that took its place, day after day, in the audiences the Commoner addressed, stood the rigors of the tour even better, many will tell you, than her robust husband.

Throughout the days of travel and hurry, of meeting thousands and being jostled about among tens of thousands, she kept well groomed, she looked attractive, and most important, she kept her temper. Kept her temper even when the gibes and jeers of a hostile audience assailed her husband, and hurled themselves against her ears.

She was always a friend of the newspaper correspondents. Just a few weeks ago, when two or three press representatives were introduced to her, as she sat in her wheel chair on the piazza of the Rogers home, she extended her hand in greeting, smiled cordially and said:

"You are reporters? I am glad, indeed, to know you. I have been meeting reporters all my life."

Then, too, we must not forget that Mrs. Bryan is an author. She wrote the biographical sketch of her husband's life which precedes his volume entitled "The First Battle." That work itself was largely inspired and suggested by her. Much of its active preparation she superintended.

But Mary Baird Bryan was not simply a pleasant, industrious and companionable political secretary to her husband. During the busiest hours of the campaigns she took personal charge of her home and of her three children, Ruth, William Jennings, Jr., and Grace.

If her husband's schedule were an arduous one there at Fairview, so was hers. Up at five, and busy with household duties. An hour or so at the university. Then down to the basement workshop, there to help her husband. About three in the afternoon she was free to take part in the civic and political interests of the town. Perhaps it was a meeting of the Farmers club; perhaps a visit to the office of The Commoner, where she, like her husband, knew everybody. Maybe it was being hostess to a delegation of important official visitors, or to a group of equally important, very humble unofficial guests. Or, maybe, a meeting of the Woman's club.

Mrs. Bryan was one of the organizers of the "Sorosis" club in Lincoln. At the meetings of women, Mrs. Bryan's words were always listened to with interest for they were sure to be informative. But she was always judiciously careful not to speak "for the family," and often as not she would remain silent when some question was being discussed, when she knew that her words might be interpreted as coming from Bryan and might reveal some confidential secret of which she knew.

Mrs. Bryan, during those crowded days, received a goodly share of mail herself. All manner of notes asking aid, charity, support, were received by her. Each of them she answered, referred to the proper channels, or otherwise took care of. As indicative of the variety of requests she was in the habit of receiving, there is the story of the young lady, of whom Mrs. Bryan had never heard, who wrote in and asked for a "pink silk dress."

Then there was the letter from a man in a western city, telling, tragically enough, of how he had been crippled for life in an election-day quarrel when he heroically defended Mr. Bryan from an abusive attack. This letter was sent over to a charity organization. A few days later it was revealed that Mrs. Roosevelt had received a similar letter. Only in her note the gentleman, of course, said it was Theodore Roosevelt whom he had championed.

The Bryans had three children, all of them now alive.

Ruth Baird Bryan, the oldest, is married to Major John Owen.

William Jennings Bryan, Jr., the middle child, while attending the University of Nebraska, met Miss Helen Virginia Berger of Milwaukee. They were married in 1909.

Grace Dexter Bryan, the younger daughter, is Mrs. Richard Hargraves.

At the Democratic national convention in New York in 1924, Bryan sought out the newspaper men one night. As he was one of the central figures of that convention, any news he might give out was sure to be significant. So the men rushed about him, pencils poised.

Mr. Bryan, with a bit of a twinkle in his eye, said, "Boys, I've a piece of news that you'll want."

Then he reached over, took a pencil away from one young man's hand, wrote for a minute on a piece of paper, and handed over the bulletin.

"A great granddaughter was born today to Mr. Bryan. The

parents are William P. Meeker and Kitty Owen Meeker, Mr. Bryan's oldest grandchild."

Then he walked away before the newspaper men could recover their wits quickly enough to congratulate him.

CHAPTER XVIII

Conventions of 1904 and 1908

St. Louis Convention—Seconds Nomination of Senator Cockrell—
"I Have Kept the Faith"—Denver Convention—Monopolies—
Dining-room Anecdote—Salem—Chicago Speech—Election Eve—
Speech to Neighbors—Election Returns—Taft Wins, Bryan De-
feated.

The 1904 Democratic convention, held at St. Louis, was for
Bryan more or less of an interlude, during which he gathered momentum to make his next and last presidential fight, following the
1908 convention at Denver. During this time, too, the somewhat
vague ideas as to what should be done about the trust question
were crystallizing, in many sections of the country, into a definite
Bryan ideal.

At the St. Louis convention the Commoner seconded the nomination of Senator F. M. Cockrell for presidential nominee and opposed
the convention's choice of Alton B. Parker. Later, however, the
Nebraskan went out and stumped for Parker.

But the St. Louis convention is important, from the point of
view of Bryan's connection with it, for his famous "I have kept the
faith" speech. It was made when he seconded Senator Cockrell's
nomination. Some extracts from it follow:

"Eight years ago a Democratic national convention placed in
my hand the standard of the party and commissioned me as its
candidate. Four years later that commission was renewed. I come
tonight to this Democratic national convention to return the commission. You may dispute whether I have finished my course, but
you cannot deny that I have kept the faith.

"As your candidate I did all that I could to bring success to the

232

At Home in Florida—Bryan and his wife photographed on the lawn of
their home at Cocoanut Grove, a suburb of Miami, Florida, where he
lived for the last few months preceding his death.

Brothers and Sisters—(left to right) Charles W. Bryan. Mrs. T. S. Allen, Mrs. J. B. Baird. and William Jennings Bryan, in 1924. when Charles W. was vice-presidential nominee.

party; as a private citizen I feel more interested in a Democratic success today than I ever did when 1 was a candidate.

"The reasons that made the election of a Democrat desirable were stronger in 1900 than in 1896, and the reasons that make the election of a Democrat desirable are stronger now than they were in 1900.

"The gentleman who presented New York's candidate dwelt upon the dangers of militarism, and he did not overstate those dangers.

"Let me quote the most remarkable passage ever found in a speech nominating a candidate for the Presidency.

"Governor Black, of New York, in presenting the name of Theodore Roosevelt to the Republican convention of this year used these words:

" 'The fate of nations is still decided by their wars. You may sing in your schools the gentle praises of the quiet life; you may strike from your books the last note of every martial anthem, and yet out in the smoke and thunder will always be the tramp of horses and the silent, rigid, upturned face. Men may prophesy and women pray, but peace will come here to abide forever on this earth only when the dreams of childhood are the accepted charts to guide the destinies of men.'

"Will you Democrats of New York present a graver indictment against President Roosevelt than that? Can you of the south present a more serious accusation? I do not ask concerning the character of the President. He may have every virtue; his life may be exemplary in every way; but if he shares the views of the man who placed him in nomination; if he believes with his sponsor that wars must settle the destinies of nations; that peace is but an idle, childish dream; that woman may pray for it; that men may prophesy about it; but that all this talk of 'orderly tribunals and learned referees' is but an empty sound—if he believes these things he is a dangerous man for our country and for the world. I believe he ought to be defeated; I believe he can be defeated.

"If we are going to have some other god besides this modern Mars, presented to us by Governor Black, what kind of a god is it to be? Must we choose between a god of war and a god of gold?

"If there is anything that compares in hatefulness with militarism on the one side it is plutocracy, and I insist that the Democratic party ought not to be compelled to choose between militarism on the one side and plutocracy on the other.

"I have not come to ask anything of this convention. Nebraska asks nothing but to be permitted to fight the battles of democracy; that is all. Some of you call me a dictator. It is false. You know it is false. How have I tried to dictate? I have said that I thought certain things ought to be done. Have you not exercised the same privilege? Why have I not a right to suggest? Because I was your candidate, have I forfeited the right to make suggestions? Sirs, if that condition were attached to a nomination for the Presidency, no man worthy to be President would ever accept a nomination. For the right of a man to have an opinion and to express it is more important and more sacred than the holding of any office however high.

"I desire to second the nomination of a man whose name has already been presented, and I second his nomination, not because I can assert to you that he is more available than any other person who might be named, but because I love the man and because on the platform we have adopted there is no good reason why any democrat in the east should vote against him. I second the nomination of Senator Cockrell of Missouri.

"The great issue in this country today is 'democracy versus plutocracy.' I have been accused of having but one idea—silver. A few years ago it was said that I had only one, but then it was tariff reform. But there is an issue greater than the silver issue, the tariff issue, or the trust issue. It is the issue between democracy and plutocracy—whether this is to be a government of the people, administered by officers chosen by the people, and administered in behalf of the people, or a government by the moneyed element of the country in the interest of predatory wealth. This issue is growing.

"I ask you to help us to meet this issue. You tell me that the Republican candidate stands for militarism. Yes, but he also stands for plutocracy. You tell me that he delights in war. Yes, but there is another objection to him, and that is that he does not enforce the law against a big criminal as he does against a little criminal. The laws must be enforced. The government must be administered according to the maxim: 'Equal rights to all and special privileges to none.'

"Let me warn you that if the Democratic party is to save this nation, it must save it, not by purchase, but by principle. That is the only way to save it. Every time we resort to purchase, we encourage the spirit of barter. Under such a system the price will constantly increase, and the elections will go to the highest bidder. If the Democratic party is to save this country, it must appeal to the conscience of the country. It must point out impending dangers; and if the party will nominate a man, I care not from what part of the country he comes, who is not the candidate of a faction, who is not the candidate of an element, but the candidate of the party, the party will stand by him and will drive the Republican party from power.

"I simply submit these suggestions for your consideration. I am here to discharge a duty that I owe to the party. I knew before coming to this convention that a majority of the delegates would not agree with me in regard to the financial plank. I knew that there would be among the delegates many who voted against me when I sorely needed their help. I am not objecting to the majority against me, nor to the presence of those who left us in 1896 and have since returned; I am here, not because I enjoy being in the minority, but because I owe a duty to the more than six million brave and loyal men who sacrificed for the ticket in recent campaigns. I came to help to get them as good a platform as I could; I have helped to get them a good platform. I came to help to get as good a candidate as possible, and I hope that he will be one who can draw the factions together—one who will give to us who believe in positive, aggressive, Democratic reforms, something to hope for, something to fight for,—one who will also give to those who have differed from us on the money question something to hope for, something to fight for. And I close with an appeal from my heart to the hearts of those who hear me: Give us a pilot who will guide the Democratic ship away from the Scylla of militarism without wrecking her upon the Charybdis of commercialism."

So much for the St. Louis convention.

Four years later, at the Denver convention of 1908, we see Bryan making a tremendous fight against the trusts. This fight, most logically, would have been inevitable back in his 1900 campaign. But the Spanish-American war came along just then and focalized Democratic public opinion, and especially Bryan's, on the issue of anti-imperialism.

Back in 1899, Bryan, in a visit to Colorado, had said in an inter-view that his suggested remedy for the trust difficulty was the mandatory licensing of a corporation before it could do business outside the state in which it was organized. This remedy was suggested by him at an anti-trust conference held in Chicago in the fall of that year. At that conference, Bryan delivered a speech which began with the sentence later to become a slogan, and still later, a part of the Democratic platform.

"I begin with the declaration," Bryan stated, "that a monopoly in private hands is indefensible from any standpoint and intolerable."

That sentence, or its variant, "A private monopoly is indefensible and intolerable," appeared in the Democratic platform in 1900, again in 1904, and word for word, in this platform on which Bryan ran for the Presidency in 1908.

Pandemonium reigned at Denver the day that Bryan, still able to get the multitudes to cheer for him, if they wouldn't all vote for him, was nominated as the Democratic standard bearer.

The following paragraph from his speech of acceptance in this campaign is reproduced here because it has been so widely quoted:

"There is a Divine law of rewards. When the Creator gave us the earth, with its fruitful soil, the sunshine with its warmth, and the rains with their moisture, He proclaimed, as clearly as if His voice had thundered from the clouds: 'Go, work, and according to your industry and your intelligence, so shall be your reward.' Only where might has overthrown, cunning undermined, or government suspended this law, has a different law prevailed. To conform the government to this law ought to be the ambition of the statesman; and no party can have a higher mission than to make it a reality wherever governments can legitimately operate."

Then began the campaign.

Back in 1896, during the first campaign, enemies had twitted the "boy orator" for being a none too financially successful lawyer. Now, twelve years later, enemies denounced him for his wealth. As a matter of fact, neither indictment was true.

In 1896, his account books showed a pleasant enough record for an attorney who was both young and a comparative stranger. And in 1908, though the Fairview home was adequate, comfortable, well equipped, it was no palace of luxury. Nor was it at all disproportionate to the money which he had gathered through his energies as editor, writer and lecturer.

At the very start of the campaign an amusing incident occurred.

The members of the Democratic national committee visited their candidate at his Fairview home on the 14th of July, 1908. Mrs. Bryan and her daughter, Grace, personally superintended the serving of the luncheon to this committee. Fried chicken, salad and vegetables from the farm; peaches and apples from the orchards, were on the menu. Few things that made their way to the table that day had not come right from Fairview.

As the men were ushered into the dining room Bryan, smiling, turned to them and said:

"My dining room will seat only forty-six. The dining room at the White House is larger."

This campaign, while not such a whirlwind of motion as the 1896 one, kept the candidate pretty much on the alert. Nor was public reaction dimmed to his appeal. He visited his birthplace, Salem, Illinois, August 27, 1908. His train pulled in at 6:30 in the morning, but there was scarcely a soul in the town who did not turn out to meet his distinguished townsman. Bryan went to the old cemetery to place wreaths of flowers on the graves of his mother and his father. On his way to the train, a committee of citizens gave him $400 as a contribution to his campaign expenses.

The seventh of September found him in Chicago, addressing 15,000 workingmen in an enthusiastic meeting at which labor and the trusts were the main themes.

Said Bryan, in that speech:

"There is in politics as in electricity, an invisible and intangible something that has as much influence on the masses of the people as have the platforms of political parties.

"Four year ago a man who was against me told me he had had a talk with one of his employes, who was a Bryan man. The employer asked the man why he was for Mr. Bryan. In doing so, all of the issues of the campaign were enumerated, but the employe answered, 'I'll tell you why I am for Mr. Bryan. I think he is on my side.'

"I'll tell you, my friends, that more people are influenced by an argument like that than by any other, and a man speaks in vain who can't convince his hearers that he is on their side.

"If I spoke before a body of trust magnates, the longer I spoke the less votes I'd get. The thing to do is to convince your hearers that you are on their side. The Democratic party is on the people's side in this campaign. The Democratic party is on the laboring man's side in this campaign.

"The trust and the labor organization cannot be described in the same language. The trust magnates have used their power to amass swollen fortunes, while no one will say that the labor organization has as yet secured for its members more than their share of the profits arising from their work. But there are fundamental differences. The trust is a combination of dollars; the labor organization in an association of human beings. In a trust, a few men attempt to control the product of others; in a labor organization, the members unite for the protection of that which is their own—namely, their own labor, which, being necessary to their existence, is a part of them.

"The trust deals with dead matter; the labor organization deals with life and with intellectual and moral forces. No impartial student of the subject will deny the right of the laboring man to exemption from the operation of the existing anti-trust law.

"If the labor organization needs to be regulated by law, let it be regulated by a law which deals with man as man, and not by a law that was aimed to prevent the cornering of a commodity or the forestalling of the market."

There was an accelerated finish. Fairview was the scene of wild excitement during the days just preceding the election. Photographers, venders of special Bryan souvenirs, crowds of people, political visitors, everybody was making a beaten track to the little town of Normal.

On the eve of election day Bryan made a speech to his neighbors. But its words have more than a local meaning:

"My friends, I am at the end of my third presidential campaign. Tomorrow, 15,000,000 voters will decide whether I am to occupy the seat that Washington and Jefferson and Jackson and Lincoln occupied. You will have your part in my victory or in my defeat. It may be that the election will turn on Nebraska, and it may be that Nebraska will turn on votes so few in number that the city of Lincoln may decide the result. If fate decrees that my name shall be added to the list of Presidents, and Nebraska added to the list of states that have furnished Presidents, I shall rejoice with you. If, on the other hand, the election shall be against me, I can feel that I have left nothing undone that I could have done to bring success to my cause. And I shall find private life so full of joy that I shall not miss the Presidency.

"I have been a child of fortune from my birth. God gave me into the keeping of a Christian father and a Christian mother. They implanted in my heart the ideals that have guided my life. When I was in law school, I was fortunate enough, as I was in my college days to fall under the influence of men of ideals who helped to shape my course; and when but a young man, not yet out of college, I was guided to the selection of one who, for twenty-four years, has been my faithful helpmate. No presidential victory could have brought her to me, and no defeat can take her from me. I have been blessed with a family. Our children are with us to make glad the declining years of their mother and myself. When you first knew me, they called me, in derision, 'The Boy Orator of the Platte.' I have outlived that title, and my grandchildren are now growing up about me. I repeat, that I have been fortunate, indeed. I have been abundantly rewarded for what little I have been able to do, and my ambition is not so much to hold any office, however great, as it is to know my duty and to do it, whether in public life or as a private citizen.

"If I am elected, I shall be absent from you but four years. If I am defeated, you will help me to bear my defeat. And I assure you that the affection that my countrymen have shown is to me dearer than all earthly office. I shall be content, if I can deserve the continuation of that affection. I have been touched by the demonstrations that have been given in other parts of the country, but in twelve years and in three campaigns, I have never had a welcome anywhere more generous, more enthusiastic than you have given in Lincoln tonight."

And when the votes were counted, the tally gave 7,678,908 votes to William Howard Taft, as against the 6,409,104 which William Jennings Bryan received. Taft had 321 electoral votes, to his opponent's 162.

Again Bryan was the good loser.

CHAPTER XIX

Faith and Religion

His Favorite Verse—Progressive in Politics, Fundamentalist in Religion—Joins Presbyterian Church, Though Parents Are Baptists—Attends Methodist Church at Normal, Nebraska—Views on Denominationalism—Conspicuous Part in General Assemblies of Presbyterian Church—D. L. Moody—Religious Customs—Advice to High School Students—America's Faults—Belief in Foreign Missionaries—Passionate Belief in Bible—Bible by His Side at Death.

When William Jennings Bryan, a junior in college, won an oratorical contest and was awarded a volume of the poems of William Cullen Bryant, he marked his favorite verse in his favorite poem and gave the book as his first gift to Mary Baird, the girl he was to marry.

That underscored stanza was a part of Bryant's poem, "Ode to a Waterfowl." It reads as follows:

He who, from zone to zone,

Guides through the boundless sky thy certain flight,

In the long way that I must tread alone,

Will lead my steps aright."

Bryan underscored those words with pencil in the book. And they, in turn, underscored themselves in spirit in Bryan's heart and soul. They formed the basic theme of his life. As recently as two months before he died, the Commoner while attending the general assembly of the Presbyterian church at Columbus, Ohio, said this:

"People often ask me why I can be a progressive in politics and a fundamentalist in religion.

"The answer is easy. Government is man-made and therefore imperfect. It can always be improved. But religion is not a man-

244

made affair. If Christ is the final word how may anyone be progressive in religion?

"I am satisfied with the God we have, with the Bible and with Christ."

Bryan, you will recall, inherited a strong religious tradition. His father, Judge Silas Bryan, sitting on the bench in court, used to bow his head and offer up a prayer when the noon hour came around each day. Judge and Mrs. Bryan were Baptists but when Bryan was about fourteen he attended a series of Presbyterian camp-meetings held near his home at Salem. During the course of these meetings he became desirous of affiliating with the Presbyterian church. His parents offered no objection. With their full consent, he joined the church of his choice and became a member of the Cumberland Presbyterian church. When he went away to college he joined the First Presbyterian church at Jacksonville. Upon removing to Lincoln, he brought his letter to the Westminster church of Lincoln, of which he was a member until he moved down to Florida.

But when he moved out to Fairview, the church nearest his farm was the Methodist church of Normal, so he and his family became regular attendants there. In doing this, Bryan was only putting into practice his belief regarding denominationalism.

"Are you a denominationalist?" he was once asked.

"No," he replied, and went on to explain.

"Denominations help to organize religion, and anything to be successful in these days must be organized. But creed, to my mind, is not paramount."

At the same time, however, Bryan took an active and zealous part in the affairs of the Presbyterian church. He was one of the outstanding laymen of that faith, and for the few years immediately preceding his death he was a conspicuous figure, the most conspicuous figure, at the annual Presbyterian general assembly. For three years he came as a commissioner from the Presbytery of Florida.

At the assembly in Indianapolis he missed being elected moderator of the General Assembly of the Presbyterian church by only a handful of votes.   His successful opponent was the Rev. Dr. Charles F. Wichart, President of the University of Wooster. It was a fight between the fundamentalists and the modernists, and the modernists won.

The following year, at Grand Rapids, Mich., Mr. Bryan made the speech nominating the Rev. Dr. Clarence Edward Macartney, pastor of the Arch Street Presbyterian church, Philadelphia, as moderator.   Dr. Macartney, a thorough fundamentalist, was elected. Bryan was made a member of the national council of the Presbyterian church.

At the Assembly at Columbus, Ohio, in May, Bryan fought the modernists and was credited with being largely responsible for the permanent judicial commission rendering a decision that positive belief in the Virgin was a prerequisite to the licensing of any young man to preach as a Presbyterian minister.

Some persons considered that Bryan was responsible for the defeat of the fundamentalist ticket at Columbus because he occasioned a split in the fundamentalist vote. The night before the election Bryan gave a statement to the press supporting for the office the Rev. Dr. William O. Thompson, President of Ohio State University. At the last moment Dr. Thompson withdrew. There was not time for the fundamentalists to get together on one candidate and two fundamentalists were nominated. This resulted in the election of the Rev. Charles R. Erdman, a professor in Princeton Theological Seminary and pastor of the First Presbyterian church at Princeton, N. J., who, although a fundamentalist, ran on a "peace" ticket.

As a youth Bryan addressed religious meetings. When elected to Congress he gave up this work temporarily. Again in 1900, after two defeats for the Presidency, he returned to his platform work. But during the intervening period he had really been preaching the gospel. For his speeches are all interlarded with quotations from the Scriptures. Back in a tariff speech of 1892, his text was "Better is a little righteousness, than great revenues without right."

And his very manner of delivering a political speech often smacked of pulpit delivery. There is a story illustrating this. It is to the effect that Bryan once pointed out that the late Dwight L. Moody preached as a lawyer presents a case to the jury. Whereupon Moody remarked that if preachers would preach as forcibly as Bryan talked politics they would make more converts.

His speeches, whether religious or political, had the incisive quality of both the lawyer and the preacher.

As middle life bore in upon him, the politician swung more and more articulately around to the thesis that political issues should be moral issues. All through the early days there had been definite foreshadowings of this stand, but, latterly, these fore-shadowings translated themselves into aggressive tenets. They climaxed themselves in Bryan's fervent fight for the right of the Tennessee legislature to pass an anti-evolution law.

Not only Bryan's principles, but his practices, were deeply religious. He held family worship every day. He said grace at every meal; at dinner at home the family joined audibly in the words of thanks. Nobody ever. heard him swear. He never drank nor smoked. Virtually all of his adult life he taught a Sunday school class. First in the tiny Methodist church at Normal near his farm. Later, when his wife's failing health influenced them to move to Florida, he taught a Bible class in a grove at Miami. There, every Sunday morning, he would fan himself and expound

the Scriptures to hundreds of residents and tourists. This class
was one of the prides of his life.

In Congress, when the House held a Sunday session, Bryan
would leave his seat for an hour, no matter how anxious he was
to take part in the debate, and go over to a church on Capitol Hill,
there to lecture on the Divinity of Christ. During the heated,
stressful times immediately before the presidential elections, Bryan
even then refused to campaign on Sunday.

Bryan's most famous non-political speech is "The Prince of
Peace." The speech, based on deep religious convictions, was given
all through this country and all over Europe. But the audience
whom Bryan best loved to address, with this as a message, was an
audience of young men. He always liked to talk to youth. The
following excerpt from a speech he made to a body of high school
students at a Billy Sunday meeting in Boston, is typical:

"This audience recalls a day in my life forty-two years ago
and more when I was a high school boy, for I was only fourteen
when I became a member of a Christian church by conversion. I
look back to that day as the most important day of my life. It
has had far more to do with my life than any other day, and the
Book to which I swore allegiance on that day has been more to
me than any party platform.

"I share in the joy you give to the older generation in coming
tonight to put your hearts under the influences of a great appeal.
Students, if you will count the books which you will have to study
before you complete the prescribed course, you will find that it takes
a multitude of books to train the human mind; and when you have
studied them all, that mind is but the agent of something greater
than the mind itself. The mind is but an instrument used by the
heart, and it takes only one Book to train the heart that ought to
be the master of the mind. All your school books will not save
your life from failure if your heart goes wrong; if your heart

goes right it can take a head, however dull, and make it useful to society.

"You come, therefore, to hear something more important than they teach in the schools. You come to learn a truth that ought to enter into the mind and sink into the heart of every student, namely, that there is no reason why any boy or girl should ever make a failure of life.

"All your learning will not keep you from failing. Learning has no power to save a human being from sin. You come tonight to consider the claims of a Book that can save you, that can add to every joy that comes through the body or the mind, that can refine every pleasure known to the physical man or to the mental man. You have come tonight to learn of that larger life into which the great evangelist will invite you as he presents to you the only Book that is good always and everywhere—the Book that will guide your foot-steps when you are young, and throw light upon your path during mature years, and the only Book one cares to have beside him as the evening of life approaches."

Once again, speaking in Oakland, California, before a joint meeting of the Baptist Young People's Union of North America, and the National Education association, Bryan summed up the faults of the American people by charging that they worshipped the gods of wealth, fashion, fame, physical comfort, travel, passion, chance and drink.

The greatest of the ten commandments, he declared, was "Thou shalt have no other gods before me."

Again and again, in slightly different phrases, came this recurrent theme, the inevitability of immortality. Here is one variation of the statement.

"Science with its skepticism, never has discovered that God wasted. No single atom of the myriad which make creation up exists without its purpose. That the coldest of the material students all agree. Why, then, should the soul be wasted? Is it to be considered less in the eternal scheme of things because it is superior to all other things which have been made? It seems to me so utterly improbable that God has failed to make provision for a future life for us as to become impossible. Personally, I am certain we shall live again as I am that we live today. If an invisible germ of life in every grain of wheat has power to persist through twice ten thousand generations, I shall not doubt that my own soul has power to live on when my earthly body shall have been dissolved to dust."

Foreign missionaries, too, came in for their share of Bryan's attention. Back eight years or so before the World War he maintained that Bibles, not bullets, would bring about the peace of the world.

At a meeting of the Presbyterian brotherhood of Chicago, held there February 14, 1909, Bryan upheld the work of foreign missionaries thiswise:

"The Christian religion is responsible more than any other thing for this nation's position in the world, its progress and the greatness of its future. They say our missionaries abroad make mistakes which get us into trouble with other nations, and when some unfortunate mistake is made we hear learned discussions about the dangers of sending out missionaries.

"It is not surprising that missionaries do make occasional mistakes. We have no class of men in this country specially educated in diplomacy whom we can send abroad as missionaries. Is there any class of men who do not make mistakes? Is it to be wondered at, therefore, that missionaries surrounded by heathens do sometimes err?"

At this same meeting Bryan took occasion to rebuke the men of Chicago for their failure to support the work of the reformers.

Eclipse Only Temporary—"The eclipse is like the recent defeat of the Democratic party," said Bryan as he saw the moon blot out the sun, January 24, 1925.

Welcome to Dayton—Bryan arrives for the evolution trial and is greeted by an enthusiastic crowd, who hail him as their champion.

Counsel for the State—Bryan standing in front of the Rogers home (the house in which he died), surrounded by his associates in the Scopes prosecution.

After looking about the room, jammed to the doors with men, the speaker said this:

"I have been wondering how it is possible that there can be so much in this city that needs correction when I see so many Presbyterian men and those of other denominations coming out in such bad weather to show their interest in the heathen of foreign lands. I cannot help reflecting on the vast amount of work that is yet to be done at home. But the work we do abroad only strengthens us here, and the evidence we collect through our foreign missionaries serves to make our faith in our country stronger and increases our activities.

"There is more altruism in the world today than ever before and Christianity is the cause. Go to the lands where Buddhism, Mohammedanism, or Confucianism reigns supreme and you will find that except for the few things they have borrowed from the Christians they have stood still for 2,000 years or more. Christianity has lifted up nations in Europe that ten centuries ago were sunk in the mire of obloquy. History shows it is Christianity that has helped to civilize nations."

Then, of course, it is self-evident that Bryan read the Bible, that he knew it, that he believed it absolutely. Of his adherence to a literal belief in the Bible, more in other chapters. But no consideration of the faith and religion of William Jennings Bryan could conclude without a stressing of the part the Bible paid in his life; personally, because he read it every day; professionally, because it dove-tailed in to all his political activities; rhetorically, because its quotations are to be found, hundreds and thousands of times in the syllables, written, delivered or merely spoken informally by the Commoner.

And, dramatically. For it was in valiant defense of the Bible, that Bryan waged his last great battle in the little Tennessee town.

And, the battle over, Bryan was sitting in his room that Sunday afternoon. The open Bible lay at his side. He had been reading it when he put it down, slipped over to the bed and lay down for that sleep which carried him, so gently, over into death.

CHAPTER XX

"The Prince of Peace"

Had rather Talk on Religion than Politics—This His Most Famous Lecture—Heard by Millions Throughout the Nation—Stand
on Evolution—Plausibility of Miracles—The Watermelon Illustration—Why Christ is Truly the Prince of Peace.

Literally millions of people have heard this best known of
Bryan's lectures, "The Prince of Peace." It was not written
all at once, but it grew and developed at each repetition. In its
final form it became Bryan's presentation of his religious tenets,
and especially of the evidence supporting Christ's title of "The
Prince of Peace."

It was Bryan's most popular Chautauqua lecture, and week
after week and year after year he gave it before vast audiences.
He preferred to give it before gatherings of men, young men
especially, because he felt that its message was aimed particularly at that class of hearers. Not only did he give it all
over the United States, but on his tour of the world he delivered it at Tokio, Manila, Bombay, Cairo, Jerusalem, Montreal,
Toronto, and in other cities.

The outstanding portions of that famous speech follow here:

"I offer no apology for speaking upon a religious theme, for it
is the most universal of all themes. I am interested in the
science of government, but I am more interested in religion than
in government. I enjoy making a political speech—I have made
a good many and shall make more—but I would rather speak
on religion than on politics. I commenced speaking on the
stump when I was only twenty, but I commenced speaking in
the church six years earlier—and I shall be in the church even

255

after I am out of politics. I feel sure of my ground when I make a political speech, but I feel even more certain of my ground when I make a religious speech. If I addressed you upon the subject of law I might interest the lawyers; if I discussed the science of medicine I might interest the physicians; in like manner merchants might be interested in comments on commerce, and farmers in matters pertaining to agriculture; but no one of these subjects appeals to all.

"Man is a religious being; the heart instinctively seeks for a God. Whether he worships on the banks of the Ganges, prays with his face upturned to the sun, kneels towards Mecca or, regarding all space as a temple, communes with the Heavenly Father according to the Christian creed, man is essentially devout.

"There are honest doubters whose sincerity we recognize and respect, but occasionally I find young men who think it smart to be skeptical; they talk as if it were an evidence of larger intelligence to scoff at creeds and to refuse to connect themselves with churches. They call themselves 'Liberal,' as if a Christian were narrow minded. Some go so far as to assert that the 'advanced thought of the world' has discarded the idea that there is a God. To these young men I desire to address myself.

"Religion is the foundation of morality in the individual and in the group of individuals. Materialists have attempted to build up a system of morality upon the basis of enlightened self-interest. They would have man figure out by mathematics that it pays him to abstain from wrong-doing; they would even inject an element of selfishness into altruism, but the moral system elaborated by the materialists has several defects.

"First, its virtues are borrowed from moral systems based upon religion. Second, as it rests upon argument rather than upon authority, the young are not in a position to accept or reject. Third, one never knows just how much of his decision is due to reason and how much is due to passion or to selfish interest. And, fourth, one whose morality rests upon a nice calculation of benefits to be secured spends time figuring that he should spend in action.

"Morality is the power of endurance in man; and a religion which teaches personal responsibility to God gives strength to morality.

"There are difficulties to be encountered in religion, but there are difficulties to be encountered everywhere. If Christians sometimes have doubts and fears, unbelievers have more doubts and greater fears. I passed through a period of skepticism when I was in college, and I have been glad ever since that I became a member of the church before I left home for college, for it helped me during those trying days.

"It was at this period that I became confused by the different theories of creation. But I examined these theories and found that they all assumed something to begin with. Well, I have a right to assume, and I prefer to assume a Designer back of the design—a Creator back of the creation; and no matter how long you draw out the process of creation, so long as God stands back of it you cannot shake my faith in Jehovah. We must begin with something—we must start somewhere—and the Christian begins with God.

"I do not carry the doctrine of evolution as far as some do; I am not yet convinced that man is a lineal descendant of the lower animals. I do not mean to find fault with you if you want to accept the theory; all I mean to say is that while you may trace your ancestry back to the monkey if you find pleasure or pride in doing so, you shall not connect me with your family tree without more evidence than has yet been produced. I object to the theory for several reasons.

"First, it is a dangerous theory. If a man links himself in generations with the monkey, it then becomes an important question whether he is going towards him or coming from him —and I have seen them going in both directions. The mind is greater than the body and the soul is greater than the mind, and I object to having man's pedigree traced on one-third of him only—and that the lowest third.

"But there is another objection. The Darwinian theory represents man as reaching his present perfection by the operation of the law of hate—the merciless law by which the strong crowd out and kill off the weak. If this is the law of our development then, if there is any logic that can bind the human mind, we shall turn backward towards the beast in proportion as we substitute the law of love. I prefer to believe that love rather than hatred is the law of development. I fear that some have accepted Darwin's theory in the hope of escaping from the miracle, but why, my friends, should the miracle frighten us?

"Christ cannot be separated from the miraculous; His birth, His ministrations, and His resurrection, all involve the miraculous, and the change which His religion works in the human heart is a continuing miracle. Eliminate the miracles and Christ becomes merely a human being and His Gospel is stripped of divine authority.

"The miracle raises two questions: 'Can God perform a miracle?' and, 'Would He want to?' The first is easy to answer. A God who can make a world can do anything He wants to do with it. The power to perform miracles is necessarily implied in the power to create. But would God want to perform a miracle?—this is the question which has given most of the trouble. The more I have considered it the less inclined I am to answer in the negative. To say that God would not perform a miracle is to assume a more intimate knowledge of God's plans and purposes than I can claim to have.

"The fact that we are constantly learning of the existence of new forces suggests the possibility that God may operate through forces yet unknown to us, and the mysteries with which we deal every day warn me that faith is as necessary as sight. The miracle is not more mysterious than many of the things with which man now deals—it is simply different. The miraculous birth of Christ is not more mysterious than any other conception—it is simply unlike it; nor is the resurrection of Christ more mysterious than the myriad resurrections which mark each annual seed-time.

"I was eating a piece of watermelon some months ago and was struck with its beauty. I took some of the seeds and dried them and weighed them, and found that it would require some five thousand seeds to weigh a pound; and then I applied mathematics to that forty-pound melon. One of these seeds, put into the ground, when warmed by the sun and moistened by the rain, takes off its coat and goes to work; it gathers from somewhere two hundred thousand times its own weight, and forcing this raw material through a tiny stem, constructs a watermelon. It ornaments the outside with a covering of green; inside the green it puts a layer of white, and within the white a core of red, and all through the red it scatters seeds, each one capable of continuing the work of reproduction. Where does that little seed get its tremendous power? Where does it find its coloring matter? How does it collect its flavoring extract? How does it build a watermelon? Until you can explain a watermelon, do not be too sure that you can set limits to the power of the Almighty and say just what He would do or how He would do it. I cannot explain the watermelon, but I eat it and enjoy it.

"Everything that grows tells a like story of infinite power. Why should I deny that a Divine hand fed a multitude with a few loaves and fishes when I see hundreds of millions fed every year by a hand which converts the seeds scattered over the field into an abundant harvest?

"I was thinking a few years ago of the Christmas which was then approaching and of Him in whose honor the day is celebrated. I recalled the message, 'Peace on earth, good will to men,' and then my thoughts ran back to the prophecy uttered centuries before His birth, in which He was described as the Prince of Peace.

"I have thought of this prophecy many times during the last few years, and I have selected this theme that I might present some of the reasons which lead me to believe that Christ has fully earned the right to be called The Prince of Peace—a title that will in the years to come be more and more applied to Him.

"All the world is in search of peace; every heart that ever beat has sought for peace, and many have been the methods employed to secure it. Some have thought to purchase it with riches and have labored to secure wealth, hoping to find peace when they were able to go where they pleased and buy what they liked.

"Some have sought peace in social distinction, but whether they have been within the charmed circle and fearful lest they might fall out, or outside, and hopeful that they might get in, they have not found peace. Some have thought, vain thought, to find peace in political prominence; but whether office comes by birth, as in monarchies, or by election, as in republics, it does not bring peace.

"I am glad that our Heavenly Father did not make the peace of the human heart to depend upon our ability to buy it with money, secure it in society, or win it at the polls, for in any case but few could have obtained it, but when He made peace the reward of a conscience void of offense towards God and man, He put it within the reach of all.

"To those who have grown gray in the Church, I need not speak of the peace to be found in faith in God and trust in an over-ruling Providence.

"Christ promoted peace by giving us assurance that a line of communcation can be established between the Father above and the child below. And who will measure the consolations of the hour of prayer?

"And immortality! Who will estimate the peace which a belief in a future life has brought to the sorrowing hearts of the sons of men?

"Christ gave us proof of immortality and it was a welcome assurance, although it would hardly seem necessary that one should rise from the dead to convince us that the grave is not the end. To every created thing God has given a tongue that proclaims a future life.

"If the Father deigns to touch with Divine power the cold and pulseless heart of the buried acorn and to make it burst forth from its prison walls, will He leave neglected in the earth the soul of man, made in the image of his Creator? If He stoops to give to the rosebush, whose withered blossoms float upon the autumn breeze, the sweet assurance of another springtime, will He refuse the words of hope to the sons of men when the frosts of winter come?

"In Cairo I secured a few grains of wheat that had slumbered for more than thirty centuries in an Egyptian tomb. As I looked at them this thought came into my mind: If one of those grains had been planted on the banks of the Nile the year after it grew, and all its lineal descendants had been planted and replanted from that time until now, its progeny would today be sufficiently numerous to feed the teeming millions of the world. If this invisible germ of life in the grain of wheat can thus pass unimpaired through three thousand resurrections, I shall not doubt that my soul has power to clothe itself with a body suited to its new existence when this earthly frame has crumbled into dust.

"A belief in immortality not only consoles the individual, but it exerts a powerful influence in bringing peace between individuals. If one actually thinks that man dies as the brute dies, he will yield more easily to the temptation to do injustice to his neighbor when the circumstances are such as to promise security from detection. But if one really expects to meet again, and live eternally with, those whom he knows today, he is restrained from evil deeds by the fear of endless remorse.

"Again, Christ deserves to be called The Prince of Peace because He has given us a measure of greatness which promotes peace. When His disciples quarrelled among themselves as to which should be greatest in the Kingdom of Heaven, He rebuked them and said: 'Let him who would be chiefest among you be the servant of all.'

"Service is the measure of greatness; it always has been true; it is true today, and it always will be true, that he is greatest who does the most of good. Nearly all of our controversies and combats grow out of the fact that we are trying to get something from each other—there will be peace when our aim is to do something for each other. The human measure of a human life is its income; the divine measure of a life is its outgo, its overflow—its contribution to the welfare of all.

"Christ also led the way to peace by giving us a formula for the propagation of truth. Not all of those who have really desired to do good have employed the Christian method—not all Christians even. In the history of the human race but two methods have been used. The first is the forcible method, and it has been employed most frequently.

"The other is the Bible plan—'Be not overcome of evil but overcome evil with good.' And there is no other way of overcoming evil.

"My faith in the future—and I have faith—and my optimism—for I am an optimist—my faith and my optimism rest upon the belief that Christ's teachings are being more studied today than ever before, and that with this larger study will come a larger application of those teachings to the every-day life of the world, and to the questions with which we deal.

"But this Prince of Peace promises not only peace but strength. Some have thought His teachings fit only for the weak and the timid and unsuited to men of vigour, energy and ambition. Nothing could be farther from the truth. Only the man of faith can be courageous. Confident that he fights on the side of Jehovah, he doubts not the success of his cause.

"What would have been the fate of the Church if the early Christians had had as little faith as many of our Christians of today? And if the Christians of today had the faith of the martyrs, how long would it be before the fulfillment of the prophecy that 'every knee shall bow and every tongue confess?'

"I am glad that He, who is called the Prince of Peace—who can bring peace to every troubled heart and whose teachings, exemplified in life, will bring peace between man and man, between community and community, between State and State, between nation and nation throughout the world—I am glad that He brings courage as well as peace so that those who follow Him may take up and each day bravely do the duties that to that day fall.

"As the Christian grows older he appreciates more and more and more the completeness with which Christ satisfies the longings of the heart, and, grateful for the peace which he enjoys and for the strength which he has received, he repeats the words of the great scholar, Sir William Jones:

'Before thy mystic altar, heavenly truth,
I kneel in manhood, as I knelt in youth,
Thus let me kneel, till this dull form decay,
And life's last shade be brightened by thy ray.'"

CHAPTER XXI

Conventions of 1912 and 1916

Wants "True Democrat"—Resolution Against Wall Street Startles
Convention—Withdraws Second Clause of It—It Passes—Mrs.
Taft in Gallery—Changes from Clark to Wilson—Wilson Wins—
Bryan Declines Vice-Presidency in "Valedictory"—1916 Conven-
tion—Hides in Improvised Chicken Coop—Suspend Rules to
Permit Him to Talk—Praises Wilson—Assails Those Advocating
Intervention in Mexico—"Power of Christ" Speech.

The most spectacular victory William Jennings Bryan ever won,
was won, ironically enough, for another man.

The scene of the victory was the Democratic national convention
of 1912, held at Baltimore. It was here that Bryan brought about
the defeat of Champ Clark, then speaker of the House, as the
presidential nominee and secured the triumph of party choice for
standard-bearer for Woodrow Wilson, then governor of New Jersey.

A few months before the convention Bryan announced that he
would not be a candidate but that he was "ready to enter upon a
campaign in behalf of a true Democrat with even more vigor than
that with which I have fought at any time in my own behalf."

That "true Democrat," Bryan felt, was Woodrow Wilson, whose
"progressive policies" had already attracted the interest of the Commoner.

His first attack on the "interests" was an oratorical bomb fired
into Wall street.

On the eve of the nomination of a presidential candidate, on
June 27, Bryan offered his famous resolution declaring the convention's freedom from the influence of J. Pierpont Morgan, Thomas
F. Ryan and August Belmont. The latter two occupied seats as
delegates on the floor of the convention.

265

No more sensational event, it is said, ever took place in a national political convention. Bryan's proposal burst like a bombshell over the 2,000 delegates and alternates and the thousands of visitors, just as the body was settling down to the business of nominating speeches.

Bryan himself appeared on the platform by the side of his friend, Permanent Chairman Ollie James, and amid a profound silence read the resolution:

"Resolved—That in this crisis in our party's career, and in our country's history, this convention sends greeting to the people of the United States, and assures them that the party of Jefferson and Jackson is still the champion of popular government and equality before the law. As proof of our fidelity to the people we hereby declare ourselves opposed to the nomination of any candidate for President who is the representative of, or under any obligation to, J. Pierpont Morgan, Thomas F. Ryan, August Belmont, or any other member of the privilege-hunting and favor-seeking class.

"Be it further resolved—That we demand the withdrawal from this convention of any delegate or delegates constituting or representing the above named interests."

Then, amid the astonished silence of the throng, Bryan began his argument for the resolution:

"This is an extraordinary resolution, but extraordinary conditions need extraordinary remedies," he asserted. "We are now engaged in the conduct of a convention that will place before this country the Democratic nominee, and I assume that every delegate in this convention is here because he wants that nominee elected.

"And it is in order that we may advance the cause of our candidate that I present this resolution. There are questions of which a court takes judicial notice, and there are subjects upon which we can assume that the American people are informed, and there is not a delegate in this convention who does not know that an effort is being made right now to sell the Democratic party into bondage to the predatory interests of this country.

"It is the most brazen, the most insolent, the most impudent attempt that has been made in the history of American politics to dominate a convention, stifle the honest sentiment of a people and make the nominee the bond slave of the men who exploit the people of this country.

"I need not tell you that J. Pierpont Morgan and Thomas F. Ryan and August Belmont are three of the men who are connected with the great money trusts of this country, who are as despotic in their rule of the business of the country and as merciless in their command of their slaves as any man in the country.

"Someone has said that we have no right to discuss the delegates who come here from a sovereign state.

"I reply that if these men are willing to insult 6,500,000 Democrats we ought to speak out against them and let them know we resent the insult.

"I, for one, am not willing that Thomas F. Ryan and August Belmont shall come here with their paid attorneys and seek secret counsel with the managers of this party. No sense of politeness or courtesy to such men will keep me from protecting my party from the disgrace that they inflict upon it.

"Now, my friends, I cannot speak for you. You have your own responsibility, but if this is to be a convention run by these men; if our nominee is to be their representative and tool, I pray you to give us, who represent constituencies that do not want this, a chance to go on record with our protest against it. If any of you are willing to nominate a candidate who represents these men——"

Bryan was interrupted by prolonged cheering and applause.

Continuing, he said: "Or who is under obligation to these men, do it and take the responsibility. I refuse to take that responsibility.

"Some have said that we haven't a right to demand the withdrawal of delegates from this convention. I will make you a proposition. One of these men sits with New York and the other sits with Virginia. I make you this proposition. If the state of New York will take a poll of its vote and a majority of them—not Mr. Murphy, but a majority of the delegates—I repeat that if New York would, on roll call, where her delegates can have their names recorded and printed, ask for the withdrawal of the name of Mr. Belmont, and if Virginia will on roll call protest against the withdrawal of Mr. Ryan, I will then withdraw the last part of the resolution.

"In answer to the argument that this resolution should not be introduced here to disturb harmony, I commend to the gentleman from Virginia the Bible doctrine: 'If thy right hand offend thee, cut it off.'

"My reputation will not be worth defending when it becomes necessary to defend it from the charges of a friend of Thomas F. Ryan. I now withdraw——"

A chorus of mingled cheers and jeers greeted this statement.

"Vote, vote," came a shout.

"—And I'm sure if it's worth while to cut off the right hand to save the body it's worth cutting off Ryan and Belmont and Morgan to save the Democratic party."

When Bryan came down from the platform his friend and former secretary, Robert F. Rose, tugged at his coat sleeve and whispered, "What became of the passage about Taft?"

Bryan turned toward one corner of the balcony and said, "Why, didn't you see that Mrs. Taft was in the gallery?"

While Bryan had been talking on the resolution the convention boiled over. From Virginia, the state which had sent Ryan as a delegate, and from New York, where Belmont sat, came angry

Scopes, Father and Son—John Thomas Scopes the young school teacher defendant in the trial of Tennessee's anti-evolution law, standing with his father. Thomas Scopes, who attended his son's trial in Dayton.

© Underwood & Underwood photo.

Darrow Arrives—The noted defense attorney reaches Dayton to take part against Bryan in the Scopes trial. He is welcomed by Scopes, Attorney Neal, and enthusiastic adherents.

demonstrations. Ryan and Belmont, however, sat silent, imperturbable.

But around these men raged a storm of indignation that rapidly spread to surrounding delegations, and soon the whole hall was plunged into an unprecedented roar.

The proposition urging the withdrawal of Ryan and Belmont was charged with being an invasion of the rights of sovereign states, and then the boos and catcalls, jeers and hisses, were mingled with hand-clapping, cheers and stamping of feet such as set a record for demonstrations.

After a bitter debate, Bryan withdrew the second paragraph of the resolution, the one with the teeth in it, demanding the withdrawal from the convention of the delegates Ryan and Belmont. His reason for this, he said later, was that:

"Many of our Democrats sincerely objected to the second resolution on the ground that it was an invasion of a right of the state, and I did not want to put them into a position where their reasons for voting against the double resolution would be the subject of discussion.

"Others were likely to use it as an excuse for voting against the first part of the resolution and I thought it best not to give them that excuse, and the purpose was served anyhow in a condemnation of the men and the system they represent."

The roll was called on the modified resolution amid a turbulence which the chairman was utterly unable to quell. Foes of Bryan, regarding his withdrawal of the second part of the resolution as a boomerang, all voted for the first part. So the resolution was adopted by a vote of 889 to 196. Two did not vote and one was absent.

Among the 889 delegates who voted with him were Ryan and Belmont themselves; and in fact the entire New York delegation which cast its ballot, apparently in a sardonic mood, with an eye to hurling ridicule at the Nebraskan.

Senator Reed of Kansas City put in nomination, Champ Clark.

Ex-Judge John W. Westcott of Camden, N. J., placed Woodrow Wilson in nomination.

On the first ballot Clark got 440½ votes and Wilson received 324. Then the fight began.

Clark led for 27 ballots and once had a clear majority of nine. At the end of the tenth ballot, when the New York delegation cast its 90 votes for Clark there was a tumultuous demonstration. The Clark men paraded around the hall, led by Miss Genevieve Clark, the candidate's daughter. The cheering lasted 23 minutes.

The high spot, oratorically, of the balloting was when Bryan changed from Clark, for whom he had been instructed, to Wilson. The nub of his speech is contained in the following paragraph from it:

"The delegates for whom I speak stand ready to carry out the instructions given, in the spirit in which they were given and upon the conditions under which they were given; but these delegates will not participate in the nomination of any man whose nomination depends upon the vote of the New York delegation. Speaking for myself and those who join me, we, therefore, withhold our vote from Mr. Clark as long as New York's vote is recorded for him, and I hereby notify the chairman and this convention that I desire recognition to withdraw these votes from any candidates to whom New York's votes are thrown. The position that we take in regard to Mr. Clark we will take in regard to any other candidate whose name is now, or may come before the convention. We shall not be parties to the nomination of any man, no matter who he may be or from what section of the country he comes, who will not, when elected, be absolutely free to carry out the anti-Morgan-Ryan-Belmont resolution and make his administration reflect the wishes and hopes of those who believe in a government of the people, by the people, and for the people.

"Now, I am prepared to announce my vote, with the understanding that I stand ready to withdraw my vote from the candidate for whom I now cast it if Mr. Murphy casts the ninety votes of New York for him. I cast my vote for Nebraska's second choice— Governor Wilson."

Bryan's determined support of the governor of New Jersey turned the tide in the bitter, long-drawn-out fight. The Nebraskan persisted in his opposition and his reiterated pleas against the "domination of the party by Wall street." The attack finally broke up the ranks of the Clark followers, and at dawn, finally, the convention designated Wilson as the nominee.

Then there was talk of running Bryan as Wilson's team-mate.

In declining to allow the use of his name as vice-presidential candidate, the Peerless Leader delivered what he called his valedictory:

"Mr. Chairman and members of the convention: You have been so generous with me in the allowance of time that I had not expected to transgress upon your patience again, but the compliment that has been paid me by the gentleman from the District of Columbia justifies, I hope, a word in the form of a valedictory.

"For sixteen years I have been a fighting man. Performing what I regarded as a public duty, I have not hesitated to speak out on every public question that was before the people of the nation for settlement, and I have not hesitated to arouse the hostility and the enmity of individuals where I felt it my duty to do so in behalf of my country.

"I have never advocated a man without gladness, and I have never opposed a man except in sadness. If I have any enemies in this country those who are my enemies had a monopoly of hatred. There is not one single human being for whom I feel a hatred.

"Nor is there any one American citizen in my own party, or in any other, that I would oppose for anything, except I believed that in not opposing him I was surrendering the interests of my country, which I hold above any person.

"I recognize that a man who fights must carry scars and I decided long before this campaign commenced that I had been in so many battles and had alienated so many, that my party ought to have the leadership of one who had not thus offended and who thus might lead with greater hope of victory.

"And tonight I come with joy to surrender into the hands of the one chosen by this convention a standard which I carried in three campaigns, and I challenge my enemies to declare that it has ever been lowered in the face of the enemy. The same belief that led me to prefer another for the Presidency rather than to be a candidate myself leads me to prefer another for second place rather than to be a candidate myself.

"It is not because the Vice-Presidency is lower in importance than the Presidency that I decline. There is no office in this nation so low that I would not take it if I could serve my country by accepting it.

"I believe that I can render more service to my country when I have not the embarrassment of a nomination and have not the suspicion of a selfish interest—more service than I could as a candidate, and your candidates will not be more active in this campaign than I shall be.

"My services are at the command of the party, and I feel a relief now that the burden of leadership is transferred to other shoulders."

The Republican party had already been split by the fight between Taft and Roosevelt at Chicago, and the nomination of Roosevelt as the candidate of the National Progressive party followed soon after the Baltimore convention. A sweeping victory came to Wilson at the polls and so it was that William Jennings Bryan, thrice defeated for President, was responsible for the election to the position of chief executive of Woodrow Wilson.

On the 5th of March, 1913, President Wilson, in recognition of the tenacious service the man from Nebraska had rendered him at the convention made him Secretary of State, which position he held until he resigned on June 8th, 1915.

The 1916 convention was held at St. Louis. Bryan went as a newspaper correspondent. But he was projected forward into importance by the will and the insistence of the crowd.

At one time when, for political reasons, Bryan did not wish to be in the fore-ground and did not wish to make a speech he had to go to the officials in charge of the seating arrangements to see if he could get into a secluded corner. As he sat in his seat in the press stand the crowd spied him and stampeded for him. It was during the platform fight and Bryan did not want to interfere or talk at that time. So they rigged up a chicken coop contrivance for him under the press stand. Here he sat and reported the proceedings until he thought it was "safe" for him to emerge.

But he did make one speech which took the convention by storm. Under a suspension of rules he was permitted to speak after the delegates had roared their approval. Senator James introduced Bryan as "one of the leading citizens of the world and America's greatest Democrat."

"We are here," Bryan announced, "to begin the fight of 1916. And a party united in every state will face the enemy.

"Today the Democratic party is able successfully to defend every action of the administration. Our President, our Senate, and our House are responsible for the greatest constructive program the Republic has ever known. We have put more laws of importance to the people on the statute books than any half dozen Republican administrations.

"No President since Jackson has had to face such a tremendous attack on the part of predatory wealth as Woodrow Wilson. Attempts were made to start a panic to prevent some of our legislation. The Secretary of the Treasury took his evidence to the White House—not to Wall street—and the panic was prevented.

"The currency law we passed has broken the grip of Wall street on the politics of the United States. For many years one hundred men in Wall street have had the power to swing our national elections as they pleased. One who has felt their power must be pardoned if he rejoices at their downfall.

"Republicans talked of regulating monopoly. But the regulators were regulated by the men who raised Republican campaign funds. The Democratic party laid the ax to the root of the tree of private monopoly.

"The Republicans in their platform lacked the courage either to admit the values of the currency law or to denounce it.

"This convention is not controlled, as was that in Chicago, by the experts of the favor seeking corporations. The Republicans dare not attack the income tax law. It has taken the burden from the bent backs of the poor and put it where it belongs. We dare the Republicans to attack it.

"The Republicans talk of the tariff. It is merely a matter of habit with them. They have put behind the tariff question so much energy that the tariff agitation runs now by sheer momentum. Our tariff law is the best the country has ever known.

"Then came the great war in Europe. Even that could not bring a panic in the United States. We inherited from a Republican administration an insurrection in Mexico. In the State Department is a telegram from Huerta stating: 'I have overthrown the government.' The Republicans dare not attack our policy towards Mexico.

"Ask any mother and she will thank the President that her son has not been sent to die in Mexico. A few men who own ranches and mines in Mexico are anxious to use American soldiers to collect profit on their Mexican investments. But the President will not intervene. If he did they would demand that he go to Panama.

"I have differed with the President on some points of his policy in dealing with the great war," Bryan continued, "but I agree with the American people in thanking God that we have a President who has kept—and will keep—us out of war.

"For two years our President has borne a burden such as few men have ever been called on to carry. Then, does not the honor of being peacemaker belong to this President and to the party which selected him?

"We have a record which we can go to the country on without fear or blush.

"No Democrat can be without pride in the record of his party. I love my party not only for what it has done, but for what it will and must do in the future.

"Who can better claim the honor of bringing the warring nations to peace than an administration which has already made treaties with half the world which make war a remote possibility?

"The United States faces the greatest opportunity ever offered a nation since time began. And what party shall take the lead in that great work but the Democratic party—the party which puts the brotherhood of man as only next to the fatherhood of God.

"I stand with the Democrats of the nation in declaring that we must give Woodrow Wilson a chance to bring the world to peace."

Let us close this consideration of Bryan's part in the St. Louis convention with his famous "Power of Christ" speech:

"There is a picture which has attracted attention wherever it has been seen—the picture of Christ before Pilate. Pilate represented the power of the Roman government, and back of him were the legions of Rome. Before Pilate, helpless, unarmed, stood the Apostle of Love. For His triumph, they nailed Him to the tree, and those who stood around mocked and jeered and said, 'He is dead!' But that, instead of being the end, was only the beginning.

"In a few centuries the power of Cæsar was gone and his legions forgotten. The power of Christ, however, increased until hundreds, yes, thousands of millions of people, have taken His name with reverence upon their lips; millions have been ready to die rather than surrender the faith that He put into their hearts. He has become the great factor of all history, the glowing figure of all time.

"Today Christ and Pilate again stand face to face, and Force and Love are again striving for mastery and dominion. The old world represented force. It built its hope of peace on fear and threats of violence. Each nation attempted to terrorize other nations in peace, and in their efforts they engendered hatreds that ended in war.

"If the nations now at war had spent one-tenth as much through trying to cultivate friendship as they have spent in cultivating hatred, there would be no war in Europe today."

CHAPTER XXII

Secretary of State

Serves At Difficult Period—Wilson and Bryan Not Always In
Agreement—The Thirty Treaties—"Nothing Is Final Between
Friends"—"They Shall Beat Their Swords Into Plowshares"—
"A Message from Bethlehem"—Controversy with Japan—Mexican
Trouble—Grape Juice—Reply to Criticism of His Lecturing—
Friction with the President.

Bryan entered into his duties as Secretary of State on March 5,
1913. It was generally understood that President Wilson had bestowed the portfolio on him in recognition of his services at
Baltimore, which won Wilson the Democratic nomination and later
the Presidency.

The two years and three months during which Bryan held this
office were years of difficulty, marked by international unrest which
resulted in the outbreak of the great war in Europe. As his term
in office grew longer, it became more difficult, as the position of
the United States and her policy toward Germany became increasingly complicated. The trouble with Mexico and the Japanese alien
land controversy in California were affairs that required delicate
handling and they caused the Secretary of State added anxiety.

In the diplomatic administration of these questions, it early became apparent that Bryan and the President often did not think
along the same lines. Their aims were the same, but their methods
differed. Two men with deeper convictions and greater tenacity
of purpose in carrying out those convictions, than Bryan and Wilson, scarcely could have been brought together. The situation was
bound some day to end as it did in June of 1915, when Bryan felt
in duty bound to give up the Secretaryship.

The office of Secretary of State offered Bryan an opportunity to put into practice some of the ideals and ideas he long had preached. On his entry into the cabinet he at once began to negotiate with foreign powers all over the world, to make treaties of peace and arbitration. He secured the approval of the President, of the cabinet, and the Foreign Affairs committee of the Senate, and then laid before the representatives of nearly all the powers, the principles of a treaty which he believed would go far toward preventing future wars.

These treaties which Bryan proposed depended on several major tenets: That there must be no war until the expiration of a set period for investigation; that the principle of investigation must apply to all disputes; that a permanent board of inquiry should be maintained, to be composed of five members, one chosen by each side from among its own citizens, one chosen by each side from the citizens of the other country, and one to be selected by agreement; that the aid of the board might be invoked by either party at any time, or the board might act on its own initiative; and lastly that each party to the treaty, once the investigation was concluded, might act independently as it saw fit.

The gist of the treaty provisions may be drawn from the text of the first clause in Article 1 of the treaty which was negotiated with Great Britain:

"The high contracting parties agree that all disputes between them, of every nature whatsoever, other than disputes the settlement of which is provided for and in fact achieved under the existing agreements between the high contracting parties, shall, when diplomatic methods of adjustment have failed, be referred for investigation and report to a permanent international commission, to be constituted in the manner prescribed in the next succeeding article; and they agree not to declare war or begin hostilities during such investigation and before the report is submitted."

It was the element of time and delay on which Bryan counted

to make such treaties a potent factor in bringing about permanent peace among nations. An investigation of just a few days might have prevented the World War, said some international experts; and, by the treaties, Bryan sought to put such a buffer of time and consideration, between countries hostile to each other over some matter in dispute.

Nearly all the nations of the world, through Bryan's negotiations, undertook the consideration of these treaties, and before Bryan had been long in office he had concluded treaties with the following powers: Great Britain, France, Italy, Spain, Russia, Greece, Sweden, Norway, Denmark, Portugal, Holland, the Argentine Republic, Ecuador, China, Paraguay, Chile, Brazil, Uruguay, Peru, Venezuela, the Dominican Republic, Switzerland, Costa Rica, Persia, Bolivia, Nicaragua, Honduras, Panama, Guatemala, and Salvador, thirty countries in all. Germany and Japan were the notable exceptions who did not enter into such a compact with the United States.

With a characteristic touch, Bryan sent a paperweight to each of the diplomats who had signed the treaties with him. It was of steel, nickel plated. The metal was from melted swords and the paperweight was in the form of a plowshare. On the beam of the plow was an inscription of the motto which Bryan believed would ultimately lead to international harmony: "Nothing is final between friends." On the blade of the plow was the quotation from Isaiah, 2:4, "They shall beat their swords into plowshares."

And on Christmas Day, 1914, members of the diplomatic corps in Washington received from the Secretary of State a booklet written by him, entitled "A Message from Bethlehem." In it, Bryan discussed war and peace and the thirty treaties, saying:

"It is believed that these treaties will go far towards making war a remote possibility, for it will be difficult for nations to engage in war after a year's deliberation. Diplomacy is the art of keeping cool and the period provided for investigation not only permits the subsidence of passion and the restoration of reason, but it gives time for the operation of that public opinion, which more and more condemns the use of force and exalts the processes of reason. Time also enables impartial judges to separate questions of fact from questions of honor—a most important task, since the line between the two is quite sure to be obscured when anger and prejudice are aroused. Instead of using the ultimatum, we are adopting the motto: 'Nothing is final between friends.'"

These treaties were not accomplished without some criticism from those who thought them a weak and foolish means of bringing about peace. Colonel Roosevelt was one of their most outspoken critics. He asserted that the navy had done more toward peace than all the treaties ever drawn up, and he declared that the Bryan pacts represented as "high a degree of fatuity as is often achieved in these matters."

Bryan made reply in a speech at Columbus, Kan., saying:

"It has been said that these treaties are little treaties and harmless because they do not bind. Thank God, Roosevelt does not speak for the American people, who regard our treaty obligations as binding. These treaties require a year's investigation before declaring war. A leading diplomat has said that a week's investigation would have averted the European war. Our new treaties will cause nations to act, not in the heat of wrath, but in sober, good judgment."

During the controversy with Japan over the anti-alien land question in California, Bryan journeyed to the coast where he worked tirelessly to bring about a satisfactory settlement. He conferred with the governor of the state and spoke several times before the state legislature. Relations between the United States and Japan were somewhat strained during the period. The outcome of the controversy was the drafting and passage of a new measure, known as the Webb bill. It modified somewhat the restrictions against the Japanese, but even then did not entirely satisfy them, and a protest was evoked from Tokio.

During his tenure of the Secretaryship, Bryan was a great stickler for secrecy. As a rule, he refused to give out the slightest inkling as to what negotiations were going on with foreign powers until the whole matter had been concluded. He worked untiringly on the details of the questions brought before him rather than entrust them to his subordinates.

It was during Bryan's term of office that the trouble with Mexico arose over an insult to the American flag and the refusal of Huerta to fire in apology a salute to the flag. The President dispatched American troops to Vera Cruz, which was captured April 12, 1914. Later, the troops and warships were withdrawn, Huerta was deposed, and a constitutional government set up under Carranza, who received the support of the administration.

Bryan's home life in Washington won the respect and admiration of officials and diplomats. He and Mrs. Bryan were fond of entertaining, and gave frequent dinner parties, luncheons, and garden parties. One feature of the Secretary's entertainment caused much comment when he first announced it. Since he had been opposed to intoxicating drinks all his life, Bryan declared when he first reached the capital that nothing except grape juice should appear on his table, and he kept his word.

Another source of much comment was Bryan's continuance of his lecturing. He appeared often on the Chautauqua circuit, and his absences from Washington were criticized. But he did not give up the lectures. In reply, he declared that the salary of $12,000 he received as a cabinet official was insufficient to meet the demands of the office and that he was forced to supplement his income by his usual means. In a statement to the public he said:

"I am glad to have the criticism brought to my attention. I

believe in criticism of public officials. Criticism is helpful. If a man makes a mistake criticism enables him to correct it; if he is unjustly criticized the criticism helps him. I have had my share of criticism since I have been in public life, but it has not prevented my doing what I thought proper to do.

"In devoting a part of my vacation to lecturing I am doing what I believe to be proper, and I have no fear whatever that any unbiased person will criticize me when he knows the facts.

"For seventeen years the sources of my income have been writing and lecturing, but each year I have made more public speeches without compensation and where I have paid my own traveling expenses, than I have where compensation was received. My earning capacity has been large, and I have made not only an income sufficient for my immediate needs but have saved on an average something more than $10,000 a year.

"In accepting the office which I now hold I gave up the opportunity to add to my accumulations, for I do not expect to increase during my term the amount I have laid aside—that is, I am willing to forego whatever advantage I might derive from the acquiring of $40,000 more, for the privilege of serving the country in this office during the coming four years. I will do more if necessary, but I do not believe that fair minded people will ask it of me.

"Therefore, until I see some reason for changing my purpose, I expect to lecture enough to bring my income up to my expenses, these lectures to be delivered during the time that other officials give to their vacations. In addition to supplementing my salary, I hope that my lectures do good—people who attend them would not do so if they did not think they received their money's worth—but I would be glad to spend my vacations resting instead of lecturing if I could do so without eating in upon the amount that I have laid away as a protection against old age.

"The number of whole week days which have been used for the lectures is, according to my recollection, seven. The rest of the lectures have been delivered at places near enough to the capital to leave in the afternoon, sometimes as late as 3:08 o'clock. I would not assume that the public was interested in these details, were it not for the fact that the representatives of a few newspapers have regarded it as a matter of great importance."

When Mr. Bryan was asked if he would lecture any more during his connection with the State Department, he replied:

"I expect to lecture whenever I deem it desirable or necessary to do so and I have not in the least altered the plans which were made at the time I assumed the duties of the office. The criticism that has been directed against my lecturing is no more bitter than the criticism I have undergone at other times and for other things during my connection with politics.

"A part of this criticism is malicious, a part of it is partisan, and a part of it is based upon misinformation. That which is malicious will answer itself, that which is partisan will be accepted as such, that which is based upon misinformation will cease when the critics are better informed.

"No man should enter public life if he objects to criticism, and he cannot stay in public life if he permits criticisms to turn him from doing what he thinks is right. He must decide his duty for himself and is answerable to the public for any mistakes he makes. I regard lecturing as an entirely legitimate field. I lectured before I was nominated for the Presidency; I lectured between campaigns; I shall continue to lecture, and I shall not believe that any person whose opinion is worth having will think the less of me because I do so. This closes the lecture subject for the present."

In a review of Bryan's career as Secretary of State, it is certain that his peace treaties are the most outstanding accomplishment. Since their negotiation, other nations have adopted the principles contained in them, and England has entered into a similar treaty with Brazil, Sweden with Chile, and Switzerland with Germany. A report of the Hague tribunal on a plan for the peaceful settlement of international disputes, prominently mentions the "Bryan treaties." It was the same principle of a delay for the purpose of inquiry that formed the heart of the league of nations platform, and the Four-Power treaty covering disputes in the Pacific is built on the lines of the Bryan treaty plan.

Even with all this taken into consideration, it is probably just, to say that Bryan did not fit well in the office of the Secretary of State. He was temperamentally unsuited to the duties, and he was unfortunate enough to serve under a man whose convictions were as tenaciously adhered to as he held to his own. This meant that both men, instead of being able to pool their efforts harmoniously toward a common purpose, were constantly having to curb their own wishes out of deference to each other.

Bryan and Wilson disagreed early on the matter of appointments, Bryan insisting much more strongly than his chief that offices should preferably be given to those who had served the Democratic party faithfully and without a break from 1896, on. Bryan was much more insistent than the President that support of nominees should depend largely on whether their principles coincided with his. The two also differed on their party platform. Bryan wrote the plank favoring a single presidential term; Wilson did not approve of it. Bryan wrote the plank favoring the abolition of tolls on American ships passing through the Panama canal. Wilson disapproval of that plank, and obtained the passage of a law which levied tolls on American ships. To Bryan's credit, he gave up his own position and supported the President in the tolls fight with all his power.

It was felt at the time that had it not been for Bryan, who declared he would stand for peace until the bitter end, the

Preparing for Battle—A character study of the defender of revealed religion, reading up preparatory to the Scopes trial. Taken on the lawn of the Rogers house. Dayton, Tenn.

A Characteristic Pose—Bryan's smile was known to millions.

Rulers of Dayton Courtroom—Judge John T. Raulston, presiding at Scopes trial, Sheriff R. B. Harris, and Captain Perkins of the Chattanooga police.

Mexican situation might have been summarily settled.   It was felt that instead of withdrawing the troops from Vera Cruz, the President might have sent more to aid them, and in a short, sharp invasion have decided the Mexican question once and for all.

From the first, Bryan's secretaryship was doomed to end in discord; it finally reached the breaking point in May of 1915.

CHAPTER XXIII

Resignation from the Cabinet

Disagreement with Wilson Over Attitude Toward Germany—Signs First Lusitania Note—Cannot Sign Second—Conference with the President—Resigns—Text of Letter and Wilson's Reply—Pleads for World Friendship—Criticism of His Action—Break with Wilson Never Healed.

Increasingly irreconcilable differences over the policy of the United States toward Germany, before the entry of America into the war, culminating in a disagreement over the second Lusitania note, brought about a breach between Bryan and President Wilson which never again was closed. Bryan resigned his portfolio as Secretary of State on June 8, 1915.

Both men were working with the same end in view—to keep the United States out of the World War. But they believed in, and followed, different sets of principles. Bryan, true to the policy which he used in making the treaties of arbitration, held forth for the soft and diplomatic answer. Wilson believed in strong language and insistent terms.

Germany had been the one great power who had refused to sign a treaty of arbitration with the United States. But a short time before, she had intimated that she might be willing to negotiate for one, and Bryan believed that she should be given the opportunity, even though she was then at war, and the United States had declared for neutrality.

The Lusitania, with citizens of the United States on board, was sunk without warning by a German U-boat on May 1, 1915. On May 13 the first protest was sent to Germany. The note was polite and almost friendly, but it insisted on the right of American citizens to travel the high seas in safety, and it demanded that ships carrying citizens of non-combatant nations must be hailed and the safety of such citizens assured, before action was taken to capture or sink the ship.

Though he did not fully agree with all that was contained in the first note, Bryan signed it. He felt that its demands were so strongly phrased that nothing but still stronger demands, instead of understanding, could come out of them. But President Wilson was determined on his policy. The country, of course, was in a turmoil of indignation at the Lusitania disaster. There were insistent cries for war. The President, in an interview with Count von Bernstorff, acquainted the German ambassador with the uncompromising stand that America would take. In language unmistakable and many times more forceful than was contained in the note, he informed von Bernstorff that there would be no discussion of any particular case until Germany had admitted the right of neutrals to ride on passenger ships, on peaceful missions, without being subject to attack without warning by German submarines.

The second Lusitania note was in preparation at this time, and Bryan could not approve of it. He knew not only what was patently in it, but he knew also, through the von Bernstorff conversation, what was back of it in the President's mind. At the cabinet meeting of June 4 to consider the second note, it was evident that there was about to be a break between these two determined men. Bryan still counseled soft words and arbitration, but he was disappointed to find that his arguments made no impression. The note drafted in the State Department and submitted by him was inadequate, he was informed, and the changes that were to be made in it were freely discussed.

Both Bryan and Wilson realized then that a parting of the ways was imminent, though both held to the last a hope that such a catastrophe might be averted. Through the nights, Bryan walked the floor of his bedroom, wrestling with the problem. Characteristically, he could find in the end no compromise between what he believed to be the right thing to do and a course that he foresaw was bound to lead the United States into the war.

A cabinet meeting was summoned for June 8 to consider a second draft of the note. Knowing that there was no chance for him to alter the President's decision, Bryan did not plan to attend. He was called to the White House by telephone. Before the cabinet met, Bryan and Wilson held a long conference. The two men were in the President's office for an hour. Finally Mr. Wilson pressed a button and summoned an old Negro servant. Wilson was, as usual, unruffled and silent; Bryan was nervous and talkative.

"Mr. Bryan would like a glass of water," the President told the old darkey. The servant brought it and handed it to Bryan. As Bryan took the glass and raised it to his lips, his hand trembled so violently that part of the water was spilled.

There was no question then of what the outcome would be. At the cabinet meeting Bryan sat apart and did not enter into the discussion. At five o'clock that night his resignation was announced. In his letter to the President, he said:

"My dear Mr. President: It is with sincere regret that I have reached the conclusion that I should return to you the commission of Secretary of State with which you honored me at the beginning of your administration.

"Obedient to your sense of duty and actuated by the highest motives, you have prepared for transmission to the German government a note in which I can not join without violating what I deem to be an obligation to my country, and the issue involved is of such moment that to remain a member of your cabinet would be as unfair to you as it would be to the cause which is nearest my heart, namely, the prevention of war.

"Alike desirous of reaching a peaceful solution arising out of the use of submarines against merchantmen, we find ourselves differing irreconcilably as to the methods which should be employed.

"It falls to your lot to speak officially for the nation; I consider it to be none the less my duty to endeavor, as a private citizen, to promote the ends which you have in view by means which you do not feel at liberty to use.

"In severing the intimate and pleasant relations which have existed between us during the last two years, permit me to acknowledge the profound satisfaction which it has given me to be associated with you in the important work which has come before the State Department, and to thank you for the courtesies extended.

"With the heartiest good wishes for your personal welfare and for the success of your administration, I am, my dear President,

"Very truly yours,

"W. J. BRYAN."

In discussing the momentous step he had taken, Bryan paid high tribute to President Wilson.

"We are on the same side so far as I know," he told questioners, "and this action of mine concerns only a difference of method in handling the German question. This difference, and the reasons therefor, I shall attempt to explain in simple language as soon as the note is sent, at which time I will cease to be Secretary of State.

"I do not see how the President, with his convictions, could have done other than he is doing. And I could not do otherwise. A man can only do what he believes to be right. We part official company the best of friends."

In his reply accepting Bryan's resignation President Wilson wrote:

"My dear Mr. Bryan: I accept your resignation only because you insist on its acceptance; and I accept it with much more than deep regret, with a feeling of personal sorrow. Our twenty years of close association have been very delightful to me.

"Our judgments have accorded in practically every matter of official duty and of public policy until now; your support of the work and purposes of the administration has been generous and loyal beyond praise; your eagerness to take advantage of every great opportunity for service it offered has been an example to the rest of us; you have earned our affectionate admiration and friendship. Even now we are not separated in the object we seek, but only in the method by which we seek it.

"It is for these reasons my feeling about your retirement from the Secretaryship of State goes so much deeper than regret. I sincerely deplore it. Our objects are the same and we ought to pursue them together. I yield to your desire only because I must, and wish to bid you Godspeed in the parting. We shall continue to work for the same causes, even when we do not work in the same way.

"With affectionate regard, sincerely yours,

"WOODROW WILSON."

A storm of criticism descended on Bryan for his act. The press of the country, for the majority, condemned him for deserting when the ship was weathering a gale. Others, realizing his sincerity and knowing the strict bounds of conscience by which he limited his acts, were more lenient. Many felt that he had acted not only honestly, but wisely, by quitting in time, when he learned that not only was he in opposition to the sentiments of the President, but to the sentiments of the nation as a whole, as well.

Subsequent to his resignation, Bryan issued several statements explaining his attitude in the matter. One of these was directed toward clarifying the matter of the wording of the note over which the rupture took place. Bryan had written his resignation after viewing the second draft of the Lusitania note. Before he had time to hand his resignation to the President, the note had been altered and its terms softened. But Bryan explained that the change was not sufficient to justify him in withdrawing his resignation. He had seen the altered draft, he said, and might have changed his mind had he so desired.

Another statement explained that he and President Wilson had broken over two principles; first, on the suggestion of investigation by an international commission; and second, as to a warning to Americans not to travel on belligerent vessels, or ships bearing cargoes of ammunition.

A third letter to the public was a plea for world peace through international friendship. With the most disastrous war in history going on in Europe and with the United States daily becoming more and more closely enmeshed, Bryan was not afraid to come out with a suggestion that it was time swords should be beaten into plowshares. No one ever accused him of lack of courage in his convictions.

"You now have before you the text of the note to Germany— the note which it would have been my official duty to sign had I remained Secretary of State," he declared. "I ask you to sit in judgment upon my decision to resign rather than to share responsibility for it.

"I am sure you will credit me with honorable motives, but that is not enough. Good intentions could not atone for a mistake at such a time, on such a subject, and under such circumstances.

"If your verdict is against me, I ask no mercy; I desire none, if I have acted unwisely. A man in public life must act according to his conscience, but however conscientiously he acts he must be prepared to accept without complaint any condemnation which his own errors may bring upon him; he must be willing to bear any deserved punishment, from ostracism to execution. But hear me before you pass sentence.

"The President and I agree in purpose; we desire a peaceful solution of the dispute which has arisen between the United States and Germany. We not only desire it, but with equal fervor we pray for it, but we differ irreconcilably as to the means of securing it.

"If it were merely a personal difference it would be a matter of little moment, for all the presumptions are on his side—the presumptions that go with power and authority. He is your President. I am a private citizen without office or title—but one of the hundred million of inhabitants.

"But the real issue is not between persons; it is between systems, and I rely for vindication wholly upon strength of the position taken.

"Among the influences which governments employ in dealing with each other there are two which are pre-eminent and antagonistic—force and persuasion. Force speaks with firmness and acts through the ultimatum; persuasion employs argument, courts investigation, and depends upon negotiation. Force represents the old system—the system that must pass away. Persuasion represents the new system—the system that has been growing, all too slowly, it is true, but growing for nineteen hundred years.

"In the old system, war is the chief corner stone—war, which at its best is little better than war at its worst; the new system contemplates a universal brotherhood established through the uplifting power of example.

"If I correctly interpret the note to Germany it conforms to the standards of the old system rather than to the rules of the new, and I cheerfully admit that it is abundantly supported by precedents—precedents written in characters of blood upon almost every page of human history. Austria furnishes the most recent precedent; it was Austria's firmness that dictated the ultimatum against Serbia which set the world at war.

"Every ruler now participating in this unparalleled conflict has proclaimed his desire for peace and denied responsibility for the war, and it is only charitable that we should credit all of them with good faith.

"They desired peace, but they sought it according to the rules of the old system. They believed that firmness would give the best assurance of the maintenance of peace, and, faithfully following precedent, they went so near the whirlpool that they were one after another sucked into the contest.

"Never before have the frightful follies of this fatal system been so clearly revealed as now. The most civilized and enlightened —aye, the most Christian—of the nations of Europe are grappling with each other as if in a death struggle. They are sacrificing the best and bravest of their sons on the battlefield; they are converting their gardens into cemeteries and their homes into houses of mourning; they are taxing the wealth of today and laying a burden of debt on the toil of the future; they have filled the air with thunderbolts more deadly than those of Jove, and they have multiplied the perils of the deep.

"Adding fresh fuel to the flame of hate, they have daily devised new horrors, until one side is endeavoring to drown non-combatant men, women, and children at sea while the other side seeks to destroy non-combatant men, women, and children on land.

"And they are so absorbed in alien retaliations and in competitive cruelty that they seem, for the time being, blind to the rights of neutrals and deaf to the appeals of humanity. A tree is known by its fruit. The war in Europe is the ripened fruit of the old system.

"This is what firmness, supported by force, has done in the old world. Shall we invite it to cross the Atlantic? Already the jingoes of our own country have caught the rabies from the dogs of war. Shall the opponents of organized slaughter be silent while the disease spreads?

"As a humble follower of the Prince of Peace, as a devoted believer in the prophecy that, 'They that take the sword shall perish with the sword,' I beg to be counted among those who earnestly urge the adoption of a course in this matter which will leave no doubt of our government's willingness to continue negotiations with Germany until an amicable understanding is reached, or at least until, the stress of war over, we can appeal from Philip, drunk with carnage, to Philip, sobered by the memories of an historic friendship and by a recollection of the innumerable ties of kinship that bind the fatherland to the United States.

"Some nation must lead the world out of the black night of war into the light of that day when 'swords shall be beaten into plowshares.' Why not make that honor ours? Some day—why not now?—the nations will learn that enduring peace can not be built upon fear—that good will does not grow upon the stalk of violence. Some day the nations will place their trust in love, the weapon for which there is no shield; in love, that suffereth long and is kind; in love, that is not easily provoked, that beareth all things, believeth all things, hopeth all things, endureth all things; in love, which though despised as weakness by the worshipers of Mars, abideth when all else fails."

The Lusitania crisis ended with the third note, sent on July 22, which concluded with the statement that if Germany, without warning, sank any more vessels carrying American passengers, it would be considered a "deliberately unfriendly act." President Wilson himself inserted those words in the note which had been drafted by Secretary Franklin K. Lane. Robert Lansing, former counsel to the Department of State, was given the portfolio in Bryan's place.

Though Bryan and the President parted with such outward expressions of good will, the break between them never was mended again. It was riven open in 1920 when Bryan openly opposed Wilson's stand on the league of nations. The rift was hopelessly widened when the Wilson forces, in the convention of 1920, threw Bryan's league plank out of the party platform.

CHAPTER XXIV

Patriotism and Pacifism

Bryan's Stand Before and After War Is Declared—Early Views
on Peace in General—Thousands Cheer Him at Madison Square
Garden—Statement Explaining His Criticisms of President Wil-
son's Preparedness Policy—London Peace Congress Speech, 1916
—War—Bryan's Offer of Service—Commoner's Editorial—Chi-
cago Chautauqua Meeting, a Pro-War Address—Pendulum Swings
Again After War—League of Nations Clash with Wilson—Patriot
Higher Than a Partisan.

"Gladly would I have given my life to save my country from
war, but now that my country has gone to war, gladly will I give
my life to aid it."

This declaration by William Jennings Bryan prefaced a lecture
he delivered in Albany, Georgia, on the 6th of April, 1917.

But it might also be used as the declaration of Bryan's life;
of his reconciliation of the zeal of a peace-loving citizen with the
service of an energetic patriot, in time of war. As a young man
Bryan, you will remember, volunteered for service in the Spanish-
American war, serving with the rank as a colonel in command of
a regiment. But after the war, with the exigency removed, Bryan
became an advocate of peace, personal and partisan.

The pendulum swung far in favor of peace. There was his
famous lecture, "The Prince of Peace." There were scores of other
articles, editorials, informal talks. During his membership in President Wilson's cabinet, with the portfolio of Secretary of State,
Bryan bended his energies to the consummation of thirty peace
treaties. Later, the ideal of peace, and his idea of how that ideal
should be achieved, compelled him, he believed, to resign from the
position of Secretary of State and break with Wilson, the man
whose nomination he had really brought about.

So much for Bryan's attitude before the United States actually declared war. Once our country had given her ultimatum, the pendulum of Bryan's pacifism swung just as far, just as sincerely, and just as energetically, in the direction of active patriotism.

It is with these seemingly antithetical points of view that this chapter is concerned. Only Bryan found nothing inconsistent in the two swings. For, as he expressed himself in the pronunciamento at the beginning of this chapter, he would gladly have given his life to keep his country from war, but once war was declared, he would as gladly have given his life to aid the immediate and successful prosecution of that war.

First, let us consider that earlier, more detached viewpoint when, in "The Price of a Soul," Bryan is talking, more or less generically, of the value of peace, and of the righteousness which is both the cause and, sometimes the result, of peace.

In this speech he says, in part:

"I challenge the doctrine, now being taught, that we must enter into a mad rivalry with the Old World in the building of battleships —the doctrine that the only way to preserve peace is to get ready for wars that ought never to come! It is a barbarous, brutal, unChristian doctrine—the doctrine of the darkness, not the doctrine of the dawn.

"Nation after nation, when at the zenith of its power, has proclaimed itself invincible because its army could shake the earth with its tread, and its ships could fill the seas, but these nations are dead, and we must build upon a different foundation if we would avoid their fate.

"Carlyle, in the closing chapters of his 'French Revolution' says that thought is stronger than artillery parks and at last molds the world like soft clay, and then he adds that back of the thought is love. Carlyle is right. Love is the greatest power in the world.

The nations that are dead boasted that their flag was feared; let it be our boast that our flag is loved. The nations that are dead boasted that people bowed before their flag; let us not be content until our flag represents sentiments so high and holy that the oppressed of every land will turn their faces toward that flag and thank God that there is one flag that stands for self-government and the rights of man.

"The enlightened conscience of our nation should proclaim as the country's creed that 'righteousness exalteth a nation' and that justice is a nation's surest defense. If ever a nation was called to put God's truth to the test, it is ours; if there ever was a time it is now. With an ocean rolling on either side, and a mountain range along either coast that all the armies of the world could never climb, we ought not to be afraid to trust in 'the wisdom of doing right.'

"Our government, conceived in freedom and purchased with blood, can be preserved only by constant vigilance. May we guard it as our children's richest legacy, for what shall it profit our nation if it shall gain the whole world and lose 'the spirit that prizes liberty as the heritage of all men in all lands everywhere?' "

Then came the conflict over in Europe. In the summer of 1915 Bryan made some fervent peace talks. He swept people off their feet. In Madison Square Garden, on the 24th of June of that year, a tremendous audience cheered themselves into a frenzy of enthusiasm as he spoke to them. Twelve thousand men and women managed to jam into the hall. Their shouts of approval were taken up by the thousands milling about the building. The police director in charge of arrangements estimated, conservatively, that 100,000 applauded Bryan that night as he made an address on "National Honor" at the mass meeting held under the auspices of the Friends of Peace society.

In the course of the talk Bryan said:

"Tonight, I plead against war with Germany. Should similar circumstances arise with France, England, or Russia, I would plead just as ardently against war with any of those countries."

As the former "Boy Orator of the Platte" banged his fist on the railing of the speaker's platform, his teeth clicked together; his body vibrated; his eyes flashed. Those in the Garden leaped to their feet. They waved American flags. They shouted and they whistled. They stamped their feet, and they shrieked. The crowd outside took up the cries and there was a scene of wild commotion.

Then a quieter interlude, when Bryan affirmed his faith in the conviction that the people of the nation would unanimously back the President in case of war. But he denounced the men who, he asserted, called upon the nation to take up arms immediately.

"I appeal to you," and he spread his arms expansively, as he looked down at the audience, "to make your views known to the President, that he may be strengthened against the insolent clamor of those who ridicule peaceful methods, and, as if infuriated by the scent of blood, are bellowing for war. I appeal to you to cast your influence, not in favor of either side, but in favor of peace for the United States and against war with any of the belligerent nations."

A few months later the fight on preparedness became acute. Bryan disagreed with President Wilson's attitude and said so in editorial and speech. But, he maintained, this was legitimate, consistent, and what the President wanted, in order that he might feel the pulse of the nation.

On the 6th of November, from Washington, Bryan issued a statement outlining his position on the defense fight, and maintaining that he was both friend and critic of the President.

First, he explained his relations with Wilson.

"I have no plans formulated," the statement read. "I am doing what I believe to be the duty of every citizen to do. How can the

President know what the people think unless individuals express themselves? Why should those who differ be silent? The editors of metropolitan newspapers who daily fling incense before the special interests do not hesitate to express an opinion as to what the country needs. Why should a country editor like myself be denied the privilege?

"Why should a Democrat's friendship for the President be questioned when he differs with the President on an issue like this, which has nothing in the history of the country or the party to commend it? The President's appeal was not to members of his party, but to the people of all shades of opinion.

"When did it become unpatriotic for a citizen to differ with a President? When did it become disloyal for a Democrat to differ with a Democratic President on an issue which the President declared to be non-partisan?

"The President said he would ask those who differed with him to express their opinion. He certainly will be the last to complain because his request is complied with."

Then, more specifically, Bryan went on to a consideration of the preparedness question to which he was definitely opposed.

After concluding his explanation of his right, in general, to disagree with his President on a non-partisan question, Bryan went on to a consideration of why he did disagree on this preparedness issue.

"A great many persons," he continued, "no one can definitely state the number, but they are quite a multitude, believe that we cannot insure the nation against war by adopting the policy which led Europe into war. It is more reasonable to assume that peace can be promoted between nations by the same philosophy which promotes peace between individuals in communities.

"We are now spending $250,000,000 a year for preparedness. A great many think that this is enough, and are opposed to any increase at present. The burden of the proof is on those who say the increase is necessary, and it will be hard to prove this, in view of the President's statement that 'we are not threatened from any quarter, but our relations with all nations are friendly; that everybody knows of our capacity for defense, and that there is no fear among us.' "

A few months later, and at the London Peace Congress we find Bryan saying these words:

"I will not disguise the fact that I consider this resolution (presenting the peace treaty plan, afterwards incorporated in the thirty peace treaties) a long step in the direction of peace, nor will I disguise the fact that I am here because I desire this Interparliamentary Union to take just as long a step as possible in the direction of universal peace. We meet in a famous hall; looking down upon us from these walls are pictures that illustrate not only the glory that is to be won in war, but the horrors that follow war. There is a picture of one of the great figures in English history (pointing to the fresco by Maclise of the death of Nelson). Lord Nelson is represented as dying, and around him are the mangled forms of others. I understand that war brings out certain virtues. I am aware that it gives opportunity for the display of great patriotism; I am aware that the example of men who give their lives for their country is inspiring; but I venture to say that there is as much inspiration in a noble life as there is in an heroic death, and I trust that one of the results of this Interparliamentary Union will be to emphasize the doctrine that a life devoted to the public, and overflowing, like a spring, with good, exerts an influence upon the human race and upon the destiny of the world as great as any death in war. And, if you will permit me to mention one whose career I watched with interest and whose name I revere, I will add that in my humble judgment, the sixty-four years of spotless public service of William Ewart Gladstone will, in years to come, be regarded as

Lawyer Again—Bryan reverts to his old profession in the Scopes case. The argument against the defense's expert testimony.

Hoisting Darrow With His Own Petard—Bryan quotes from Darrow's defense of Loeb and Leopold in his argument in court.

© Underwood & Underwood photo.

Father and Son—William Jennings Bryan, Sr., and William Jennings Bryan, Jr., fight shoulder to shoulder to uphold Tennessee's anti-evolution law.

rich an ornament to the history of this nation as the life of any man who poured out his blood upon a battlefield."

Then one profound day came the entry of the United States into the World War. And Bryan's pendulum of pacifism swung, with a full, vigorous sweep, clean over to the side of patriotism. A positive, aggressive patriotism, not one quiescently philosophic.

Immediately after the country's declaration of war the erstwhile exponent of peace sent the following telegram to Woodrow Wilson. Dated April 6, from Tallahassee, Florida, it read as follows:

"Believing it to be the duty of each citizen to bear his part of the burden of war and his share of its perils, I hereby tender my services to the government. Please enroll me as a private whenever I am needed. Assign me to any work that I can do until called to the colors. I shall, through the Red Cross, contribute to the comfort of soldiers in the hospitals, and through the Young Men's Christian Association, aid in guarding the morals of the men in camp."

A few days later, on the 16th, Bryan, then fifty-seven years old, went to the White House to reiterate the offer he had telegraphed his chief.

Following the interview, Bryan dictated a statement declaring his intention to support the government in any war plans on which it might decide. He declined, however, to discuss conscription specifically.

In all future speeches, pending a call from the government for his services, the former Secretary of State pledged himself to lay especial stress on the exigencies of the food situation. In conjunction with food conservation, as well as with his own temperance beliefs, Bryan said he would endorse any plan to prohibit the use of grain for making liquor during the war.

The following editorial appeared in The Commoner in a few months:

"We must win. Defeat is inconceivable—it would be indescribably unfortunate, if it were possible. We can not allow any foreign nation to determine the destiny of the United States—especially a nation committed, as Germany is, to arbitrary government and militarism.

"Neither can we afford to have our allies overcome—that would bring upon us the disasters of defeat or the burden of carrying on the war alone.

"We are in the war by the action of Congress—the only body authorized to take the nation into war. The quickest way to peace is to go straight through, supporting the government in all it undertakes, no matter how long the war lasts nor how much it costs."

And a few weeks later in a message of patriotism that thrilled thousands at a Chautauqua meeting in Chicago, the Commoner used his silver tongue to get across an impassioned plea for a quick victory.

"Now is no time for dissension," the resonant voice urged.

"It is not only our duty to back up the President and the government in this trying hour, but it is our duty to back them up in whatever they undertake during the war."

The audience, excited by his pro-war declarations, rose to its feet and cheered and screamed and yelled its approval.

"No one can say," he continued, "how long this war will last. But one fact more important than a guess is, that no matter whether long or short, the quickest way out of it is straight through it."

And there was another demonstration.

"And the more anxious a person is for peace the more loyally he should support this government of ours. Every person who is praying for peace should be giving of every aid he or she is capable in support of the United States, for we shall have peace when this nation has triumphed and not before."

Then, commending to the audience the work of the Red Cross,

the Young Men's Christian Association and the Knights of Columbus, Bryan said:

"For these noble agencies will make the lot of our soldiers easier and surround them with the right kind of influences. We should all do everything possible in the line of food production and food conservation, and then furnish all the money we can for the successful prosecution of the war, both by taxation and loans.

"To sustain this government is the solemn duty of every person who stands for the best form of government ever conceived by the mind of man, and toward which the world is moving. For, as a result of this present war, after the nation has triumphed, as it will triumph and deserves to triumph, autocracy will be overthrown in this world."

Finally the war was ended; the Allies and America had won.

Once more President Wilson and former Secretary of State Bryan had an open clash, and again, over peace procedure. The first difference of opinion had come in June, 1915, when Bryan, feeling that he could not sign the note dealing with the submarine issue that had been prepared for transmission to Berlin, resigned from the President's cabinet.

The next clash came on the evening of January 9, 1920, when both men spoke at the Jackson Day dinner in Washington. The President condemned reservations to the league of nations covenant advanced by the late Senator Henry Cabot Lodge. Bryan took sharp issue with the President. He repudiated Wilson's famous Article X and went so far as to advocate a compromise with the Republicans.

The echo of that clash, only the echo was more decisive than the original, came when the Wilson administration leaders by an overwhelming majority vote defeated Bryan's league plank in the 1920 Democratic convention, placing the Wilson plank in the platform.

And then, once again, as recently as January, 1924, the pendulum began to swing over to pacifism. It didn't fling itself back quite so far, perhaps, as it had in years gone by. The gentle swing started with Bryan's plea that our nation purchase a "priceless peace with a worthless debt," and was made in an address at Memphis, Tennessee.

Bryan advocated cancellation of war loans made by the United States to her allies on condition that the debtor nations disarm and join in a movement for world peace.

"These debts are worthless," he said. "The best thing America can do is to trade a worthless debt for a priceless peace. We should tell these debtor nations that when they disarm they can tear up their notes to us."

And, in closing this consideration of Bryan's patriotism and pacifism, we can not do better than direct attention to that autobiographical philosophy expressed by Bryan in his "Price of a Soul":

"The patriot must desire the triumph of that which is right, more than the triumph of that which he may think to be right if he is, in fact, mistaken; and so the partisan, if he be an intelligent partisan, must be prepared to rejoice in his own or his party's defeat, if by that defeat his country is the gainer."

CHAPTER XXV

The Reforms

Political Prophet, if Unsuccessful Candidate—Republicans "Stole His Clothes" Charge—Prohibition—Grape Juice—"Don't Bury Democratic Party in Drunkard's Grave"—Prohibition and the War—Woman Suffrage—Popular Election of Senators—Income Tax Amendment—Eight Hour Day—Government by Injunction—Publicity of Campaign Contributions—Establishment of Department of Labor.

When Bryan, thrice defeated for President but political prophet of amazing successes, lay dead in his coffin, and messages of condolence were pouring in from all parts of the world, it was for John W. Davis, candidate for President in 1924, to epitomize the Commoner's achievements, by stating:

"I think it only fair to say that few men, if any, have lived to see so many of the policies they advocated enacted into law."

They laughed at Bryan; they cartooned him up and down the land, for the grape juice and all; they made him the central figure of vaudeville skit and whimsical verse. On some of his proposed issues, time has given a true if cruel perspective and what seemed so vastly important at the moment, the free silver issue for instance, has tapered off into something so remote from a vital problem that it is difficult for this political generation to comprehend the zeal with which the question was fought out, back in 1896.

But in other reforms, Bryan played a winner. True, he never got to the White House, and these reforms in which his friends claim for him the initial credit were all enunciated, in the final analysis, by others. But a survey of his writings and utterances years ago, demonstrates beyond a doubt that he was a prophet of no small success in some of his proposed readjustments.

311

Indeed, so many of the causes championed by Bryan were later written into the government of the United States that once, during the administration of Theodore Roosevelt, when the two men were attending the same dinner, Bryan, with a twinkle in his eye, charged Roosevelt with having "stolen his clothes."

Then Bryan told how an old colored lady grew desperately ill, and sent for a white doctor living near by, when her own colored doctor had proved woefully inadequate.

The white physician said:

"Well, aunty, you had to send for me after all, didn't you? What did that old fraud do for you? Did he find out what was the matter with you? Did he take your temperature?"

Aunty replied, " 'Deed, sir, I don't know what all he done took. I ain't had time look 'round yit, but dem no 'count niggahs liable take anything."

Bryan wasn't sure that Roosevelt had left him even his temperature.

The beginnings of Bryan's stand on prohibition came, of course, years before their first general enunciation. Himself a total abstainer, the Commoner never approved of liquor. But it was about 1909, after his third defeat for the Presidency, that the Peerless Leader, refusing to stay "dead," launched his plan of forcing prohibition to the front as a Democratic issue. Shrewd political observers in his own, and in the Republican party, then proclaimed that Bryan's dry idea would sound his death knell.

But he persisted. In an issue of The Commoner in November, 1909, we find him letting go this broadside at the saloon and its relation to human liberty:

"The liquor dealers, recognizing that their obvious pecuniary interest would lessen the weight of any argument which they might publicly advance, are making their fight under cover of organizations purporting to represent those who use liquor. Well-meaning

men have been misled into believing that every attempt to lessen
the evils of intemperance is a fanatical attack on personal liberty.

"What is meant by 'personal liberty'? Does it mean a person
has a right to drink in any quantity at any time and in any place,
no matter what injury he may inflict upon others? If not, with
whom rests the right to fix limitations? The right to drink does
not necessarily include the right to demand the establishment of a
saloon."

In December, 1909, with Bryan championing the dry issue
vigorously, the defeat of the prohibition constitutional amendment
in Alabama moved many political leaders to declare that William
Jennings Bryan had come out for prohibition as a national issue
"too late to do himself and his perennial ambitions any good."

One of the more acrimonious of his attackers, a Senator, said
this:

"It looks as if Bryan had been anywhere from two to four years
too late in embracing the prohibition creed for the purpose of turning it to political uses. The fact is, that the reaction from the local
option wave of legislation has set in, and you may be prepared
to see the movement come to a dead stop and much of the legislation already enacted repealed. That is indicated not only by the
outcome of the Alabama contest but by the temper of the people
in other southern prohibition states. The prohibition movement is
on the wane, because the people are coming to their senses. They
find that there is just as much liquor sold in blind tigers under
prohibition as in open saloons under license.

"I wasn't surprised to find Bryan taking up with the movement, for he is to be classed with the purely emotional creatures.
I suppose he thinks he can get the nomination from the prohibition
party, too, and be swept into office in 1912, but he is due for a sad
awakening."

But Bryan went right on fighting.

In 1915, in the course of a total abstinence speech delivered at New York, he acclaimed water in this fashion:

"All hail to the drink of drinks—to water, the daily need of every living thing! It ascends from the earth in obedience to the summons of the sun, and descends in showers of blessings. It gives forth of its sparkling beauty to the fragrant flower; its alchemy transmutes base clay into golden grain; it is the radiant canvas upon which the finger of the Infinite traces the rainbow of promise. It is the beverage that refreshes and brings no sorrow with it. Jehovah looked upon it at creation's dawn and said 'It is good.' "

About the same time, disturbed by what he characterized as "the way some of the Democratic editors of the country have misinterpreted" his stand in favor of both prohibition and woman's suffrage, Bryan, then the Secretary of State, made it plain in an editorial in The Commoner that he did not favor these measures as national enactments, but rather, by state legislation.

But he added that his hostility to the liquor business was great enough, and his belief in the rights of woman suffrage strong enough, to cause him to vote for either amendment, should they be presented as federal acts.

His "grape juice" stand, during his incumbency as Secretary of State, is outlined in another chapter. It can be mentioned here, however, that it was the subject of jest up and down the countryside, but that Bryan stood the ridicule valiantly.

In fact, one of his favorite stories related to the time, back in 1884, when he made a speech at a tiny Illinois schoolhouse. As he drove up in his buggy, the story goes, one Timothy Flynn came up, led the orator to one side, pulled out a bottle and said,

"Won't you have something to drink?"

Bryan said, "No, thank you."

Timothy was insistent, "Better have a little," he urged.

Bryan maintained that he "didn't care for any."

"Oh, just a drop," Timothy importuned.

"No, I don't use it,"—Bryan's audiences were always laughing by the time he got to this point.

"Then," Bryan would say, "Timothy laid his hand upon my shoulder, and I can hear his voice now, full of pathos, as he said, 'Well, do the best you can, anyway.'"

In March, 1918, Bryan stood on the steps of the Art Institute in Chicago and exhorted ten thousand to favor prohibition. Michigan boulevard was thronged with listeners and traffic was blocked as the crowds surged about the building and spilled out into the street.

A few months later, at the Billy Sunday tabernacle in Philadelphia, more than twelve thousand came up the trail and signed the pledge. The burden of Bryan's theme, at this meeting, was that men cannot afford to drink, from financial or physical reasons. The physical discomfort, he argued, fails to compensate for any possible pleasure. Again, men owe to their progeny life without any inherited weakness, and lastly, "man is his brother's keeper and he is morally wrong in drinking, for the example it sets the weak."

In January, 1917, Bryan sent five thousand Illinois Democrats into a spasm of enthusiasm down at Springfield, Illinois, when he literally screamed out, "You shall not bury the Democratic party in a drunkard's grave."

He charged that his own defeat for the Presidency in 1908 was brought about by the organized liquor forces. His speech was directed to a non-partisan spirit and urged everybody to work to make the state capital dry at the April election.

The entry of the United States into the war gave Bryan additional ammunition for his dry arguments. A speech delivered by him in March, 1918, to a group of railroad shop workers assembled at a Y. M. C. A. in Chicago, was highly typical of the pleas he was making all over. A few sentences from that speech follow:

"At no time in the world's history has America needed 100 per cent men more than at present. On the battle-line abroad where is now in progress probably the greatest battle in history, and here at home, during the harder strain of war, our men must be up to their fullest powers of achievement. Muscles must be strong and eyes steady. Any traffic which contributes to unsteadiness or bad condition is an enemy of the nation and a hazard to the entire Allied cause. Such is strong drink used either by soldiers or civilians. It is a poison that unnerves and shatters. I agree with the British statesmen who put alcohol as the greatest curse of the world today.

"Knowing that we cannot spare a loaf of bread and that every loaf wasted is a help to the enemy, the brewers of the nation deliberately go ahead and throw away this grain manufacturing a poisonous drink."

In that same month Bryan was elected president of the National Dry federation which, the following February, presented him with a silver cup in token of his work for the cause.

This, one of his most impassioned pleas, was made shortly before the national prohibition amendment was passed:

"The sentiment in favor of prohibition, local, state and national, is growing because increased intelligence and an awakening conscience unite in condemning the license system.

"No community would permit the existence of an institution which, merely for profit, cut off fingers, toes, hands and feet; why then should any community permit the existence of the saloon which, for the money to be made by it, cripples the body, enfeebles the brain, and destroys the morals?

"No community would license a person to scatter the germs of hog cholera among hogs; why then should any community license a saloon to spread disease and death among human beings, and, through tainted blood, close the door of hope to innocent children before they see the light of day?"

The second reform which Bryan advocated, and which was written into the Constitution of the United States, was the cause of woman suffrage.

Immediately the issue was projected into the lime-light of national publicity, Bryan took a staunch stand on it, declaring that he would claim no privileges for himself that he would not ask for his wife.

When the suffrage amendment was submitted to the voters of Nebraska in 1914, Bryan took an active part in the campaign for its passage. One of his most famous speeches follows, in part:

"I shall support the amendment. I shall ask no political rights for myself that I am not willing to grant to my wife.

"The first objection I remember to have heard was that as woman cannot bear arms she should not have a voice in deciding questions that might lead to war, or in enacting laws that might require an army for their enforcement.

"This argument is seldom offered now for the reason that as civilization advances laws are obeyed because they are an expression of the public opinion, not merely because they have powder and lead behind them.

"Second. It is urged by some that woman's life is already full of care and that the addition of suffrage would either overburden her or turn her attention away from the duties of the home.

"The answer made to this is that the exercise of the franchise might result in a change of thought and occupation that would relieve the monotony of woman's work and give restful variety to her activities.

"Third. Many well meaning men and women affirm that suffrage would work a harm to woman by lessening the respect in which she is held.

"This argument would have more weight had it not been employed against every proposition advanced in favor of the enlargement of woman's sphere. This objection was once raised to the higher education, but it is no longer heard. The same objection was offered each time the door has opened, and woman, instead of suffering degradation, has risen.

"As for myself, I am not in doubt as to my duty. I desire to present the argument to which I give the greatest weight. Without minimizing other arguments advanced in support of the extending of suffrage to woman, I place the emphasis upon the mother's right to a voice in molding the environment which shall surround her children—an environment which operates powerfully in determining whether her offspring will crown her latter years with joy or 'bring down her gray hairs in sorrow to the grave.'

"I am not willing to stay the mother's hand if she thinks that by the use of suffrage she can safeguard the welfare of those who are dearer to her than her own life.

"Politics will not suffer by woman's entrance into it. If the political world has grown more pure in spite of the evil influences that have operated to debase it, it will not be polluted by the presence and participation of woman.

"Neither should we doubt that woman can be trusted with the ballot. She has proved herself equal to every responsibility imposed upon her; she will not fail society in this emergency."

An additional reason for Bryan's support of the measure was that he felt that the adoption of the woman suffrage amendment would greatly aid the cause of prohibition and of world peace.

The third great political change which Bryan championed, and which later was incorporated in our Constitution, was the popular election of senators. Back in 1890 he ran for Congress on a platform which contained, verbatim, this plank:

"We favor an amendment to the Federal Constitution which will take the election of the United States Senators from the state legislatures and place it in the hands of the people where it belongs."

In 1892, during his first term, he voted for the resolution proposing such an amendment, the first to be passed by either House on this issue. No action was taken at that time, but at the next, the 53rd session, the resolution was passed by the House. The Senate opposed it.

In the Democratic platform of 1900, Bryan saw to it that one plank stood for the popular election of Senators. This plank was on deck again in 1904, in 1908 and in 1912. In 1910, with the Democrats again in control of the House, a resolution, for the sixth time, was passed. This time the Senate agreed and the amendment was submitted to the states. It was shortly ratified. And William Jennings Bryan, as Secretary of State, had the opportunity, in April, 1913, of signing his name to the last official document that made his beloved amendment a part of the Constitution, the amendment which he had begun to advocate when, as a young man of thirty, he was first running for Congress out in Nebraska.

Then there is the income tax amendment. Bryan's 1896 platform contained a plank in favor of this measure. After many a fight, this measure was ratified in 1913, but just two months too soon for Bryan to affix his signature to it, as the head of the State Department.

In his "Royal Art," Bryan declares the income tax is not only more fair in principle than a tax upon consumption but, "through the exemption which it contains," it "in a measure, equalizes the injustice done by the indirect forms of taxation, since those who escape the income tax are the very ones who pay more than their quota through indirect taxation."

This is the big quartette of reforms that were translated into law.

But there were many other measures and phases of measures to which Bryan gave the energy of his vitality, the flood of his oratory, and the persistency of his vigilance.

There was the eight-hour day. Said Bryan in a campaign speech in 1916:

"I put myself on record as in favor of an eight-hour day years ago. I believe in it. These laboring men are a part of our community; they are a part of our business life; they are part of our political life, and they have a right to live up to all the possibilities of American citizenship. If you drive the laboring man from his bed to his work, and from his work back to his bed again, how is he to know the comforts of home life? And how is he to prepare himself for the discharge of the duties of citizenship? It is a farce to say to the laboring man that he is a citizen, and then allow him to be denied opportunity to prepare himself to enjoy the things you give him. The eight-hour day is now a fact, and it has been established under the leadership of a President who wisely used the opportunity presented."

Then, too, there was his opposition to government by injunction. At a Labor Day speech in Chicago, in 1908, he argued:

"All that is sought is the substitution of trial by jury for trial by judge, when the violation of the court's decree must be established by evidence.

"Not only is the prosecution for contempt a criminal prosecution, but there is even more reason for a jury than in the ordinary criminal case. In the criminal court the judge acts in a judicial capacity only. He is not responsible for the law which is being enforced in his court, and therefore he has no personal grievance against the defendant, and, not being the prosecutor in the case, he does not feel a personal interest in the result of the trial; but in a contempt proceeding the judge is the lawmaker and the public prosecutor as well as the judge."

Again, as a political prophet, we find record, from his acceptance speech in 1908, of his insistence that the white light of publicity should shine, unobstructed, upon all partisan campaign contributions.

For in asserting that an election is a public affair, he said:

"The people, exercising the right to select their officials and to decide upon the policies to be pursued, proceed to their several polling places on election day and register their will. What excuse can be given for secrecy as to the influences at work? If a man, pecuniarily interested in 'concentrating the control of the railroads in one management,' subscribes a large sum to aid in carrying the election, why should his part in the campaign be concealed until he has put the officials under obligation to him? If a trust magnate contributes $100,000 to elect political friends to office with a view to preventing hostile legislation, why should that fact be concealed until his friends are securely seated in their official positions?

"This is not a new question; it is a question which has been agitated—a question which the Republican leaders fully understand —a question which the Republican candidate has studied, and yet he refuses to declare himself in favor of the legislation absolutely necessary, namely, legislation requiring publication before the election."

Once again, to record a foreshadowing of success, in that 1908 Labor Day speech we find Bryan saying this:

"A long step toward the elevation of labor to its proper position in the nation's deliberations is to be found in the establishment of a Department of Labor, with a cabinet officer at its head. The wage-earners deserve this recognition, and the executive is entitled to the assistance which such an official could render him. I regard the inauguration of this reform as the opening of a new era in which those who toil will have a voice in the deliberations of the President's council chamber."

True, the most deeply motivating theory in Bryan's life, the free silver issue, is the one which, above all others, was not carried into actuality; was not heralded as necessary; was pushed aside so definitely that now it is entirely and forever out of the line of vision.

But, granting all that, it is still possible, it seems, to state in the words of John W. Davis:

"I think it only fair to say that few men, if any, have lived to see so many of the policies they advocated enacted into law."

Triumph in Court—Following Bryan's impassioned plea against admission of scientific witnesses on Scopes' behalf, Judge Raulston rules against them.

Council of War—A conference during the Scopes trial. Left to right—William J. Bryan, Jr., Bryan and Judge Ben F. McKenzie.

© P. & A. photo.

Religion vs. Science—In other words. Bryan against Darrow. on the afternoon Bryan took the witness stand to be questioned by the great defense lawyer.

CHAPTER XXVI

Conventions of 1920 and 1924

Bryan's Power Declines—Breaks with Wilson Over League—
Jackson Day Dinner Speech—Prohibition Issue—Dry Plan Defeated—"My Heart Is in the Grave with Our Cause"—Klan Issue
in 1924—"Daybreak Prayer"—Speech Supporting McAdoo—"Oil"
—His Man Defeated—Back to Miami.

For Bryan, the years between his resignation as Secretary of State and the opening of the 1920 Democratic convention in San Francisco marked the decline of his hitherto tremendous sway over the destinies of his party. He was one of the most notable figures at the San Francisco convention and at the New York convention of 1924; at both conclaves he was a storm center, eloquent as ever, fighting as earnestly. But the old power that had won him the affectionate title of the Peerless Leader was definitely gone.

First, his interest in social reforms; and next, his increasing devotion to the cause of religion, were occupying more and more of his time and were engaging more and more of his activity. Though he remained to the end, ever a factor to be reckoned with in the political life of the country, yet his heart was not in politics as it had been from the early years out in Nebraska until his break with President Wilson caused him to resign from the cabinet.

The first month of 1920 saw the gulf between the Democratic War President and his former Secretary of State grow still wider.

The disagreement grew out of the fight between Wilson and the Senate over the ratification of the peace treaty and its league of nations covenant. President Wilson, of course, was insisting that the treaty be ratified without any essential change and he desired that the issue be determined by popular vote.

In the President's stand Bryan saw a great danger to the Democratic party. He believed that the President's refusal to accept any compromise was placing the party in the position of opposing a popular sentiment which called for acceptance of the treaty with reservations.

On Jackson Day, January 8, the break was made plain. Twin dinners of celebration were being held in Washington, one at the Willard and the other at the Washington hotel. A letter from President Wilson was read to the Democratic leaders at each of the dinners. It called again for immediate ratification; it condemned again the reservations to the treaty advocated by Senator Lodge; and it called for a reference of the issue to the people in the coming Presidential election.

Over at the Washington hotel, Bryan was pleading just the opposite view. He came out openly for a compromise on the reservations and asserted that the Democratic party would meet disaster did they appeal to the people on a platform of unqualified ratification. As Wilson had condemned the Lodge reservations, so Bryan condemned Wilson's Article X. To all intents he advised surrender to the Republican anti-administration faction. His plea came before the reading of the Wilson letter at the banquet he attended. It was not cordially received. Stony silence greeted it on the part of most of his hearers. Wilson's letter they received with cheers.

Bryan's speech shocked them with its boldness. He spoke as follows:

"Seldom has such an opportunity for great service come to any party as now presents itself to our party. But opportunity brings responsibility. Much is required of those to whom much is given. A soldier is a soldier until his day of opportunity comes—after that he is either a hero or a coward.

"So with the party; opportunities improved become stepping

stones to success; opportunities neglected are millstones about the party's neck.

"The opportunities now offered are as large as the nation and as wide as the world. In this hour, when we take counsel together for the coming campaign, it is the duty of each member of the party, as I take it, to present the situation as he sees it, without stopping to inquire whether his views are shared by others.

"One can not call a mass meeting to determine what to think; the theory of democracy is that all think and give expression to their thought, and then conclusions are reached by comparison of views.

"Permit me, therefore, to present the more important of these opportunities as I see them. The nations are entering upon a new era; old systems are passing away; democracy is dawning everywhere.

"Our nation is the only great nation in a position to furnish the moral leadership required. The nations of Europe are busy with their own problems; our people are the only ones disinterested enough to be trusted by all, and the Democratic party is the party whose ideas best fit it for the task of leadership in such a work.

"A Democratic President was the spokesman of the United States in holding out to a war-worn world the hope of universal peace, and he brought back from Paris the covenant of a league of nations that provides means for settling international disputes without a resort to force. He did the best he could, and succeeded better than we had any right to expect, when we remember that he fought single-handed against the selfish interests of the world.

"The Republican party, in control of the Senate, instead of ratifying at once, or promptly proposing changes that it deemed necessary, has fiddled while civilization has been threatened with conflagration. It could have adopted its reservations as well five months ago as later, but it permitted endless debate while suffering humanity waited.

"The Democratic Senators stood with their President for ratification without reservation, and I stood with them, believing that it was better to secure within the league, after it was established, any necessary changes, than to attempt to secure them by reservations in the ratifying resolutions.

"But our plan has been rejected, and we must face the situation as it is. We must either secure such compromises as may be possible, or present the issue to the country. The latter course would mean a delay of at least fourteen months, and then success only in case of our securing a two-thirds majority in the senate.

"We cannot afford, either as citizens or as members of the party, to share with the Republican party responsibility for further delay; we can not go before the country on the issue that such an appeal would present.

"The Republicans have a majority in the Senate and therefore can, by right, dictate the Senate's course. Being in the minority, we cannot demand the right to decide the terms upon which the Senate will consent to ratification.

"Our nation has spent 100,000 precious lives and more than $20,000,000,000 to make the world safe for democracy, and the one fundamental principle of democracy is the right of the majority to rule. It applies to the Senate and to the House as well as to the people.

"According to the Constitution, a treaty is ratified by a two-thirds vote, but the Democratic party can not afford to take advantage of the constitutional right of a minority to prevent ratification. A majority of Congress can declare war. Shall we make it more difficult to conclude a treaty than to enter a war?

"Neither can we go before the country on the issue raised by Article X. If we do not intend to impair the right of Congress to decide the question of peace or war when the time for action arises, how can we insist upon a moral obligation to go to war which can have no force or value except as it does impair the independence of Congress? We owe it to the world to join in an honest effort to put an end to war forever, and that effort should be made at the earliest possible moment.

"A Democratic party can not be a party of negation; it must have a constructive program. It must not only favor a league of nations, but it must have a plan for the election of delegates and a policy to be pursued by those delegates.

"What plan can a Democratic party have other than one that contemplates the popular election of those delegates who, in the influence they will exert, will be next in importance to the President himself?

"And what policy can the Democratic party have within the league of nations other than one of absolute independence and impartiality between the members of the league?

"Our nation's voice should at all times be raised in behalf of equal and exact justice between nations as the only basis of permanent peace; it should be raised in defense of the right of self-determination and in proclaiming a spirit of brotherhood as universal as the peace which we advocate.

"We have domestic problems, also, which offer an opportunity to render large service, and one objection to thrusting the treaty into the campaign is that it would divert attention from questions demanding immediate consideration . . ."

So the San Francisco convention opened on June 28 with the league issue the paramount one; with prohibition added to lend still more ground for discord; and with Bryan, as usual, a focal point in the battle. He may not have been a candidate, but probably he was the most talked of man at the convention.

On a piece of scratch paper, with a pencil, he wrote fifty-nine words that were to throw the convention into a furore:

"We heartily congratulate the Democratic party on its splendid leadership in the submission and ratification of the prohibition amendment to the Federal Constitution and we pledge the party to the effective enforcement of the Volstead law honestly and in good faith, without any increase in the alcoholic content of permitted beverages, and without any weakening of its other provisions."

His hotel suite, the day before the convention opened, was always crowded. The management had to place a long row of chairs in the corridor outside his door to accommodate those who wished to wait to see him. It was almost like the old days over again.

But his high spirits were to be short-lived. As a delegate from Nebraska he had a place on the resolutions committee and it was here that he received his first blow. His substitute for the Wilsonian league of nations plank of the platform was rejected by a large majority.

Bryan pleaded eloquently before the committee.

"The adoption of my plank will not mean a repudiation of the President," he was reported to have said. "It will open the peace of the world, will give Mr. Wilson the opportunity to direct the first participation of the United States in the league of nations, and make him for the remainder of his term the moral leader of the world."

But his argument was of no avail. The "Virginia plank," calling for ratification of the treaty without nullifying reservations and the declaration that "honor and integrity are dependent upon America's participation in the league," was adopted. The defeat of Bryan's plank followed, after a stormy session on the floor of the convention.

Bryan offered four amendments to the platform, but all were rejected by the delegates. His proposed dry plank was snowed under by a vote of 929½ against, to 155½ for. He proposed an amendment calling for an anti-profiteering plank, one providing for a declaration against universal military training, and one demanding the creation of an industrial board, patterned on the principle of the Bryan treaties, to settle labor disputes. But these last three, also were rejected.

Bryan was at his best when he took the platform to defend his dry plank. He flayed the liquor interests.

"The eighteenth amendment is in the Constitution to stay," he cried. "The liquor traffic is dead. It is a corpse and decency requires the corpse be covered up, buried. I thank God a Democratic convention has courage as well as prinicple. They are dead that sought the young child's life."

Bourke Cockran followed, to defend his plank calling for modification of the Volstead act. It was a masterful speech. Bryan sat smiling as he in turn was lambasted. After the vote was over, turning down both his amendment and Cockran's, someone asked Bryan how he felt.

"Pretty well for a mangled corpse," was his reply.

James M. Cox, governor of Ohio, was finally nominated as Democratic candidate for President. While the bands still were playing and the people cheering, Bryan walked from the convention hall.

"My heart is in the grave with our cause," he said, "and I must pause until it comes back to me. The nomination of Cox cannot be interpreted in any other way than a victory for the wets, although of course there were other forces behind him."

For the first time, he failed to do any stumping for his party's presidential candidate. The reason for his action, he said, was that he did not agree with Cox on many issues and he did not want to debate with the candidate of his own party, who was finally defeated by Warren G. Harding.

During the interim between the convention of 1920 and that

of 1924, Bryan turned still further away from active politics, devoted more of his time to lecturing, and took a greater interest in the affairs of the Presbyterian church. In 1923 he was defeated for moderator of the Presbyterian General Assembly after an exciting contest, but he was elected vice-moderator at the Assembly of 1924.

He had established his legal residence in Miami, Fla., so when the convention of 1924 came around, he was sent to New York as a delegate from the Palmetto State. Again he was a member of the resolutions committee that fought and wrangled over the issue of whether or not to bring the name of the Ku Klux Klan into the party platform. During one meeting of the committee when the Klan issue was under discussion Bryan dropped to his knees and urged his fellow members to join him in prayer that they might be guided aright. He vigorously opposed bringing the name of the Klan into the resolution; he demanded that the "three menacing words" of its title be kept out.

He was reminded by a delegate from Brooklyn that there had been three menacing words in his own platform of 1896—"sixteen to one."

"That's too long past to be brought against me now," Bryan replied, smiling. "There is a statute of limitations even in politics."

Probably one of the most famous of Bryan's public prayers, to become known as the "Daybreak Prayer," was offered by him while the Klan issue was still before the resolutions committee. The committee met on a Friday night to take up this question, which had been left to the last. Member after member spoke; there was bitterness and antagonism, and it cropped out at the slightest excuse.

Bryan was acting chairman. Judge John H. McCann of Pennsylvania made a speech attempting to soften the attitude of the members. The meeting lasted late. It was six o'clock in the morning before the committee was ready to call a halt. Bryan spoke to Judge McCann; the judge, he remarked, was a Catholic; he was a Protestant. Bryan suggested that the two of them close the session with prayer. While all stood, Judge McCann recited the Lord's prayer. Bryan followed with this prayer of his own:

"Our Heavenly Father, we come into Thy presence conscious that Thou art infinite in wisdom, love and power, while we are limited in knowledge and prone to err.

"Thou dost care for Thy children, and hast promised to reveal Thyself and Thy will to those whose hearts are open to Divine suggestion.

"We need Thy counsel, Lord. We are carrying great responsibilities and dealing with mighty problems that vex and trouble us. We are subject to prejudice and passion and unconscious bias.

"Cleanse our minds from all unworthy thoughts and purge our hearts of all evil desires. Show us Thy way, and help us to know what Thou would'st have us say and do and be.

"We would consecrate ourselves wholly unto Thee and Thy service. 'Thy kingdom come, Thy will be done, on earth as it is in Heaven.'

"Help us to advance in our day and this day the brotherhood Thou didst establish. May it include all mankind.

"So guide and direct us in our work today that the people of our party and of our country and of the world may be better for our coming together in this convention and in this committee.

"Bless us, not for ourselves, but that we may be a blessing. We ask in Jesus' name. Amen."

Throughout the struggle over the Klan issue, after it had been brought onto the floor of the convention, Bryan sought for compromise and harmony. On the famous day back in '96 he had issued a challenge to battle; in New York he issued a call for peace. His influence resulted finally in the decision of the convention to keep the "three menacing words" out of the platform. Bryan, it is to be understood, did not support the Klan, but he believed that nothing but disharmony and bitter feeling could result from making mention of that organization, or any other specific organization, in the platform.

The Democratic convention of 1924 will go down in history because of the terrifically long drawn out deadlock which lasted until the 103rd ballot and the nomination of John W. Davis of West Virginia. Throughout most of the fight, it was a struggle between William G. McAdoo of California and Governor Al Smith of New York. Bryan was supporting McAdoo. It was at the conclusion of the thirty-eighth ballot that he was granted permission to explain his vote and he took the rostrum.

The scene that followed was one of the most remarkable ever staged at any convention. It was one of the most riotous. Bryan began:

"Mr. Chairman, members of the convention, I greatly appreciate the privilege you have accorded me, and I hope when I am through you will feel that I have improved the time for the benefit of the Democratic party. I have only one desire, and that is that we shall win this next election, and I only desire that because I see no other hope for the nation except in the victory of the Democratic party.

"We have met here as representatives of the party in the entire nation and no one who is accustomed to national conventions will fail to appreciate the wisdom of bringing together representatives of the party from all the states and territories.

"All of us are liable to be influenced by environment. Man's ideal of what is to be is half and half environment. No one can listen to the earnest plea made in behalf of different candidates without realizing how much acquaintance with life and record has to do with the formation of opinion; and as I have listened to the pleadings of the friends of the various candidates I have felt that possibly if we could have a campaign long enough for every voter to get as well acquainted with the proposed candidate as those who advocate him, it would be easier to make a selection and come to an agreement.

"I do not claim any advantage over any one else. I am one in a thousand and ninety-eight delegates, one in twelve of the Democrats of Florida, and I ask no one to accept my opinion on my authority. I only ask that they consider the reasons that have led me to the conclusions that I have reached, and give to those reasons such weight as each one may think that they deserve.

"I think that is the spirit in which we all should meet, and with this introduction I want to submit a word in regard to a number of candidates, not in criticism, for I shall not mention any candidates whom I would have to criticize. I only want to speak of some whom I would be glad to commend, and when I have done that, I want to speak of something more important than candidates. I want to get the lesser things out of the way before I take up the things of supreme importance.

"In the first place I want to say to you that the Democratic party has candidates in abundance. We could call the roll of states and find in every state a Democrat worthy to be President of the United States. I have not time to call the roll, but if it becomes necessary I will furnish the list, and there will be more than one in many of the states who, in my judgment, would, with credit, fill the White House.

"I am only going to mention a few and you will understand the reasons why I select these. They are going to be scattered over the country. I want to show you how rich our party is in great and worthy Democrats.

"We have a man in Florida. He is the president of our state university. His name is Dr. A. A. Murphree. (Voice: "We want Smith; we want Smith"; laughter, applause, and cheers.) He is a

Democratic scholar (hisses and boos.) He is a scholarly Democrat. (Voice: "Never heard of one.")

"Those who have not informed themselves upon the nation's great men ought to be silent until they have had a chance to inform themselves. This gentleman lives way down in Florida, and if any of you think that Florida is too small to have a President, I want you to know we are bigger than Vermont (Voice: "What is the matter with Smith?") and better than Vermont. He would fill the office with credit to himself and with honor to his party and the nation.

"I mention him as the first on the list, and as I travel north from Florida to North Carolina I mention one of the best Democrats in the United States, Josephus Daniels. He made a magnificent Secretary of the Navy. He is sound on every question, and he would grow every day in the campaign as people knew him better. That is my second man.

"My third is another southern man, Joseph Robinson of Arkansas (cheers and applause.) He is the leader of the minority in the Senate, a splendid leader, measures up to every requirement of the Presidency.

"Here are three men from the south. This is probably the last convention of my party in which I shall be a delegate (applause), and I want my friends—don't applaud, I may change my mind (laughter, applause, and cheers)—I want to pay back today the debt of gratitude that I owe to the south.

"I lived in the north when I was thrice nominated for the Presidency. (A voice: "It will never be again.") The south helped to nominate me in three campaigns. The south helped as far as they could in the giving of electoral votes. More than that, the south has helped this nation secure every economic reform that has been secured in sixty years.

"Some people have said that you cannot nominate a man from

the south. I remind you that we have had two wars since the Civil war, and the sons of those who wore the gray and the sons of those who wore the blue marched side by side and were ready to die together on the battlefield.

"I remind you that the south furnished as many soldiers for the late war as it furnished to the Confederacy. I remind you that the south furnished more money to do our part in the world war than it furnished to the Confederacy (A voice: "Why shouldn't it?"; applause.)

"It is time that we should hush forever the voice that would exclude the south from poll participation in our party's welfare and in the welfare of our nation.

"The man who says that the north will not vote for a southern man libels the north. I call you to witness that Kansas, which possibly has a larger percentage of ex-Union soldiers in it in proportion to population than any state of the Union, elected as a governor of that state Senator Harris, who went from Virginia to Kansas, and who was a Confederate soldier before he went to Kansas from Virginia.

"What Kansas has done any other state would do. I had the pleasure of seconding the nomination of an ex-Confederate soldier twenty years ago in our national convention. I believed then that he would poll as many votes as an ex-Confederate soldier as he would have polled if he had lived in a state farther north. I believe it today.

"What this nation wants is a man whose heart beats in sympathy with the common people, and we don't care where he was born or where he lives.

"I mentioned three southern men, and now I want to mention some northern men. (A voice: "Don't forget New Jersey." Another voice: "What is the matter with Underwood?" Another voice: "He's all right.")

"My first northern man is Samuel Ralston of Indiana. He is a Democrat. He is a progressive Democrat. He has a noble record of work done for his state and for his nation through the Democratic party.

"My next man from the north is E. T. Meredith of Iowa. He was in the President's cabinet. He has been long identified with agriculture, and he knows the farmers' needs. The farmers constitute the largest group of our population, some 29 per cent, and they are the ones who are in most distress today. Their condition presents its piteous appeal to the nation and the Democratic party has tried to answer that appeal.

"If you will pardon me, my next northern man has the misfortune to be my brother. (Laughter and applause and boos.) But you need not take my word for it; take the 50,000 majority they gave him in Nebraska, which is better testimony than my word.

"Take his record. Has he protected the people from the extortion of the gasoline monopoly and from the extortion of those who control the coal supply of Nebraska? Take the verdict rendered in his favor at the last primary, 82 per cent of the votes cast at the primary, the Democratic primary, and 78 per cent of the votes cast at the primary of the independent party in that state.

"And then I go to the northwest, and I mention the name of a man from Montana, Thomas J. Walsh. He is your presiding officer. As a lawyer he has no superior, as a stateman he has few equals, and as an investigator he is above them all.

"Under his leadership more gigantic corruption has been disclosed than in any previous investigation. He raised the lid and let the American people see how the Republican machine worked when well oiled. (Cries of "McAdoo! McAdoo!")

"And out of that investigation is going to come one priceless benefit to our nation. We have for a generation been trying to show the Republicans that these men who contribute large sums do not contribute for patriotic purposes, but that they are buying government favors at public auction; that by large campaign contributions they purchase legislative privileges and administrative immunity; and as a result of this investigation we are going to purify American politics and make it decent again. And T. J. Walsh will deserve more credit than any for the facts that make this possible.

"I have given you names of Democrats—(Voices: "Name the real one you have got in mind." "Atta boy!" "What's the matter with Smith?")

"Do not rush me, my friends. (Voices: "McAdoo! McAdoo!") Give me time to develop my subject in my own way. I shall not disappoint you when I am through.

"My friends, I commenced in the southeast corner of the United States, and I cross the nation to the northwest corner and give you men in these different sections. If you have any preference about sections, take your choice. (A voice: "How about Connecticut?") I could commence in the northeast and go to the southwest, and from the west and go east, and from the north and go south, and, if it is necessary, I will furnish you a list that will keep you voting until the next presidential campaign.

"But, my friends, I now want to present a brief argument for one who, I think, fits into this occasion, and I will tell you why. It is necessary that we shall make a progressive fight. We are challenged, and we cannot decline the challenge; and if they had not challenged us, we would have challenged them, for that is the issue that must be satisfied.

"I think it is necessary also that our candidate shall be a man whose record on the liquor question is such that every mother will know that every home will be protected. I have given you the names of men whose position will not be questioned on the matter of law enforcement, and there must be no question as to our candidate's position on the great progressive issue.

"The last Congress was the most progressive Congress we have had in years, and the Democratic party in that Congress made the most progressive record that the Democratic party has made since I have been acquainted with politics (Applause), and my acquaintance runs back many years.

"And, therefore, to fit our party's sentiment, to fit our party's record, to fit our party's platform, and to appeal to the only votes that we have any chance of securing, our candidate must be a progressive. (Cries of "Senator Walsh!")

"My friends, if we intend to nominate a reactionary, which I consider impossible in this convention, he could not draw Republican reactionaries from the Republican party. He could not even hold reactionary Democrats away from the Republican ticket. We have tried it before. We have allowed them to select a reactionary, and, after having disgraced us, they have deserted us on election day; and this year they shall not take us up on the mountain and promise us land that they don't own and can't deliver.

"I have mentioned men who, I think, would fit into our platform, and now I mention one who has made it possible for us to have a progressive platform and nominate a progressive candidate. (A voice: "Name yourself.")

"If he had not made the fight we would not have a progressive convention today and we could not nominate a progressive candidate. But because of his courageous leadership, we have a progressive convention in which they cannot nominate anything but a progressive candidate.

"The man who is entitled to credit for making possible a victory this year, whether you like him or not, whether you nominate him or not, but the man who has made possible the election of a progressive is William Gibbs McAdoo of California."

All his life Bryan had been accustomed to addressing hostile audiences. Never had he faced one like the one there in New York

© Underwood & Underwood photo.

A Modern Crusader—Caught in the heat and stress of the battle at Dayton, Tenn. A typical picture of Bryan in his last great fight.

In the Pulpit—Crowds hear Bryan preach in the Methodist church in
Dayton, on a Sunday during the Scopes trial July 12, 1925.

which burst into a storm of "boos" and cries of "Oil, oil, oil" at the mention of McAdoo's name. Cheers and applause mingled with the derisive shouts and turned the convention hall into a noisier bedlam than ever.

"Tell us about Doheny and McAdoo and oil," cried a New Jersey delegate. "Oil, oil," became a chant from the galleries. Chairman Walsh pounded fruitlessly for order. Through it all, Bryan leaned calmly over the rail trying to catch the questions that were being hurled at him. Hostile delegates were demanding what right he had to turn an explanation of his vote into a half hour's speech. The Commoner's eyes flashed their old fire as he engaged in colloquy with first one, then another.

"No man who allows Wall street to influence his action has any right to criticize McAdoo, who cannot be bossed by Wall street," he shot back at his tormentors, to an accompaniment of more cheers and jeers. Finally, Bryan managed to make himself heard above the noise, and he brought his speech to a close.

He finished:

"We not only have distress here but we have confusion abroad. The world looks to us. In Russia they have a class government. In Great Britain they have a laboring man for Premier. In France socialism is in control and it threatens Germany and Italy. That is the condition of the old world. I believe it has been brought about largely by the concentration of wealth that has enriched a few and has made homeless the many.

"When Lloyd George made his fight to tax the landlords, he used a sentence more powerful than any other sentence that has been used in argument I believe in a thousand years, when he said, 'Why make ten thousand owners of the soil and all the rest trespassers in the land of their birth?'

"My friends, the Republican party has been granting privileges and favors. It gave one hundred millions to Doheny, about one hundred millions to Sinclair. It tried to give ninety millions of relief from taxation to less than five thousand of the biggest taxpayers, and it gave four hundred fifty millions in relief from taxation to the profiteers. It put a burden of over three billions on the masses of the people for the benefit of protected interests.

"Here are four measures and if you will add together what they take out of the pockets of the people and give to the favored and privileged ones who bought the privileges with their campaign contributions, you will find the sum would pay the President's salary for 36,400 years. If they go on distributing their favors, piling up riches in the hands of the few and spreading destitution among the many, it will not be many generations until the quotation of Lloyd George will be echoing throughout our land.

"I am glad we met in New York. I want our Democratic party to appeal to the millionaires of New York and tell them that less than half the people who die in the United States leave enough money to make it worth while to administer on their estates. Of thirty millions of voters, less than one in four have income enough to pay a tax on.

"These men of wealth ought to know, and the Democratic party ought to tell them, that it is better to leave a good government to their children than to leave large fortunes. (Applause.) And that is what the Democratic party is prepared to do. We want to make this government so good that to be a private citizen of the United States will be better than to be a king in any other country in the world."

But the speech and the turmoil were of no avail in breaking the deadlock. It persisted until McAdoo's withdrawal and the nomination of Davis closed the convention.

The New York convention was Bryan's last appearance in politics. His influence was responsible for the nomination of his brother, Charles W. Bryan of Nebraska, for Vice-President, but the Commoner took no greatly active part in the campaign that followed and which ended in Coolidge's election. Bryan returned to his Florida home, to spend his time in lecturing, in the teaching of the Bible class of which he was so fond, and in carrying on the campaign against the doctrine of evolution, which was to reach its crisis in the Scopes trial, and end with the tragedy of his death in Dayton, Tenn.

CHAPTER XXVII

"Faith of Our Fathers"

Defense of the Bible and Tennessee Anti-Evolution Law—Arrival
In Dayton—Plans Scopes Prosecution—Champion of Tennessee
Folk—In Court—Speech Against Admission of the Defense Scientific Testimony.

Down in the little Tennessee town of Dayton, hidden in a valley among the hazy blue slopes of the Cumberlands, William Jennings Bryan achieved the acme of his career. In the prosecution of John Thomas Scopes, the Dayton teacher, for breach of Tennessee's anti-evolution law, the Great Commoner in three departments of his nature found the fullness of life.

It was the pinnacle of his physical being; for he was to die there in the little town a few days after the trial closed. It was the superlative in his public life; for never before during his career had he had so large, or so keenly interested, an audience.

Above all, it was the utmost reach of the inner life of the man himself. For during those few weeks, spent in the preparation and trial of the case, were crystallized and expressed all the ideals of this man who was famed as a politician, statesman, orator, and commoner, but the fundamental of whose life was his religious faith.

Never, in a long life marked with attack after attack, was Bryan such a target for those who disagreed with him as he was during the Scopes trial. Politics never barbed the shafts of his opponents as did this great religious controversy. Free silver, or his stand during the war, never brought forth such an onslaught of bitterness and ridicule as did his stand in Tennessee, for revealed religion against the hosts of science in whom he saw the army of an unbelief that would surely wreck civilization.

At the same time, never before in a career of leadership had he been so much the champion of those who found in him a personification of their beliefs. When he spoke in the packed courtroom against Darrow and Malone and Hays he spoke with the voices of millions of fundamental religionists behind him.

It was the logical outcome of his life, this participation in the trial of religion versus science. From Bryan, the religious orator, to Bryan, the religious prosecutor, was a natural step.

The future must render the verdict in the Scopes trial, which was but a minute manifestation of the age-old war between science and religion. Probably it will strike a balance somewhere between the two great extremes represented at that trial. By how much were Darrow and his scientific experts wrong; by how much was Bryan wrong? Years of progress alone can tell.

His critics assailed Bryan because he was "ignorant." He was not ignorant. To understand him, one must have been on the front porch of the Rogers home, where Bryan lived in Dayton, and have heard him discuss informally the issues that were at stake and his belief in them.

"A reporter came to me," he said, "saying that his editor had told him to ask me whether I thought the world was flat. I told him the question was an insult and I would not stand for such treatment. No intelligent man believes such stuff as that."

What his critics really were assailing was a tendency to shut his ears to arguments that, if accepted, might cause him to change his preconceived beliefs. Characteristically, Bryan admitted no compromise. It was all or nothing at all, as he saw it. He could not reconcile certain theories of science with his religious faith, so he disregarded the theories. It was a natural thing to do, a very human method. Those who attacked must remember that he saw the foundation, not only of his own life but of the life of his nation, threatened by the teachings of science.

There are a great majority who disagree with his policy of using the legislatures to regulate a religious matter. But there are none who knew the man who doubt the sincerity and honesty of his intentions.

Scopes was indicted for teaching from Hunter's "Biology," to children in the Dayton high school, that man evolved from a lower order of animals. The Tennessee anti-evolution statute made it a misdemeanor to teach any theory contradicting the Divine creation of man as recounted in the Bible.

Soon after the indictment, Bryan announced that he would take part in the prosecution, representing the Christian Fundamental association. The announcement was made before a meeting of the Pittsburgh Presbytery amid applauding cheers.

"We've got a lot of mind worshipers in this country," he told his hearers. "There is a shocking decline in the spiritual life of our schools and colleges. On the word of a well known scientist, the belief in a personal God and a personal immortality is dying out.

"The attack being made right now upon those who stand squarely for the Christian faith of their fathers is not an attack on orthodoxy. It is an attack on religion. Unless we can defend the doctrine that God created man and put him here for a purpose and sent Jesus Christ here to die for him, what's the church for? The church must not be made a social club. You may not applaud sentiment like this, but if you put the hypothesis of science above the word of God, I don't expect you to tolerate me.

"There are about 5,000 scientists, and probably half of them are atheists, in the United States. Are we going to allow them to run our schools? We are not! When we get through with this fight against Godless teaching in our schools you'll find that 109 million out of the 110 million people of this country are going to run the schools—not a handful of self-important scientists.

"The hand that writes the teacher's pay check is the hand that rules the schools."

Bryan's stand against evolution was not a new one. His opposition to the theory found its way into his "Prince of Peace" lecture. And back in 1911 he talked against it in interviews and on the platform. In reply to a question concerning his opinion of evolution, in that year, he declared:

"I cannot accept it. The monkey may be an acceptable ancestor for some. I do not find him so. The doctrine of evolution explains but one-third of the problem, and that the lowest of the thirds—the physical."

In 1920 at the class day exercises at Northwestern university, Bryan spoke impromptu and asserted:

"No teacher should be allowed on the faculty of any American university unless he is a Christian. And where the Bible is not taught, no other philosophy should be substituted."

The Tennesee case found him with all his argument, all his mastery of words, all the fire of his belief, ready for the crucial test.

A teacher accepting pay in dollars stamped "In God We Trust" should not be permitted to teach the children that there is no God, he declared as he prepared for the struggle.

"Christians," he said, "are compelled to build their own colleges in which to teach Christianity; why not require atheists and agnostics to build their own colleges if they want to teach atheism and agnosticism?"

Who, if not the legislatures, should have the right to determine what shall be taught in the public schools, he asked? Legislatures fix punishments for crime, they regulate marriage and divorce, the descent of property, the care of the children, and all other matters between citizens, he argued. Why, then, are they not competent to regulate the schools?

For a few weeks the Tennessee town of some two thousand inhabitants became a world center of interest. Into Dayton flocked a hundred or more newspaper men from all parts of the country. Some came from Canada. Over the wires thousands upon thousands of words were sent out to papers all over the globe. On the day Bryan took the witness stand the Western Union telegraph company reported that it had handled more than 200,000 words, and the various press services carried beside this number some 50,000 more. London papers were getting cabled dispatches of 500 to 1,000 words on every eventful day.

For into the narrow confines of the town among the hills was packed the drama of one of the oldest conflicts known to civilized man. Acting on the stage were actors whose names were known the world over. Listening, looking on, transmitting the news, was a gathering worthy of any great national convention. Round and about it all was the colorful scenery of Tennessee, its fertile valleys and wooded ridges seamed with coal; above all, its people, simple folk, sons and daughters of the soil, for the most part staunch believers in the fundamental faith, home lovers, jealous independents, sprung from old Anglo-Saxon pioneering stock. Of book learning they had little, these people; of belief in God and His revealed word, they had much.

They looked to Bryan as their spokesman, and he did not disappoint them. Those who wondered from whence Bryan drew the support to face the opposition he met through life had only to watch these people, see them crowd about him to shake his hand, listen to them, and hear their words of awed praise, to understand that here was a prophet and here, his people.

He mixed with them like one of themselves. They came to court, the men in overalls and blue shirts, the women in plain dresses of gingham and calico. Bryan appeared in shirtsleeves and often in the hot-weather shirt Mrs. Bryan had devised for him, without a collar.

He defended them against the ridicule of writers from the great cities who came to scoff at them and who called them ignorant and yokels.

"Why should the size of the town be a matter of importance in the trial of a religious case?" he said. "Christianity began in a small town, whether we date the beginning with the birth of Christ in Bethlehem or with the youth of Christ, spent in Naz-areth. Why should not this peaceful community furnish a fitting environment for the trial of a case that involves the two greatest subjects that interest mankind: Education and religion?

"The newspaper critics who have been making fun of Dayton should read the front page of the book which gave rise to this trial. The biology which the defendant was teaching has as its frontispiece a picture of a crowded city street and just below it the picture of a farm house on a quiet country road. Beneath the two pictures is a suggestion upon which the city editors might reflect with profit. This is the comment that the author of the book makes upon the two pictures contrasted: 'Compare the unfavorable, artificial environment of a crowded city with the more favorable environment of the country.'

"What is the secret of the world's interest in this little case?" Bryan asked. "It is found in the fact that this trial uncovers an attack which, for a generation, has been made more or less secretly upon revealed religion; that is, the Christian religion.

"We have no knowledge of it outside the Bible, which Christians regard as the revealed will of God. The Bible is our only standard of morality. It gives us our only conception of God and our only knowledge of Christ, the only begotten Son of God.

"Anything that attacks the Bible attacks revealed religion. A successful attack would destroy the Bible and, with it, revealed religion.

"The contest between evolution and Christianity is a duel to the death. It has been in the past a death grapple in the dark; from this time on it will be a death grapple in the light. For this trial is going to give information or be the means of bringing out information upon which this controversy will be decided.

"If evolution wins, Christianity goes—not suddenly, of course, but gradually, for the two cannot stand together. They are as antagonistic as light and darkness; as antagonistic as good and evil. Heretofore evolution has been like 'the pestilence that walketh in darkness.' Hereafter it will be 'the destruction that wasteth at noonday.'

"Opponents of Christianity understand the character of the struggle and from henceforward Christians will understand its character. Christians, believing that revealed religion offers mankind the only abiding truth will fight evolution as their only great foe.

"If they are wrong they will, of course, be defeated and be compelled to abandon the Bible as the word of God.

"If information furnished at the trial, and brought out afterward because of the trial, shows evolution to be unproven and therefore unworthy of acceptance, science will have to fall back upon demonstrated truth which has no terrors for Christianity.

"Christianity is not afraid of truth," Mr. Bryan exclaimed. "It only opposes hypotheses put forth in the name of science but unsupported by facts."

In two Sunday talks to congregations, during the course of the trial, the Commoner again defended the people of the hills.

"Christ today is the leader of the thought of the world," he declared. "He was unlettered and had no school advantages. No scholar dares add a sentence to His moral code. A dull brain with a passion for service is better than a brilliant mind with no such passion."

At his second talk he assailed the correspondents who had spoken slightingly of the people of Tennessee.

"These men who come from other states to call you yokels and bigots," he exclaimed. "I wish I had them here to set them face to face with a humanity they cannot imitate. In the end, every critic you have will be rotted and forgotten."

The Scopes trial began. Quickly it became apparent, as everyone had expected, that it was to be, not a suit at law, but the starting point for discussion of the paramount and fundamental questions which it involved.

The jury was chosen; then there was long argument on the constitutionality of the law. Judge John T. Raulston, presiding, ruled that the statute was constitutional.

With Bryan on the side of the state were Attorney General Tom Stewart, technical head of the prosecution; Former Judge Ben McKenzie, Gordon McKenzie and Herbert and Sue Hicks, William A. Thompson and Bryan's son, William Jennings Bryan, Jr.

Clarence Darrow, defender of Leopold and Loeb and probably one of the greatest defense lawyers of the country, was, of course, the leader of Scopes' counsel. With him were Attorneys Dudley Field Malone and Arthur Garfield Hays of New York, and Judge John Randolph Neal of Knoxville.

Quickly it became apparent that the contest was between the two great leaders, Bryan and Darrow. The state put in its case. The defense admitted the charges, but it sought to put a dozen famous scientists on the stand to show what evolution was, and that it could be reconciled with the Biblical story of the creation.

Here the real issues were joined. And here Bryan had his chance to make the first plea in open court. He argued, of course, that the testimony of the scientists should not be admitted.

Standing before the bar of the court in his shirtsleeves, he pleaded with that silver tongue of his for the outlawry of the theory that attacked his faith. In the stifling heat the audience listened. They crowded the seats, stood in the aisles, and overflowed into the hall. In her wheel chair, white-haired Mrs. Bryan sat and heard her husband's speech.

"Today we come to the discussion of a very important part of this case," Bryan said in opening, "a question so important that upon its decision will determine the length of this trial. In the first place, our position is that the statute is sufficient. The statute defines exactly what the people of Tennessee desired and intended and did declare unlawful, and needs no interpretation."

Mr. Bryan then reviewed the evidence given by the state's witnesses. He continued:

"That is the evidence before the court, and we do not need any expert to tell us what the law means. An expert cannot be permitted to come here and try to defeat the enforcement of a law by testifying that it isn't a bad doctrine.

"The place to prove that, or teach that, was in the legislature. My friends, if the people of Tennessee were to go into New York, the state from which this impulse comes, to resist a law, or if they went into any other state and tried to convince the people that a law they had passed ought not to be enforced just because the people who went there didn't think it ought to have been passed, it would be resented. Don't you think the people of this state knew what they were doing when they passed the law and knew the dangers of the doctrine?

"They did not want it taught to their children, your Honor. It isn't proper to bring experts in here to try to defeat the purpose of the people of this state by trying to show that this thing that they denounce is a beautiful thing that everybody ought to believe in. It isn't a place for expert testimony. We have sufficient proof in the book—doesn't the book state the very thing that is objected to, and outlawed in this state? Who has a copy of that book?"

The Court—Do you mean the Bible?

Mr. Bryan—No, sir; the biology.

A Voice—Here it is, Hunter's biology.

"No, not the Bible," Bryan continued. "You see, in this state they cannot teach the Bible. They can only teach things that declare it to be a lie, according to the learned counsel.

"The question is, can a minority in this state come in and compel a teacher to teach that the Bible is not true and make the parents of those children pay the expenses of the teacher to tell their children what these people believe is false and dangerous? Has it come to a time when the minority can take charge of a state like Tennessee and compel the majority to pay their teachers while they take religion out of the hearts of the children of the parents who pay the teachers?

"My friends, if man and monkey were in the same class called primates it would mean they came up from the same order. It might mean that instead of one being the ancestor of the other they were all cousins.

"The Christian believes that man came from above. The

evolutionist believes he must have come from below, and that he is from a lower order of animals.

"Tell me that parents have not the right to declare that children are not to be taught this doctrine—shall be detached from the throne of God and be compelled to link their ancestors with the jungles? Why, my friends, if they believe it, they go back to scoff at the religion of their parents.

"The parents have a right to say that no teacher paid by their money shall rob their children of faith in God and send them back to their homes, skeptics, infidels, agnostics, or atheists.

"This is the doctrine that they wish taught; this is the doctrine that they would force upon the schools, that they will not let the Bible be read in."

Bryan then produced Darwin's "Descent of Man."

"Evolution is not a theory," he went on, "but a hypothesis. Huxley said it could not become a theory until they found more species that had developed according to the hypothesis, and at that time there had never been found a single species, the origin of which could be traced to another species, and it is true today.

"Never have they traced one single species to any other, and yet they call us ignoramuses and bigots because we do not throw away our Bible and accept evolution as proved.

"They demand that we allow them to teach this stuff to our children; that they may come home with their imaginary family tree and scoff at their mothers' and fathers' Bible.

"Not one of them can tell you how life began. The atheists say it came in some way without a God; the agnostics say it came in some way, they know not whether with a God or not; and the Christian evolutionists say we came from away back there somewhere, but they do not know how far back.

"They want to come in with their little padded-up evolution theories that commence with nothing and end nowhere.

"They do not deal with the problems of life—they do not teach the great science of how to live—and yet they would undermine the faith of these little children in that God who stands back of everything and whose promise we have that we shall live with Him forever by and by.

"They shut God out of the world. They do not tell us where immortality began. They did not tell us wherein this long period of time between the cell at the bottom of the sea and man where man became endowed with the hope of immortality.

"They want to teach that to these children and take from them their belief in a God who stands ready to welcome His children."

"Does the evolutionary theory involve the Divine Birth, the Virgin Birth?" asked the court.

It was plain that the curiosity of Judge Raulston had been aroused.

"Yes," was the reply, "because this principle of evolution disputes the miracle and that means they eliminate the Virgin Birth—that means that they eliminate the resurrection of the body.

"Man, rising all the time, never fell. He didn't need the Savior. No reason for His coming. They eliminate belief in the Savior and every moral standard the Bible gives us."

He came to Nietzsche and the Leopold-Loeb case. He referred to Darrow's speech in this case, a copy of which he held.

"Because Leopold read Nietzsche," he said, "and adopted his philosophy as a superman, he was not responsible for taking human life. That's the doctrine they are trying to bring in here with the evolution theory."

At this point Mr. Darrow objected.

"Not a word of truth in it," he said. "Nietzsche never taught evolution. These two people were insane. In southern Illinois the other day a clergyman killed his wife. I don't blame the doctrine of the clergyman."

Bryan resuming, read from Darrow's speech in the Loeb trial where it referred to professors of universities as responsible for the murder. Darrow said he would read later the rest of it, explaining this.

"Now," Bryan resumed, "when it comes to Bible experts, do they think that they can bring them in here to instruct the members of the jury, eleven of whom are members of the church? I submit that of the eleven members of the jury more of the jurors are experts on what the Bible is than any Bible expert who does not subscribe to the true spiritual influences of what our Bible says."

Voices in audience, "Amen!"

"The beauty about the word of God is that it does not take an expert to understand it. They have translated that Bible into five hundred languages, they have carried it into nations where but few can read a word or write, to people who never saw a book, who never read, and yet can understand that Bible and they can accept the salvation that that Bible offers.

"They can know more about that book by accepting Jesus and feeling in their hearts the sense of their sins forgiven than all of the skeptical outside Bible experts that could come in here.

"Therefore, your honor, we believe that this evidence is not competent. This is not a mock trial. If we must have a mock trial to give these people a chance to get before the public with their views, then let us convene it after this case is over.

"But let this court, which is here supported by the law and by the taxpayers, pass upon this law.

© P. & A. photo

Bryan Is Dead—Friends and neighbors gather in front of the Rogers house in Dayton, Tenn.. to talk in whispers of the tragedy that occurred July 26. 1925.

© P. & A. photo.

Guard of Honor—Members of the Dayton post of the American Legion stand guard on the front porch of the Rogers house, where Bryan died and where his body lay in state. In the center, Kelso Rice, Chattanooga policeman, who accompanied the body to Washington as special guard at Mrs Bryan's request.

The Commoner's Body Arrives—The picture shows the flag-draped casket being carried up the steps of the New York Avenue Presbyterian church. Washington, D C., Thursday, July 30, 1925.

"We can bring our experts here for the Christians, more than they can bring who do not believe in Christianity. We can bring more than one who believes in the Bible and rejects evolution, and our witnesses will be just as good experts as theirs on a question of that kind.

"We could have a thousand or a million witnesses, but this case as to whether evolution is true or not is not going to be tried here; if it is carried to the state's courts it will not be tried there, and if it is taken to the great court at Washington it will not be tried there.

"No, my friends, no court, and no jury, great or small, is going to destroy the issue between the believer and the unbeliever.

"The Bible is the Word of God, the Bible is the only expression of man's hope of salvation. The Bible, the record of the son of God, the saviour or the world, born of the Virgin Mary, crucified and risen again, that Bible is not going to be driven out of this court by experts who come to testify that they can reconcile evolution with its ancestors in the jungle. with man made by God in His image and put here for purposes as a part of the Divine plan.

"The facts are simple, the case is plain, and if these gentlemen want to enter upon a larger field of educational work on the subject of evolution, let us get through with this case and then convene a mock court, for it will deserve the title of mock court if its purpose is to banish from the hearts of the people the Word of God as revealed."

At the conclusion of the plea fundamentalist and evolutionist broke into applause. Mr. Malone, in a stirring speech, answered Bryan, declaring that truth must always and eventually prevail. Attorney General Stewart closed the debate. After many hours spent in preparing his decision, Judge Raulston ruled that the experts' testimony could not go to the jury. It was allowed to go into the record for the higher courts in affidavit form.

Disappointed in their hope to get this testimony of scientific men before the nation, the defense sprang a legal coup. They called for William Jennings Bryan to take the witness stand as an expert on the Bible.

CHAPTER XXVIII

The Last Battle

Bryan against Darrow—On the Witness Stand—Defends Revealed Religion—Jonah and the Whale—The Story of the Creation—Eve and the Temptation—How the Serpent Travelled.

No court scene in the world's history ever has held—or will hold—all the dramatic qualities that were contained on the platform outside the Dayton courthouse on the afternoon Bryan took the witness stand and offered the shield of his faith to the slashing thrusts of Darrow's legal skill and agnostic philosophy.

The courtroom was the lawn and the clump of maple trees in the courthouse yard. The weight of the hundreds of spectators who had jammed their perspiring way into the regular courtroom on the second floor of the courthouse had caused fears that the building would collapse, and Judge Raulston had ordered that this greatest scene of all—bound to attract the crowds as no other event in the trial—should be held outside for safety's sake.

Crude wooden benches made of planks set across squared logs held the spectators. They filled these, then they stood. The men and women and children of the Tennessee hills crowded and banked themselves in rank on rank clear back to the courtyard fence to view and hear this battle unique in the world's annals.

It was William Jennings Bryan, champion of revealed religion, against Clarence Darrow, prophet of science.

Two men, both past middle age, both indeed nearing the day when death would decide the personal issue of which was wrong and which was right, they strove there with the multitude tensely looking on, now awed into silence, now frenziedly cheering and applauding, forgetting that this was a court of law.

It epitomized the struggle of the ages, that conflict there, the eternal war between religion and science.

The greatness of the two, their very physical bulk as they stood before the crowd, the magnitude of their personalities, their fervent vigor, reminded one of two of the giant animals that science says once lived on earth doing battle to the death.

It was a piece of clever lawyership on the part of the defense that brought the scene about. Their scientific witnesses had been ruled from the stand. Everyone thought the trial, so far as high spots went, was nearly over. Then they called for Bryan to take the witness chair. Readily, he stepped forward. He wanted, only, he said, to have a similar opportunity of questioning Darrow.

He took his seat. Darrow began his questioning. The fierce play back and forth between these two can be depicted only in the stenographic report of what followed.

The Court—Mr. Bryan, you are not objecting to going on the stand?

Mr. Bryan—Not at all.

The Court—Do you want Mr. Bryan sworn, Mr. Darrow?

Mr. Darrow—No, I take it you will tell the truth, Mr. Bryan. You have given considerable study to the Bible, haven't you, Mr. Bryan?

Mr. Bryan—Yes, sir, I have tried to. I have studied the Bible for about fifty years, or some time more than that. I studied it more lately than in my youth.

Q.—Do you claim that everything in the Bible should be literally interpreted? A.—I believe everything in the Bible should be accepted as it is given there; some of the Bible is given illustratively. For instance, "Ye are the salt of the earth."

I would not insist that man was actually salt, or that he had flesh of salt, but it is used in the sense of salt as saving God's people.

They began calmly, good-naturedly enough. But Darrow quickly got down to specific questions pertaining to Bryan's Bible faith. His questions grew pointed; Bryan's answers, more emphatic.

Q.—But when you read that Jonah swallowed the whale—or that the whale swallowed Jonah—excuse me please—how do you literally interpret that? A.—When I read that a big fish swallowed Jonah—it does not say whale——

Q.—Doesn't it? Are you sure? A.—That is my recollection of it. A big fish, and I believe it; and I believe in a God who can make a whale and can make a man and make both do what He pleases.

Q.—Now, you say, the big fish swallowed Jonah, and he there remained how long—three days—and then he spewed him upon the land. You believe that the big fish was made to swallow Jonah? A.—I am not prepared to say that; the Bible merely says it was done.

Q.—You don't know whether it was the ordinary run of fish or a fish made for that purpose? A.—You may guess; you evolutionists guess.

Q.—But when we do guess, we have the sense to guess right. A.—But do not do it often.

Q.—But you believe He made them—that He made such a fish and that it was big enough to swallow Jonah? A.—Yes, sir. Let me add: one miracle is just as easy to believe as another.

Q.—It is for me. A.—It is for me too.

Q.—Just as hard? A.—It is hard to believe for you, but easy for me.

Q.—Perfectly easy to believe that Jonah swallowed the whale? A.—The Bible says so. The Bible doesn't make as extreme statements as evolutionists do.

Q.—That may be a question, Mr. Bryan, about some of those you have known? A.—The only thing is, you have a definition of fact that includes imagination.

Q.—And you have a definition that excludes everything but imagination.

They were warming to the struggle. Mind and wit were tuning up. A sting crept into both voices.

Q.—The Bible says Joshua commanded the sun to stand still for the purpose of lengthening the day, doesn't it? And you believe it? A.—I do.

Q.—Do you believe at that time the sun went around the earth? A.—No, I believe that the earth goes around the sun.

Q.—Do you believe that the men who wrote it thought that the day could be lengthened or that the sun could be stopped? A.—I don't know what they thought. I think they wrote the fact without expressing their own thoughts.

Attorney General Tom Stewart jumped to his feet for the first of several times, to object to this questioning going on further. It wasn't proper in a law suit, he said. It wasn't. But like two fighters, you couldn't drag these two contestants apart. "I am willing," said Bryan, and the questioning went on.

Mr. Darrow—Have you an opinion, as to whether, whoever wrote the book—I believe it is Joshua—thought the sun went around the earth or not? A.—I believe he was inspired.

Q.—Can you answer my question? A.—When you let me finish the statement. You cannot measure the length of my answer by the length of your question. (Laughter in the courtyard.)

Mr. Darrow—No; except that the answer will be longer. (Laughter in the courtyard.)

Mr. Bryan—I believe the Bible is inspired and written by inspired authors. Whether the one who wrote as he was directed to write understood the things he was writing about, I don't know.

Q.—Do you think whoever inspired it believed that the sun went around the earth? A.—I believe it was inspired by the Almighty and He may have used language that could be understood at that time, instead of using language that could not be understood until Darrow was born. (Laughter and applause.)

Q.—So it might have been subject to construction, might it not? A.—That is your construction. I am answering your question.

Q.—Don't you believe that in order to lengthen the day it would have been construed that the earth stood still? A.—I would not attempt to say what would have been necessary, but I know this: that I can take a glass of water that would fall to the ground without the strength of my hand and, to the extent of the glass of water, I can overcome the law of gravitation and lift it up, whereas, without my hand, it would fall to the ground. If my puny hand can overcome the law of gravitation, the most universally understood, to that extent, I would not set a limit to the power of the hand of the Almighty God that made the universe.

Q.—I read that years ago, in your "Prince of Peace." Can you answer my question directly? If the day was lengthened by stopping either the earth or the sun, it must have been the earth? A.—Well, I should say so.

Q.—We know also the sun does not stand still? A.—Well, that is relatively so, as Mr. Einstein would say.

Q.—I ask you if it does stand still? A.—You know as well as I know.

Q.—Better. You have no doubt about it? A.—No. And the earth moves around.

Q.—Yes ? A.—But 1 think that there is nothing improper if it will protect the Lord against your criticism.

Q.—I suppose He needs it. A.—He was using language at that time the people understood.

Q.—And that you call "interpretation?" A.—No, sir; I would not call it interpretation.

Q.—I say, you would call it interpretation at this time, to say it meant something then? A.—You may use your own language to describe what I have to say, and I will use mine ir answering.

Bryan shot to his feet and his answer flamed out at his tormenter. His anger was stirred.

Q.—Now, Mr. Bryan, have you ever pondered what would have happened to the earth if it had stood still? A.—No. sir; the God I believe in could have taken care of that, Mr. Darrow.

Q.—I see. Have you ever pondered what would naturally happen to the earth if it stood still suddenly? A.—No.

Q.—Don't you know it would have been converted into a molten mass of matter? A.—You testify to that when you get on the stand; I will give you a chance.

Q.—You have never investigated that subject? A.—I don't think 1 have ever had the question asked.

Q.—Or ever thought of it? A.—I have been too busy on things that I thought were of more importance than that.

Q.—You believe the story of the flood to be a literal interpretation? A.—Yes, sir.

Q.—When was that flood? A.—I would not attempt to fix the date. The date is fixed, as suggested this morning.

Q.—About 2400 B. C.? A.—That has been the estimate of a man that is accepted today. I would not say it is accurate.

Q.—What do you think? A.—I do not think about things that I don't think about.

Q.—Do you think about things that you do think about? A.—Well, sometimes. (Laughter in the courtyard.)

General Stewart—I am objecting to his cross-examining his own witness.

The Witness—I want him to have all the latitude that he wants. For I am going to have some latitude when he gets through.

Mr. Darrow—You can have latitude and longitude. (Laughter.)

The Witness—These gentlemen have not had much chance—they did not come here to try this case. They came here to try revealed religion. I am here to defend it, and they can ask me any questions they please. (Applause.)

Mr. Darrow—Great applause from the bleachers.

The Witness—From those whom you call "yokels."

Mr. Darrow—I have never called them yokels.

The Witness—That is the ignorance of Tennessee, the bigotry.

Mr. Darrow—You mean who are applauding you?

The Witness—Those are the people whom you insult?

Mr. Darrow—You insult every man of science and learning in the world because he doesn't believe in your fool religion.

Darrow, beside himself, hurled out the words. Bryan's face grew red with anger. He was on his feet to cast back a reply when Judge Raulston broke it. "I will not stand for that," he cried. At last, the excitement died down.

Mr. Darrow—How long ago was the flood, Mr. Bryan? A.—Let me see Usher's calculation about it. It is given here as 2348 years before Christ.

Q.—You believe that all the living things that were not contained in the ark were destroyed? A.—I think the fish may have lived.

Q.—Outside of the fish? A.—I have no proof to the contrary.

Q.—I am asking you whether you believe? A.—I do.

Q.—You are not satisfied there is any civilization that can be traced back 5,000 years? A.—I would not want to say there is, because I have no evidence of it that is satisfactory when the scientists differ, from 24,000,000 to 306,000,000 years in their opinion, as to how long ago life came here. I want them to come nearer together before they demand of me to give up my belief in the Bible. I am satisfied by no evidence that I have found that would justify me in accepting the opinions of these men against what I believe to be the inspired word of God.

Q.—You believe that every civilization on the earth and every living thing except possibly the fishes that came out of the ark were wiped out by the flood? A.—At that time.

Q.—And that whatever human beings, including all the tribes, that inhabit the world and have inhabited the world, and who ιun their pedigree straight back, and all the animals, have come onto the earth since the flood? A.—Yes.

Q.—You do know that there are thousands of people who profess to be Christians who believe the earth is much more ancient and that the human race is much more ancient? A.—I think there may be.

Witness and questioner argued back and forth about the sources of religion, about religions, other than Christianity. The talk ran to Confucianism and Buddhism.

Q.—Do you regard them as competitive? A.—No, I think they are very inferior.

Q.—You have never in all your life made any attempt to find out about the other peoples of the earth—how old their civilizations are—how long they had existed on the earth, have you? A.—No, sir; I have been so well satisfied with the Christian religion that I have spent no time trying to find arguments against it.

Q.—Were you afraid you might find some ? A.—No, sir; and I am not afraid now that you will show me any; I have all the information I want to live by and die by.

Q.—And that's all you are interested in? A.—I am not looking for any more on religion.

Q.—You don't care how old the earth is, how old man is, and how long the animals have been here? A.—I am not so much interested in that.

Q.—You have heard of the tower of Babel haven't you? A.—Yes, sir. That was about 100 years before the flood, Mr. Darrow, according to this chronology.

Q.—That would be 4155 years ago. Up to 4155 years ago every human being on earth spoke the same language? A.—Yes, sir, I think that is the inference that could be drawn from that.

Q.—Do you know how many languages are spoken on the face of the earth? A.—No. I know the Bible has been translated into 500. Those are all the principal languages.

Q.—There are a great many that are not principal languages. And you say that all those languages of all the sons of men have come on the earth not over 4150 years ago? A.—I have seen no evidence that would lead to me to put it any further back than that.

Q.—Mr. Bryan, could you tell me how old the earth is? A.—No, sir, I couldn't.

Q.—Could you come anywhere near it? A.—I wouldn't attempt to. I could possibly come as near as the scientists do, but I had rather be more accurate before I give a guess.

The questioning turned to the age of the earth; Mr. Bryan

believed it was much older than 4,000 years. Then to the story of creation in Genesis.

Q.—Do you think the earth was made in six days? A.—Not six days of twenty-four hours.

Q.—Doesn't it say so? A.—No, sir.

Gen. Stewart—I want to interpose another objection. What is the purpose of this examination?

Mr. Bryan was on his feet. He shouted out over the heads of the audience.

"The purpose is to cast ridicule on everybody who believes in the Bible, and I am perfectly willing that the world shall know that these gentlemen have no other purpose than ridiculing every person who believes in the Bible."

Darrow, too, was stamping about.

"We have the purpose of preventing bigots and ignoramuses from controlling the education of the United States, and you know it, and that is all," was his retort.

"I am glad to bring out that statement," cried Bryan to the court, to Darrow, and to the eager spectators below. "I want the world to know that this evidence is not for the review. Mr. Darrow and his associates have filed affidavits here stating the purpose, as I understand it, is to show that the Bible story is not true.

"I am not trying to get anything into the records. I am simply trying to protect the word of God against the greatest atheist or agnostic in the United States. (Prolonged applause.) I want the papers to know I am not afraid to get on the stand in front of him and let him do his worst. I want the world to know that agnosticism is trying to force unbelief on our colleges and on our schools, and the people of Tennessee will not permit it to be done."

"The reason I am answering," Mr. Bryan declared, "is not

for the benefit of the Supreme court. It is to keep these gentlemen from saying I was afraid to meet them, and let them question me; and I want the Christian world to know that any atheist, agnostic, unbeliever, can question me any time as to my belief in God and I will answer him."

"Your Honor," he continued, "they have not asked a question legally, and the only reason they have asked any question is for the purpose—as the question about Jonah was asked—for a chance to give this agnostic an opportunity to criticize a believer in the word of God; and I answered the question in order to shut his mouth so he cannot go out and tell his atheist friends that I would not answer his question. That is the only reason in the world."

Bryan was furiously indignant. He paced the platform and shook his finger in Darrow's face. Never, probably, in his whole career had he publicly displayed such feeling. The crowd was rocked with emotion and when Bryan finished his sympathizers cheered and applauded wildly.

Dudley Field Malone, Darrow's associate counsel, made a stirring speech in reply, scoring Bryan for his attack on Darrow. Malone, too, drew wild applause. It took resolute pounding of the bailiff's gavel to restore order and let Mr. Darrow continue.

Mr. Darrow—Do you believe that the first woman was Eve? A.—Yes.

Q.—Do you believe she was literally made out of Adam's rib? A.—I do.

Q.—Did you ever discover where Cain got his wife? A.—No, sir; I leave the agnostics to hunt for her.

Q.—Where she came from you do not know. All right. Does the statement, "The morning and the evening were the first day," and the "morning and evening were the second day" mean anything to you? A.—I don't think it necessarily means a twenty-four-hour day. I do not think it does. But I think it would be just as easy for the kind of God we believe in to make the earth in six days or in six years, or in six million years, or in six hundred million years. I do not think it important whethei we believe one or the other.

Q.—Do you think those were literal days? A.—My impression is they were periods.

Q.—Have you any idea of the length of the periods? A.—No, I haven't.

Q.—Do you think the sun was made on the fourth day? A.—Yes.

Q.—The creation might have been going on for a very long time? A.—It might have continued for millions of years.

Q.—Do you believe the story of the temptation of Eve by the serpent? A.—I do.

Q.—Do you believe that after Eve ate the apple or gave it to Adam—which ever way it was—that God cursed Eve, and at that time decreed that all womankind henceforth and forever should suffer the pains of childbirth in the reproduction of the earth? A.—I will believe just what the Bible says.

Q.—And you believe that came about because Eve tempted Adam to eat the fruit? A.—Just as it says.

Q.—And you believe that is the reason that God made the serpent to go on his belly after he tempted Eve? A.—I believe the Bible as it is, and I do not permit you to put your language in the place of the language of the Almighty. You read that Bible and ask me questions, and I will answer them. I will not answer your questions in your language.

Q.—I will read it to you from the Bible: "and the Lord God said unto the serpent, because thou has done this, thou art cursed above all cattle, and above every beast of the field; upon thy belly shalt thou go and dust shalt thou eat all the days of thy life." Do you think that is why the serpent is compelled to crawl upon its belly? A.—I believe that.

Q.—Have you any idea how the snake went before that time? A.—No, sir.

Q.—Do you know whether he walked on his tail or not? A.—No, sir. I have no way to know. (Laughter.)

Q.—Now, you refer to the bow that was put in the Heaven, after the flood, the rainbow. Do you believe in that? A.—Read it.

Q.—All right, Mr. Bryan, I will read it for you.

Mr. Bryan—Your honor, I think I can shorten this testimony. The only purpose Mr. Darrow has is to slur at the Bible, but I will answer his question. I will answer it all at once, and I have no objection in the world. I want the world to know that this man, who does not believe in a God, is trying to use a court in Tennessee——

Once more Bryan was out of his chair, pouring his words in a swift torrent out over the sea of rapt faces.

Mr. Darrow—I object to that.

Mr. Bryan (Continuing)—To slur at it, and while it will require time, I am willing to take it.

Mr. Darrow—I object to your statement. I am examining you on your fool ideas that no intelligent Christian on earth believes.

Once more, tumult, at that bitter attack on the great Commoner and his faith. The crowd was in a stir, adherents of Bryan, proponents of Darrow, adding their voices to the clamor on the platform. Darrow was shaking his finger in Bryan's face now, and Bryan was returning the gesture with vehemence. No stenographer could catch all the quick words. Then the judge cut in, and the gavel halted this day, one of the most eventful in American court history, as well as one of the most eventful in the life of Bryan.

Bryan's faith had been submitted to a test of fire. Men will judge according to their views as to which of the two mighty contestants won the advantage. Suffice it, that the champion of revealed religion had had the courage of his conviction, that he had submitted readily to an inquisition by one of the keenest legal minds in the country.

One of the disappointments of his life was that he never had the opportunity to submit Darrow to a like examination. The trial ended the next day. Another swift move on the part of the defense brought it to a close without even the formality of argument—the second great disappointment; for it was in making the closing speech that Bryan intended to put forth one of the finest efforts of his life.

But it was otherwise ordered. Scopes was swiftly declared guilty, as had been expected, and his case was prepared for presentation to the higher courts.

Bryan did not have even the opportunity of giving out his closing speech in person. Death took him, and the speech printed further on in this book was given out posthumously.

How much that last afternoon on the witness stand had to do with bringing on that death more quickly will, of course, never be known. Bryan felt tired after that strenuous day, he confessed. It must of necessity have sapped much of his wearied strength.

Guarding the Bier—Veterans of the Spanish-American war standing guard about the casket of the Great Commoner.

Last Tribute—Scene at the funeral services in Washington. Hundreds packed the church; other hundreds were left outside in the rain.

At Rest—Soldiers from Fort Myer carrying the casket to the grave in Arlington cemetery while crowds of mourners stand in the rain.

Where Bryan Sleeps—Site of the grave of the Great Commoner in Arlington National cemetery with the amphitheater in the background.

CHAPTER XXIX

He Lay Down to Sleep

Sunday afternoon, July 26, 1925—Grief of Mrs. Bryan— All Dayton, the Nation Mourns—Pilgrimage from the Hills—Memorial Services—Sermon of the Rev. Dr. Jones.

In the midst of his last great labor, which was to be a nation-wide campaign for laws protecting the Bible, William Jennings Bryan lay down to sleep. It was during the afternoon of Sunday, July 26, 1925. He died while he slept, of heart trouble.

Death was dramatic for the Great Commoner as so many events of his life had been. The drama of the Scopes trial was over; another drama, of the fight to protect revealed religion, was to follow. It was just a lull in the fight when the end came.

He was still in Dayton, scene of the trial. The man who knew palaces and stately mansions died as he had lived—the Commoner—in a simple cottage, the home of Richard Rogers, Dayton druggist, where the Bryans had resided during the trial.

Apparently full of health, enthusiastic over his plans for the future, Bryan had gone to his room to take a nap after a hearty luncheon. It was about one-thirty in the afternoon when he retired; he had asked to be wakened about four o'clock. Mrs. Bryan sent William McCartney, the family chauffeur and companion to Bryan, in to wake him.

But the Commoner was to wake no more on earth. Doctors were called, but they could do no more than confirm scientifically what everyone knew. Bryan was dead.

Mrs. Bryan was on the front porch when McCartney went in. He cried out to her that something had happened. She made her way to her husband's side, calling him. He didn't answer

379

and she fell across the bed, crying. After the first outburst of grief, she gathered herself together and courageously shared the duties attendant on the sudden tragedy.

The news spread through Dayton and the surrounding country like wildfire. The people could hardly believe that the man whom they had come to regard almost as a patron saint had died so suddenly. Crowds gathered in front of the Rogers house, then quietly dispersed when they learned that the widow was under the doctor's care for a time. But they gathered again in knots at the street corners and along the sidewalks, to talk in hushed voices of this loss, which was to them as keen almost as the death of a member of their own families.

There had been no immediate foreshadowing of the end, though on looking back later, it seemed that Bryan had felt for some time that he had not a great deal longer to live.

At the Democratic convention in New York in the summer of 1924, it was recalled, he had told Former Senator Gilbert M. Hitchcock of Nebraska that he felt "his life was fast coming to an end, that he had overtaxed himself so much, and he could not stand fatigue as he used to."

And those who heard him talk at Pikeville, a town near Dayton, during the trial, remembered that he had spoken there of fatigue in explanation of the shortness of his speech. He had felt the great heat very keenly during the trial and had become worn and thin. But never had the fire of the crusader burned more fiercely.

Before he went in to take that last nap, he had protested in answer to anxious inquiries, that he had never felt better. Even during the few days of comparative interim he had been busy. He had completed the preparation of the speech which was to have been his final argument in the prosecution of Scopes and had visited Chattanooga to see about having it printed, now that he was unable to give it in court in person. On the day before his death he had made a trip to Winchester, Tenn., a trip that rivaled a day of any of his political tours for the number of people he addressed.

At ten o'clock in the morning, on the way to Winchester, he had spoken to a great throng at Jasper. At Fairgrounds, later in the day, he addressed an audience of 8,000. Returning from Winchester, Bryan's train was like his campaign special of 1896. The journey turned spontaneously into a back platform speaking tour. At town after town the Great Commoner made speeches.

He was in excellent spirits and enjoyed the cheering and the wild applause as he pleaded for battle against the forces of unbelief. He hailed the conviction of Scopes as a great victory for the cause of Christianity and a staggering blow to the "powers of darkness." His audiences would not let him go. At the town of Cowan he spoke for twenty minutes. The schedule of his train was thoroughly disjointed.

Altogether, it was estimated, Bryan covered 200 miles and talked to more than 50,000 people on the day before he died. On the morning of his death he had attended the service at the Southern Methodist church in Dayton. He had expected to go to Nashville and Knoxville in a day or so to deliver more addresses. Mrs. Bryan was planning a trip to Idaho where her husband was to join her later.

Following his death, Mrs. Bryan expressed her husband's wish that he be buried in the National cemetery at Arlington, and arrangements were begun for the funeral.

But first the people of Dayton were to have opportunity to do honor to their beloved friend and revered leader.

On the Monday after his death, Bryan's body lay in state in the bronze coffin in the front room of the Rogers home while his humbler followers came to gaze for the last time on the face of their champion. Gathered as watchers about the coffin were Bryan's associates in the Scopes prosecution. Telegrams and letters of sympathy by the hundred were pouring in from all parts of the United States and of the world. Six members of the Dayton post of the American Legion were selected to stand guard at the coffin.

But Mrs. Bryan refused their offer to go on with the body to Washington as a military guard of honor.

"We are simple people," she said, "and we want all arrangements simply made."

Out of respect to the dead Commoner who lay in their midst the flags of Dayton flew at half mast and all the shops were closed, while on the front window of Robinson's drug store, where took place the discussion that grew into the Scopes trial, this proclamation, issued by the mayor of Dayton, was pasted:

"He fell while in the line of duty to the cause nearest his heart. All Dayton mourns his untimely death."

There was greater show at the formal services at Washington which followed, and at the burial in Arlington cemetery, but there were no sincerer tributes than were paid by the plain folk of Tennessee. Two days after Bryan's death, and the day before his body left in a special car for the capital, simple memorial services were held under the maples in front of the Rogers house.

All Dayton was there, and down from the Cumberland hills came the neighboring folk. They laid aside their work in cornfield and orchard. On foot, a-mule back, jostling behind rude wagons, or in automobiles, they came from their farms. They formed a hushed parade of honor down Dayton's main streets. They spoke in simple terms of him as they had heard him during the past weeks. Easily, naturally, as if the man who had been three times candidate for the Presidency of the United States

and once was Secretary of State, had been a neighbor of theirs—
as indeed he had—they paid him homage.

Lightly, they trod as they left the sidewalk and mounted the
four cement steps that led to the front door of the Rogers home.
Softly, they passed through the screen door and into the little
room where lay the flag-draped coffin. Whispering ceased as
they edged up to the casket and gazed fixedly down at the placid
features of the man whom, but a few days before, they had
heard and cheered as he defended their faith and his own.

Out on the lawn in front of the cottage the mourners gathered
for the service. The Rev. Charles R. Jones, pastor of the Dayton
Methodist church, preached the memorial sermon. So simple
it was, so sincere, and so typical of the way in which not only
the people of Dayton, or of Tennessee, but people throughout
this nation felt toward the Great Commoner, that it is given here
to close this chapter:

"One of the young men associated with Mr. Bryan in this
law suit of which the whole world has heard," Rev. Jones began,
"made this remark to me the other day. He said, 'Brother
Jones, there is one verse of Scripture in the Bible, the most
applicable one to Mr. Bryan's life, in my opinion, in the great
Book, 'Well done thou good and faithful servant.'

" 'Well done thou good and faithful servant.' If the truth has
ever been said of any man, this can be said of William Jennings
Bryan. If there ever has been a faithful servant in the cause
of the kingdom of Jesus Christ, the Great Commoner was that
man.

"In introducing Mr. Bryan the first Sunday he spoke in our
little city I remember to have said of him: 'I believe that he is
the voice of one crying in the wilderness, make strong his paths.'

"Then last Sunday morning he came in and down the aisle
and took the front pew. He sat upon the front pew just in front

of the preacher and when the congregation stood I said 'We will remain standing while Brother Bryan leads us in prayer.'

"He started out approaching the Father with these words, 'Dear Heavenly Father,' in a conversational tone, as if he were seated by your side or my side, in friendly conversation. And the burden of his prayer seemed to be for the guidance of the holy spirit. One of his petitions was, 'Guide us by thy holy spirit.' He prayed God's blessings upon the church of Jesus Christ and upon the Bible which he loved, and for which I verily believe he gave his gracious, his magnificent, his beautiful, his God-fearing, his victorious life.

"We often laud the motives which we read in the Holy Book, but I believe that William Jennings Bryan went to an untimely death a martyr to the cause of the living God. And as brave men have met death upon the thousands of battlefields, this most wonderful, greatest of all Christians with which this great country has been blessed, met death with a smile.

"I came upon the widow. I found her sitting in her chair, with an occasional tear. She wondered why a great man had to go now with so much work to be done. I said, 'Mrs. Bryan, workmen die, but their work goes on.' She said, 'But I wonder who will take his place. Where is the man?' I thought upon that. I could not get away from it.

"I want to say this: That Mr. Bryan did not stack arms and forever bury his leadership. He is a greater leader this afternoon than he was last Sunday morning. I turned to these lawyers whom he loved, and I believe these young men will do their utmost to carry out the great principle for which he fought and died, and if they do do it, William Jennings Bryan shall not have died in vain, so far as they are concerned.

"William Jennings Bryan is still the man in the forefront, and he shall arise as the mighty unit, hundreds, thousands and millions of men and women, boys and girls will meet the great enemy of the Bible, which is the work of God, in solid phalanx, and we shall look upon William Jennings Bryan as in death but much more alive today than ever before in the history of his life.

"I want to say here today that greater fear has followed upon the opposers of the fundamental principles of the Son of God than ever before in the history of atheism, agnosticism, and all the other damnable "isms" known to the devil and his cohorts.

"Let us arise as American people who have followed Him and who are still following Him."

CHAPTER XXX

Life After Death

The Posthumous Speech—Right of Legislatures to Control the Schools—The Menace of the Evolution Theory—Darwin as an Example—Darrow's Defense of Leopold and Loeb Used Against Him—World Motivated by Hate, not Love, if Evolution Triumphs—"Faith of Our Fathers."

The fortunes of a trial at law robbed Bryan of one of his most cherished desires, the hope of making the closing argument in the Scopes trial. The ruling that brought the trial to an unexpected close snatched from him the dreamed-of opportunity of making this one most eloquent plea for his religion against the forces of science that he believed were aligned against it.

A lawyer's fortune robbed him of this chance, but death gave it back to him in his grave. He lost the occasion of making this final argument in person, while all the newspaper-reading world had its ear attuned to the happenings in Dayton. Death achieved for him a greater occasion, a greater audience.

Had things gone as he expected, the world would have read this last speech against a background of the man's eloquent personality. It would have pictured him, there in the courtroom, using that gift of oratory which was his, as he had never used it before. When at last this speech, which follows, was given out by Mrs. Bryan, on the day after her husband's death, the world read it with an awe that never could have been achieved in any courtroom, nor by any manner of earthly eloquence.

Bryan had been working on its preparation for many days. It was ready, typed, when he lay down in that last sleep. It is printed here below, not in full—for it is very long—, but with only a few portions more suitable for the courtroom omitted.

"Demosthenes, the greatest of ancient orators, in his 'oration of the crown,' the most famous of his speeches, began by supplicating the favor of all the gods and goddesses of Greece. If, in a case which involved only his own fame and fate, he felt justified in petitioning the heathen gods of his country, surely we, who deal with the momentous issues involved in this case, may well pray to the Ruler of the universe for wisdom to guide us in the performance of our several parts of this historic trial.

"Let me in the first place, congratulate our cause that circumstances have committed the trial to a community like this and entrusted the decision to a jury made up largely of the yeomanry of the state.

"I appreciate the sturdy honesty and independence of those who come into daily contact with the earth, who, living, near to nature, worship nature's God, and who, dealing with the myriad mysteries of earth and air seek to learn from revelation about the Bible's wonder-working God. I admire the stern virtues, the vigilance and the patriotism of the class from which the jury is drawn, and am reminded of the lines of Scotland's immortal bard, which when changed but slightly, describe your country's confidence in you:

"O Scotia, my dear, my native soil!
   For whom my warmest wish to Heaven is sent,
Long may thy hardy sons of rustic toil
   Be blest with health, and peace, and sweet content!

"And, oh, may Heav'n their simple lives prevent
   From luxury's contagion, weak and vile.
Then, howe'er crowns and coronets be rent,
   A virtuous populace may rise the while,
   And stand, a wall of fire, around their much-loved isle.'

"Let us now separate the issues from the misrepresentations, intentional or unintentional, that have obscured both the letter and the purpose of the law. This is not an interference with freedom of conscience. This law does not violate any rights guaranteed by any constitution to any individual.

"It need hardly be added that this law did not have its origin in bigotry. It is not trying to force any form of religion on anybody. The majority is not trying to establish a religion or to teach it—it is trying to protect itself from the effort of an insolent minority to force irreligion upon the children under the guise of teaching science. What right has a little irresponsible oligarchy of self-styled 'intellectuals' to demand control of the schools of the United States, in which 25,000,000 of children are being educated at an annual expense of nearly $2,000,000,000?

"Christians must, in every state of the union, build their own colleges in which to teach Christianity; it is only simple justice that atheists, agnostics and unbelievers should build their own colleges if they want to teach their own religious views or attack the religious views of others."

In a clear, lawyerlike manner, he states the facts in the case against Scopes; reviews the testimony given by the state's witnesses, the boys whom Scopes taught, the superintendent of schools, and the president of the school board. He continues with his argument:

"These are the facts. They are sufficient and undisputed; a verdict of guilty must follow.

"But the importance of this case requires more. The facts and arguments presented to you must not only convince you of the justice of conviction in this case but, while not necessary to a verdict of guilty, they should convince you of the righteousness of the purpose of the people of the state in the enactment of this law. The state must speak through you to the outside world and repel the aspersions cast by the counsel for the defense upon the intelligence and the enlightenment of the citizens of Tennessee.

"Religion is not hostile to learning; Christianity has been the greatest patron learning has ever had. But Christians know that 'the fear of the Lord is the beginning of wisdom' now just as it has been in the past, and they therefore oppose the teaching of guesses that encourage Godlessness among the students.

"Neither does Tennessee undervalue the service rendered by science. The Christian men and women of Tennessee know how deeply mankind is indebted to science for benefits conferred by the discovery of the laws of nature and by the designing of machinery for the utilization of these laws. Give science a fact and it is not only invincible, but it is of incalculable service to man. If one is entitled to draw from society in proportion to the service that he renders to society, who is able to estimate the reward earned by those who have given to us the use of steam, the use of electricity, and enabled us to utilize the weight of water that flows down the mountainside?

"Who will estimate the value of the service rendered by those who invented the phonograph, the telephone and the radio? Or, to come more closely to our home life, how shall we recompense those who gave us the sewing machine, the harvester, the threshing machine, the tractor, the automobile and the method now employed in making artificial ice? The department of medicine also opens an unlimited field for invaluable service. Typhoid and yellow fever are not feared as they once were. Diphtheria and pneumonia have been robbed of some of their terrors, and a high place on the scroll of fame still awaits the discoverer of remedies for arthritis, cancer, tuberculosis and other dread disease to which mankind is heir.

"Christianity welcomes truth from whatever source it comes,

and is not afraid that any real truth from any source can interfere with the Divine truth that comes by inspiration from God himself. It is not scientific truth to which Christians object, for true science is classified knowledge, and nothing therefore can be scientific unless it is true.

"Evolution is not truth; it is merely an hypothesis—it is millions of guesses strung together. It had not been proven in the days of Darwin; he expressed astonishment that with two or three million species it had been impossible to trace any species to any other species. It had not been proven in the days of Huxley, and it has not been proven up to today. While many scientists accept evolution as if it were a fact, they all admit, when questioned, that no explanation has been found as to how one species developed into another.

"Darwin suggested two laws, sexual selection and natural selection. Sexual selection has been laughed out of the class room, and natural selection is being abandoned, and no new explanation is satisfactory even to scientists.

"Some of the more rash advocates of evolution are wont to say that evolution is as firmly established as the law of gravitation or the Copernican theory. The absurdity of such a claim is apparent when we remember that anyone can prove the law of gravitation by throwing a weight into the air, and that anyone can prove the roundness of the earth by going around it, while no one can prove evolution to be true in any way whatever.

"There is no more reason to believe that man descended from some inferior animal than there is to believe that a stately mansion has descended from a small cottage. Resemblances are not proof—they simply put us on inquiry. As one fact, such as the absence of the accused from the scene of the murder, outweighs all the resemblances that a thousand witnesses could swear to, so the inability of science to trace any one of the millions of species to another species, outweighs all the resemblances upon which evolutionists rely to establish man's blood relationship with the brutes.

"But while the wisest scientists can not prove a pushing power, such as evolution is supposed to be, there is a lifting power, that any child can understand.

"Christ is our drawing power; He said, 'I, if I be lifted up from the earth, will draw all men unto me.' and His promise is being fulfilled daily all over the world."

Bryan takes up the doctrine of evolution as set forth in Hunter's Biology, the text from which Scopes taught. He turns to the family tree contained in the book, where the various great classes of animals are represented by circles at the end of each branch, and within the circle a number, showing the approximate number of species in each animal group.

"No circle is reserved for man alone!

"He is, according to the diagram, shut up in the little circle entitled 'mammals,' with 3,499 other species of mammals. Does it not seem a little unfair not to distinguish between man and lower forms of life?

"What shall we say of the intelligence, not to say religion, of those who are so particular to distinguish between fishes and reptiles and birds, but put a man with an immortal soul in the same circle with the wolf, the hyena and the skunk? What must be the impression made upon children by such a degradation of man?

"In the preface of this book, the author explains that it is for children, and adds that 'the boy or girl of average ability upon admission to the secondary school is not a thinking individual.' Whatever may be said in favor of teaching evolution to adults, it surely is not proper to teach it to children who are not yet able to think.

"The evolutionist does not undertake to tell us how protozoa, moved by interior and resident forces, sent life up through all the various species, and can not prove that there was actually any such compelling power at all. And yet, the school children are asked to accept their guesses and build a philosophy of life upon them.

"If it were not so serious a matter, one might be tempted to speculate upon the various degrees of relationship that, according to evolutionists, exist between man and other forms of life. It might require some very nice calculation to determine at what degree of relationship the killing of a relative ceases to be murder and the eating of one's kin ceases to be cannibalism.

"But it is not a laughing matter when one considers that evolution not only offers no suggestions as to a Creator, but tends to put the creative act so far away as to cast doubt upon creation itself. And, while it is shaking faith in God as a beginning, it is also creating doubt as to a heaven at the end of life. Evolutionists do not feel that it is incumbent upon them to show how life began, or at what point in their long drawn out scheme of changing species man became endowed with hope and promise of immortal life.

"God may be a matter of indifference to the evolutionists, and a life beyond may have no charm for them, but the mass of mankind will continue to worship their Creator and continue to find comfort in the promise of their Savior that He has gone to prepare a place for them. Christ has made of death a narrow, starlit stripe between the companionship of yesterday and the reunion of tomorrow; evolution strikes out the stars and deepens the gloom that enshrouds the tomb.

"If the results of evolution were unimportant, one might require less proof in support of the hypothesis, but before accepting a new philosophy of life, built upon a materialistic foundation, we have reason to demand something more than guesses. 'We may well suppose' is not a sufficient substitute for 'thus saith the Lord.'"

The argument goes on and quotes from Darwin's "Descent of Man." Another family tree is brought forth, this time the one as the great English naturalist conceived it. Bryan picks his theory to pieces.

"Our first indictment against evolution is that it disputes the truth of the Bible account of man's creation and shakes faith in the Bible as the word of God. This indictment we prove by comparing the processes described as evolutionary with the text of Genesis. It not only contradicts the Mosaic record as to the beginning of human life, but it disputes the Bible doctrine of reproduction according to kind—the greatest scientific principle known.

"Our second indictment is that the evolutionary hypothesis, carried to its logical conclusion, disputes every vital truth of the Bible. Its tendency, natural, if not inevitable, is to lead those who really accept it, first to agnosticism and then to atheism. Evolutionists attack the truth of the Bible, not openly at first, but by using weazel words like 'poetical,' 'symbolical' and 'allegorical' to suck the meaning out of the inspired record of man's creation."

Bryan quotes further from Darwin, this time from a statement appearing in the biography of Darwin written by his son. And the argument goes on:

"When Darwin entered upon his scientific career he was 'quite orthodox and quoted the Bible as an unanswerable authority on some point of morality.' Even when he wrote 'The Origin of Species' the thought of 'a first cause, having an intelligent mind in some degree analagous to man' was strong in his mind. It was after that time that 'very gradually, with many fluctuations,' his belief in God became weaker.

"He traces this decline for us and concludes by telling us that he cannot pretend to throw the least light on such abstruse problems—the religious problems above referred to. Then comes the flat statement that he 'must be content to remain an agnostic' and to make clear what he means by the word agnostic he says that 'the mystery of the beginning of all things is insoluble by us' —not by him alone, but by everybody. Here we have the effect of evolution upon its most distinguished exponent; it led him from an orthodox Christian, believing every word of the Bible and in a personal God, down and down and down to helpless and hopeless agnosticism.

"But there is one sentence upon which I reserved comment— it throws light upon his downward pathway. 'Then arises the doubt, can the mind of man, which has, as I fully believe, been developed from a mind as low as that possessed by the lowest animals, be trusted when it draws such grand conclusions?'

"Here is the explanation; he drags man down to the brute level, and then, judging man by brute standards, he questions whether man's mind can be trusted to deal with God and immortality!

"How can any teacher tell his students that evolution does not tend to destroy his religious faith? How can an honest teacher conceal from his students the effect of evolution upon Darwin himself? And is it not stranger still that preachers who advocate evolution never speak of Darwin's loss of faith, due to his belief in evolution?

"The parents of Tennessee have reason enough to fear the effect of evolution upon the minds of their children. Belief in evolution cannot bring to those who hold such a belief any compensation for the loss of faith in God, trust in the Bible and belief in the supernatural character of Christ. It is belief in evolution that has caused so many scientists and so many Christians to reject the miracles of the Bible, and then give up, one after another, every vital truth of Christianity. They finally cease to pray and sunder the tie that binds them to their Heavenly Father.

"The miracle should not be a stumbling block to any one. It raises but three questions: First: Could God perform a miracle? Yes, the God who created the universe can do anything He wants to with it. He can temporarily suspepd any law that He has made or He may employ higher laws that we do not understand.

"Second: Would God perform a miracle? To answer that question in the negative one would have to know more about God's plans and purposes than a finite mind can know, and yet some are so wedded to evolution that they deny that God would perform a miracle merely because a miracle is inconsistent with evolution.

"If we believe that God can perform a miracle and might desire to do so, we are prepared to consider with open mind the third question, namely did God perform the miracles recorded in the Bible? The same evidence that establishes the authority of the Bible establishes the truth of the record of miracles performed."

Bryan reads into his record the confession of the scientist, George John Romanes, that he lost his belief in orthodox religion through his studies of evolution. "One of the most pathetic confessions that has come to my notice," Bryan calls it, as he goes on:

"Do these evolutionists stop to think of the crime they commit when they take faith out of the hearts of men and women and lead them out into a starless night? What pleasure can they find in robbing a human being of 'the hallowed glory of that creed' that Romanes once cherished, and in substituting 'the lonely mystery of existence' as he found it? Can the fathers and mothers of Tennessee be blamed for trying to protect their children from such a tragedy?

"If anyone has been led to complain of the severity of the punishment that hangs over the defendant, let him compare this crime and its mild punishment with the crimes for which greater punishment is prescribed. What is the taking of a few dollars from one in day or night in comparison with the crime of leading one away from God and away from Christ?

"And, it must be remembered, that we can measure the effect on only that part of life which is spent on earth; we have no way of calculating the effect on that infinite circle of life of which existence here is but a small arc.

"The soul is immortal and religion deals with the soul; the logical effect of the evolutionary hypothesis is to undermine religion and thus affect the soul. I recently received a list of questions that were to be discussed in a prominent eastern school for women. The second question in the list read 'Is religion an obsolescent function that should be allowed to atrophy quietly, without arousing the passionate prejudice of outworn superstition?'

"The real attack of evolution, it will be seen, is not upon orthodox Christianity, or even upon Christianity, but upon religion—the most basic fact in man's existence and the most practical thing in life.

"The people of Tennessee have been patient enough; they acted none too soon. How can they expect to protect society, and even the church, from the deadening influence of agnosticism and atheism if they permit the teachers employed by taxation to

poison the minds of the youth with this destructive doctrine?
And remember, that the law has not heretofore required the
writing of the word 'poison' on poisonous doctrines. The bodies
of our people are so valuable that druggists and physicians must
be careful to properly label all poisons; why not be as careful
to protect the spiritual life of our people from the poisons that
kill the soul?

"There is a test that is sometimes used to ascertain whether
one suspected of mental infirmity is really insane. He is put
into a tank of water and told to dip the tank dry while a stream
of water flows into the tank. If he has not sense enough to turn
off the stream, he is adjudged insane. Can parents justify themselves if, knowing the effect of belief in evolution, they permit
irreligious teachers to inject skepticism and infidelity in the minds
of their children?

"Do bad doctrines corrupt the morals of students? We have
a case in point. Mr. Darrow, one of the most distinguished
criminal lawyers in our land, was engaged about a year ago in
defending two rich men's sons who were on trial for as dastardly
a murder as was ever committed."

Straight at Darrow, his opponent, he throws the arguments
Darrow used to save Leopold and Loeb from the gallows: that
they should not be blamed too harshly for being influenced by
the doctrines taught them in the university, especially the doctrines of Nietzsche, in whose superman Leopold found his theory
of life.

And straight at Darrow Bryan hurls his answer:

"This is a damnable philosophy, and yet it is the flower that
blooms on the stalk of evolution. Mr. Darrow thinks the universities are in duty bound to feed out this poisonous stuff to
their students, and when the students become stupefied by it and

commit murder, neither they nor the universities are to blame. I am sure, your honor, and gentlemen of the jury, that you agree with me when I protest against the adoption of any such a philosophy in the state of Tennessee.

"A criminal is not relieved from responsibility merely because he found Nietzsche's philosophy in a library which ought not to contain it. Neither is the university guiltless if it permits such corrupting nourishment to be fed to the souls that are entrusted to its care.

"Psychologists who build upon the evolutionary hypothesis teach that man is nothing but a bundle of characteristics inherited from brute ancestors. That is the philosophy which Mr. Darrow applied in this celebrated criminal case. 'Some remote ancestor'—he does not know how remote—'sent down the seed that corrupted him.' You cannot punish the ancestor— he is not only dead, but, according to the evolutionists, he was a brute and may have lived a million years ago. And he says that all the biologists agree with him—no wonder so small a percentage of the biologists, according to Leuba, believe in a personal God.

"This is the quintessence of evolution, distilled for us by one who follows that doctrine to its logical conclusion. Analyze this dogma of darkness and death. Evolutionists say that back in the twilight of life a beast, name and nature unknown, planted a murderous seed and that the impulse that originated in that seed throbs forever in the blood of the brute's descendants, inspiring killings innumerable, for which murderers are not responsible because coerced by a fate fixed by the laws of heredity!

"It is an insult to reason and shocks the heart. That doctrine is as deadly as leprosy; it may aid a lawyer in a criminal case, but it would, if generally adopted, destroy all sense of responsibility and menace the morals of the world.

"A brute, they say, can predestine a man to crime, and yet they deny that God incarnate in the flesh can release a human being from this bondage or save him from ancestral sins. No more repulsive doctrine was ever proclaimed by man; if all the biologists of the world teach this doctrine—as Mr. Darrow says they do—then may heaven defend the youth of our land from their impious babblings.

"Our third indictment against evolution is that it diverts attention from pressing problems of great importance to trifling speculation. While one evolutionist is trying to imagine what happened in the dim past, another is trying to pry open the door of the distant future. One recently grew eloquent over ancient worms, and another predicted that 75,000 years hence everyone will be bald and toothless. Both those who endeavor to clothe our remote ancestors with hair and those who endeavor to remove the hair from the heads of our remote descendants ignore the present with its imperative demands.

"The science of 'how to live' is the most important of all the sciences. It is desirable to know the physical sciences, but it is necessary to know how to live. Christians desire that their children shall be taught all the sciences, but they do not want them to lose sight of the Rock of Ages while they study the age of the rocks; neither do they desire them to become so absorbed in measuring the distance between the stars that they will forget Him who holds the stars in His hand.

"While not more than two per cent of our population are college graduates, these, because of enlarged powers, need a 'heavenly vision' even more than those less learned, both for their own restraint and to assure society that their enlarged powers will be used for the benefit of society and not against the public welfare.

"Evolution is deadening the spiritual life of a multitude of students. Christians do not desire less education, but they desire that religion shall be entwined with learning so that our boys and girls will return from college with their hearts aflame with love of God and love of fellowmen, and prepared to lead in the altruistic work that the world so sorely needs.

"The cry in the business world, in the industrial world, in the professional world, in the political world—even in the religious world—is for consecrated talents—for ability plus a passion for service.

"Our fourth indictment against the evolutionary hypothesis is that, by paralyzing the hope of reform, it discourages those who labor for the improvement of man's condition. Every upward-looking man or woman seeks to lift the level upon which mankind stands, and they trust that they will see beneficient changes during the brief span of their own lives.

"Evolution chills their enthusiasm by substituting aeons for years. It obscures all beginnings in the mists of endless ages. It is represented as a cold and heartless process, beginning with time and ending in eternity, and acting so slowly that even the rocks can not preserve a record of the imaginary changes through which it is credited with having carried an original germ of life that appeared sometime from somewhere.

"Its only program for man is scientific breeding, a system under which a few supposedly superior intellects, self-appointed, would direct the mating and the movements of the mass of mankind—an impossible system. Evolution, disputing the miracle, and ignoring the spiritual in life, has not place for the regeneration of the individual. It recognizes no cry of repentance and scoffs at the doctrine that one can be born again.

"It is thus the intolerant and unrelenting enemy of the only process that can redeem society through the redemption of the individual. An evolutionist would never write such a story as the prodigal son; it contradicts the whole theory of evolution. The two sons inherited from the same parents and, through their parents, from the same ancestors, proximate and remote. And these sons were reared at the same fireside and were surrounded by the same environment during all the days of their youth; and yet they were different.

"If Mr. Darrow is correct in the theory applied to Loeb, namely, that his crime was due either to inheritance or to environment, how will he explain the difference between the elder brother and wayward son? The evolutionist may understand from observation, if not by experience, even though he can not explain, why one of these boys was guilty of every immorality, squandered the money that the father had laboriously earned, and brought disgrace upon the family name; but his theory does not explain why a wicked young man underwent a change of heart, confessed his sin, and begged for forgiveness.

"And because the evolutionist can not understand this fact, one of the most important in the human life, he can not understand the infinite love of the Heavenly Father who stands ready to welcome home any repentant sinner, no matter how far he has wandered, how often he has fallen, or how deep he has sunk in sin.

"Your Honor has quoted from a wonderful poem written by a great Tennessee poet, Walter Malone. I venture to quote another stanza which puts into exquisite language the new opportunity which a merciful God gives to everyone who will turn from sin to righteousness.

'Though deep in mire, wring not your hands and weep;
   I lend my arm to all who say, "I can."

No shame-faced outcast ever sank so deep,
But he might rise and be again a man.'

"There are no lines like these in all that evolutionists have ever written. Darwin says that science has nothing to do with the Christ who taught the spirit embodied in the words of Walter Malone, and yet this spirit is the only hope of human progress. A heart can be changed in the twinkling of an eye and a change in the life follows a change in the heart.

"If one heart can be changed, it is possible that many hearts can be changed—that a world can be born in a day. It is this fact that inspires all who labor for man's betterment. It is because Christians believe in individual regeneration and in the regeneration of society through the regeneration of individuals that they pray, 'Thy kingdom come, Thy will be done on earth as it is in heaven.' Evolution makes a mockery of the Lord's prayer.

"To interpret the words to mean that the improvement desired must come slowly through unfolding ages—a process with which each generation could have little to do—is to defer hope, and hope deferred maketh the heart sick.

"Our fifth indictment of the evolutionary hypothesis is that, if taken seriously and made the basis of a philosophy of life, it would eliminate love and carry man back to a struggle of tooth and claw. The Christians who have allowed themselves to be deceived into believing that evolution is a beneficent, or even a rational process, have been associating with those who either do not understand its implications or dare not avow their knowledge of these implications."

Once more the argument quotes from "The Descent of Man," to show to what a world condition we must come if the doctrine of evolution is to be logically carried out.

"Darwin reveals the barbarous sentiment that runs through

evolution and dwarfs the moral nature of those who become obsessed with it. Let us analyze the quotation just given. Darwin speaks with approval of the savage custom of eliminating the weak so that only the strong will survive and complains that 'we civilized men do our utmost to check the process of elimination.' How inhuman such a doctrine as this! He thinks it injurious to 'build asylums for the imbecile, the maimed, and the sick,' or to care for the poor.

"Even the medical men come in for criticism because they 'exert their utmost skill to save the life of every one to the last moment.' And then note his hostility to vaccination because it has 'preserved thousands who, from a weak constitution would, but for vaccination, have succumbed to smallpox.'

"All of the sympathetic activities of civilized society are condemned because they enable 'the weak members to propagate their kind.' Then he drags mankind down to the level of the brute and compares the freedom given to man unfavorably with the restraint that we put on barnyard beasts.

" 'We must therefore bear' what he regards as 'the undoubtedly bad effect of the weak surviving and propagating their kind.' Could any doctrine be more destructive of civilization? And what a commentary on evolution! He wants us to believe that evolution develops a human sympathy that finally becomes so tender, that it repudiates the law that created it and thus invites a return to a level where the extinguishing of pity and sympathy will premit the brutal instincts to again do their progressive (?) work.

"Let no one think that this acceptance of barbarism as the basic principle of evolution died with Darwin. Within three years a book has appeared whose author is even more frankly brutal than Darwin. The book is entitled 'The New Decalogue of Science' and has attracted wide attention."

From this book, among other quotations, Bryan takes the following passage:

" 'Evolution is a bloody business, but civilization tries to make it a pink tea. Barbarism is the only process by which man has ever organically progressed, and civilization is the only process by which he has ever organically declined. Civilization is the most dangerous enterprise upon which man ever set out. For when you take man out of the bloody, brutal, but beneficient, hand of natural selection you place him at once in the soft, perfumed, daintily gloved, but far more dangerous hand of artificial selection. And, unless you call science to your aid and make this artificial selection as efficient as the rude methods of nature, you bungle the whole task.'

"This aspect of evolution may amaze some of the ministers who have not been admitted to the inner circle of the iconoclasts whose theories menace all the ideals of civilized society. Do these ministers know that 'evolution is bloody business?' Do they know that 'barbarism is the only process by which man has ever organically progressed?' Do they know that 'the bloody, brutal hand of natural selection' is 'beneficient?' And that the 'artificial selection' found in civilization is 'dangerous?' What shall we think of the distinguished educators and scientists who read the manuscript before publication, and did not protest against this pagan doctrine?"

There are other quotations, each called in to demonstrate just what evolution is, just what the acceptance of evolution must do to the faith of the individual. Then the Great Commoner, never more the silver tongued orator than here, even with that tongue silenced by death, swings into his peroration.

"Can any Christian remain indifferent? Science needs religion to direct its energies and to inspire with lofty purpose those who employ the forces that are unloosed by science. Evolution is at war with religion because religion is supernatural; it is, therefore, the relentless foe of Christianity, which is a revealed religion.

"Let us, then, hear the conclusion of the whole matter. Science is a magnificent material force, but it is not a teacher of morals. It can perfect machinery, but it adds no moral restraints to protect society from the misuse of the machine. It can also build gigantic intellectual ships, but it constructs no moral rudders for the control of storm-tossed human vessels. It not only fails to supply the spiritual element needed but some of its unproven hypotheses rob the ship of its compass and thus endanger its cargo.

"In war, science has proven itself an evil genius; it has made war more terrible than it ever was before. Man used to be content to slaughter his fellowmen on a single plane—the earth's surface. Science has taught him to go down into the water and shoot up from below, and to go up into the clouds and shoot down from above, thus making the battlefield three times as bloody as it was before; but science does not teach brotherly love.

"Science has made war so hellish that civilization was about to commit suicide; and now we are told that the newly discovered instruments of destruction will make the cruelties of the late war seem trivial in comparison with the cruelties of wars that may come in the future. If civilization is to be saved from the wreckage threatened by intelligence, not consecrated by love, it must be saved by the moral code of the meek and lowly Nazarene. His teachings and His teachings alone, can solve the problems that vex the heart and perplex the world.

"The world needs a savior more than it ever did before, and there is only one 'name under heaven given among men whereby we must be saved.' It is this name that evolution degrades, for, carried to its logical conclusion, it robs Christ of the glory of Virgin Birth, of the majesty of His deity and mission, and of the triumph of His resurrection. It also disputes the doctrine of the atonement.

"It is for the jury to determine whether this attack upon the Christian religion shall be permitted in the public schools of Tennessee by teachers employed by the state and paid out of the public treasury. This case is no longer local; the defendant ceases to play an important part. The case has assumed the proportions of a battle royal between unbelief that attempts to speak through socalled science and the defenders of the Christian faith, speaking through the legislators of Tennessee.

"It is again a choice between God and Baal; it is also a renewal of the issue in Pilate's court.

"In that historic trial—the greatest in history—force, impersonated by Pilate, occupied the throne. Behind it was the Roman government, mistress of the world, and behind the Roman government were the legions of Rome.

"Before Pilate stood Christ, the apostle of love. Force triumphed; they nailed Him to the tree and those who stood round mocked and jeered and said, 'He is dead.' But from that day the power of Caesar waned and the power of Christ increased.

"In a few centuries the Roman government was gone and its legions forgotten, while the crucified and risen Lord has become the greatest fact in history and the growing figure of all time.

"Again force and love meet face to face, and the question, 'What shall I do with Jesus?' must be answered. A bloody, brutal doctrine—evolution—demands, as the rabble did 1,900 years ago, that He be crucified. That can not be the answer of this jury, representing a Christian state and sworn to uphold the laws of Tennessee. Your answer will be heard throughout the world; it is eagerly waited by a praying multitude.

"If the law is nullified, there will be rejoicing wherever God is repudiated, the Savior scoffed at and the Bible ridiculed.

"Every unbeliever of every kind and degree will be happy. If, on the other hand, the law is upheld and the religion of the school children protected, millions of Christians will call you blessed and, with hearts full of gratitude to God, will sing again that grand old song of triumph.

> 'Faith of our fathers, living still,
> In spite of dungeon, fire and sword;
> Oh how our hearts beat high with joy,
> When'er we hear that glorious word,
> Faith of our fathers—holy faith;
> We will be true to Thee till death.' "

Such is Bryan's last great address. Had he given it, as he planned, in the courtroom, the verdict of the future surely would have granted it a place beside that other great plea of 1896, the "Cross of Gold" speech. As it is, coming as it were from the lips of the man after his death, it will forever hold a place more than equal but set apart from all other utterances of the Great Commoner.

CHAPTER XXXI

Well Done, Faithful Servant

Official Announcement of Bryan's Death—President Coolidge's Tribute—Clarence Darrow—Vice-President Dawes—William H. Taft—John W. Davis—The Rev. John Roach Stratton—William C. Redfield—Germany—Judge Raulston—Tribute and Plan for Memorial School—Plans to Lead Trip to Holy Land Disclosed.

By order of President Coolidge, the death of Bryan was formally announced from Washington by Secretary of State Frank B. Kellogg. The announcement read:

"By direction of the President, the undersigned is charged with the sad duty of announcing the death on July 26, 1925, at Dayton, Tenn., of William Jennings Bryan, a distinguished citizen of the United States, formerly a representative in Congress from the state of Nebraska, a colonel in the Spanish-American war, and Secretary of State.

"In all these capacities his services were characterized by a faithfulness to duty and a devotion to public interest. His private life was one for the emulation of all American citizens. Thrice the nominee of a great political party, his death will be especially mourned by a large personal following who held him in affectionate esteem.

"As a testimony of this respect, it is ordered by the President that the national flag be displayed at half staff on the national buildings at Washington on the date of the funeral.

"FRANK B. KELLOGG."

It was but one of thousands of eulogies of the Great Commoner, to be sent by mail and telegraph to Mrs. Bryan and to be printed in the press of America.

President Coolidge sent a long telegram of sympathy to the

408

widow. The President and Mr. Bryan differed on almost every important political question, yet the two had a sincere respect and admiration for each other. Whenever Bryan was in Washington he never failed to call at the White House to pay his respects. Just a short time before Bryan's departure for Dayton he had lunched there as the guest of the President and Mrs. Coolidge.

Mr. Coolidge was sensible of the great charm of Bryan as a conversationalist and told, as he sent his message of condolence to Mrs. Bryan, of the pleasure and interest with which he had listened to Bryan's reminiscences of the man and the events which had marked the Commoner's long career.

To Mrs. Bryan the President wired:

"The sudden death of Mr. Bryan brought a sense of personal loss to Mrs. Coolidge and myself. It was only the other day he had been our guest at the White House. We wish to extend to you and your family our most heartfelt sympathy.

"Mr. Bryan has been a prominent figure in public affairs for a third of a century. He has been a leader in the advocacy of many moral reforms and was representative of the effort for purity in our political life. He was endowed with the great gift of eloquence.

"The sincerity of his motives was beyond dispute. He was three times chosen the head of a great political party and held the exalted office of Secretary of State. His career is another example of what American opportunity affords to those who have the will industriously to apply themselves.

"It would be difficult to find among his contemporaries any one with so large a circle of friends and acquaintances who had so generously bestowed upon him their esteem and confidence.

"I trust that you may be given great consolation in remembering all his worth and in the abiding faith that a Divine Providence has ordered all things well.

"CALVIN COOLIDGE."

In the death of the Great Commoner, all political and religious differences were laid away and the notable men of the United States spoke of Bryan in highest praise, forgetting for the time being whether they had fought at his side or in the ranks of the opposition.

Clarence Darrow, his latest and perhaps his most bitter opponent, declared:

"I have known Mr. Bryan since 1896, and supported him twice for the Presidency. He was a man of strong convictions and always espoused his cause with ability and courage. I differed with him on many questions but always respected his sincerity and devotion."

Said Vice-President Charles G. Dawes:

"I have been a friend of Mr. Bryan for thirty-eight years, since we started as young lawyers in Lincoln, Neb. Throughout all these years there shows his resplendent high personal character. In all he did, Mr. Bryan was in earnest. He never did unworthy or mean things. He may have been mistaken at times, as we all are, but he was trying always to do the right as he saw it."

William H. Taft, former President and present chief justice of the United States Supreme Court, wired Mrs. Bryan:

"Mrs. Taft and I extend to you our heartfelt sympathy. Mr. Bryan and I were long time friends, though usually opposed on the issues of the day. His will be a most notable figure in our political history. He has had a remarkable personal following because they believed in him, his patriotism, his political views, and they will greatly miss his courage and leadership."

The antagonism and the bitterness and the ridicule were melted away, and there showed in those who spoke only kindness and sorrow for their friend's passing.

Said John W. Davis, former ambassador to Great Britain and the Democratic candidate for President in 1924:

"The depressing news of Mr. Bryan's death must prove a great shock not only to his friends but to the country at large. I am most deeply grieved by it. No other man of his generation has been so long identified with public questions or has been so universally known throughout the United States. Although many of the things put forward by him were not accepted, I think it is only fair to say few men, if any, have lived to see so many of the policies they advocated enacted into law.

"His incalculable influence upon public thought cannot be measured, however, only by the standards of personal or political success. If he had done no more than furnish to the men of his day an outstanding example of unflinching moral courage, he would have rendered a great service to his age. This virtue earned him the respect even of those who most profoundly disagreed with him. He was never content until he had discovered what he believed was the moral right or wrong of every public question. When this had been decided he was unwavering.

"The country is poorer for his loss."

The Rev. Dr. John Roach Straton, pastor of Calvary Baptist church, New York, who was a friend of many years' standing, paid this tribute to Mr. Bryan:

"I received this sad message only a moment ago. It is a great shock to me, a shock so great that I can scarcely speak. I loved Mr. Bryan and I knew him intimately. Through our good fellowship I came to know the depths of his great soul and his noble mind. I regarded him as one of the outstanding figures of this modern world.

"Mr. Bryan was a patriot, a great patriot. If ever a man loved his country he did. He was a patriot and an intelligent one. He loved his country not only for its history but in the light of its ideals. He was one of the men who appreciated the fact that this American Republic came into being through religion. I feel that the country has suffered an irreparable loss. A Prince in Israel has fallen.

"It was fitting that the last act of his noble life should have been his glorious fight at Dayton in defense of the old religion, in support of the old faith. I was just this evening finishing a letter to him, in which I sent him a message of cheer and suggested to him that he participate in plans I had in mind for a great revival meeting in this city in the near future.

"Mr. Bryan was a real Christian, and I am sure that he has gone home to be with God forever."

William C. Redfield, Secretary of Commerce in the cabinet of President Wilson, when Mr. Bryan was Secretary of State, recalled the resignation of the Commoner and the President's effort to have him continue with the administration.

"I think I was the first person, next to the President, to hear of Mr. Bryan's resignation as Secretary of State," said Mr. Redfield. "I had an appointment with the President and he was late, an unusual incident for him, and I waited in the White House office for half an hour. Then the President came down the stairs and announced he had just left Mr. Bryan, who had resigned, and that he had tried to have Mr. Bryan reconsider and withdraw his resignation.

"Afterward Mrs. Bryan told me that her husband had walked the floor most of the night preceding his resignation to the President, trying to reach a decision as to the best course to follow, and he finally decided that it was his duty under the circumstances to retire from the Cabinet."

Mr. Redfield was shocked when informed of the death of Mr. Bryan. In his personal tribute he said he had known Mr. Bryan very well for years, had held him in the highest personal esteem and as a public figure of the highest character, though he had not always been able to agree with him and had never supported him in any of his campaigns for the Presidency.

"I have no doubt," Mr. Redfield continued, "that the outstanding public service of Mr. Bryan was in 1913, when he smoothed over the threatened difficulty between the United States and Japan. We owe to his tact and good judgment at that time the amicable adjustment which succeeded his efforts."

In Germany they mourned the man who had tried to find a way to peace in their darkest hour. President Paul Loebe of the Reichstag declared:

"We learn with sincere regret of the sudden death of Mr. Bryan, one of the most remarkable figures in the political world. Germany especially regrets his passing, since he was one of the few whose efforts during and after the war were bent toward lasting peace. His friendship during our darkest days was an inspiration. He hated war and loved peace. We have lost a friend."

Bryan, it was learned from a friend after his death, was to have gone on a long trip within a short time, leading a pilgrimage of hundreds of his followers to the Holy Land. Announcement of the journey had been planned for the very near future. It was to have been a crowning of Bryan's career.

Instead of that, the ultimate journey was from the Rogers house and the simple services in Dayton, by special train, to Washington, to the New York Avenue Presbyterian church and then to the National Cemetery at Arlington.

CHAPTER XXXII

Earth to Earth

It was a simple journey but a triumphant one, from Tennessee to the capital. Along the right of way followers of the Commoner gathered to pay him final honor. At every stop where there was sufficient time, men and women and children crowded up the steps of the private car, to enter and look reverently into the coffin with its draping of flags.

More crowds were at the station in Washington when the train bearing the body came in. In silence they expressed their sympathy to Mrs. Bryan. She smiled and thanked three stalwart attendants who lifted her from the train and carried her to a wheel chair. Her daughter, Mrs. Ruth Owen, was with her and the two went to the Lafayette hotel, to stay there during the funeral. During his lifetime Bryan preferred that hotel because no bar was included in the original plans of the building.

From the station, Bryan's body was taken to the churcn to lie there in state. From eight o'clock in the morning until ten at night, on the day before the funeral, the body lay there in the austere interior of the building. Silent, motionless veterans of the Spanish-American war stood guard by the casket where the former colonel of the 3d Nebraska volunteers of '98 slept in death.

The bare, rectangular auditorium bespoke the simplicity that had been the Commoner's in life. The only decorations, in contrast to the white rails of the balcony, the white-painted pew ends, and the white fluted columns back of the altar, were an American flag hanging from its staff at the right of the dais, and a great wreath of lilies and ivy leaves, bearing on a white card the legend, "From the Secretary of State."

On the front of the altar, directly behind the bronze casket, were inscribed the words, "In Remembrance of Me."

All day, and long after dark the sorrowing followers of the dead crusader came. Men, women, children, babes in arms—representatives of every race, nationality, creed, and political party—they filed by the casket in a steady stream of humanity. Up the front steps of the old brick edifice they marched silently, past the casket, and out by a side stairway leading to the Sunday school rooms below. It was estimated that at least two thousand persons passed by every hour; after the government offices let out there were many more than that.

Up by the right hand aisle they came to the casket, and down by the left to go out, many dabbing handkerchiefs at moist eyes, and some dropping into a rear pew for a moment, to kneel there in prayer.

The setting was the same the next afternoon, July 31, when Bryan was to be laid to rest. But added to it were the scores of floral tributes, covering the chancel, the altar, every available bit of space in the front of the church, with a banking of scent and color. Roses and lilies were everywhere. An open Bible of white flowers bearing across its pages the inscription "The Prince of Peace" was the gift of the Jackson Democratic association of which Bryan was made an honorary member back in '96.

The wreath from the Secretary of State was there and a large cross of lilies from the Bryan family stood in front of the casket. Two clusters of flowers lay on the casket itself, one a spray from the Commoner's great granddaughter, born during the 1924 convention; the other, a wreath of pink roses sent by President and Mrs. Coolidge.

Since early morning it had been raining, a steady drizzle marked by sudden downpours, but the storm had not kept away the throngs. During the morning those who had not had the chance the day before, filed past the casket in a long procession.

As two forty-five, the hour of the funeral, drew near the church began to fill. Every pew was taken long before the services began, and hundreds, not fortunate enough to obtain tickets of admission, stood uncomplainingly in the wet, outside.

In the front pews sat the active and the honorory pallbearers. The active pallbearers were: former Secretary of the Navy Josephus Daniels, Senator Duncan U. Fletcher of Florida, Col. P. M. Callahan of Louisville, Ky., Charles A. Lord of Lincoln, Neb., M. F. Dunlap of Jacksonville, Ill., and State Senator Charles E. Hull of Salem, Ill.

The honorary list included: Senators Swanson of Virginia, Ashurst of Arizona, Sheppard of Texas, McKellar of Tennessee, and Norris of Nebraska; Representatives Oldfield of Arkansas, Upshaw of Georgia, and Yates of Illinois; Gov. Donahey of Ohio, former Secretary of Labor Wilson of Pennsylvania, Bishop Thomas Nicholson of Michigan, former Senator Hitchcock of Nebraska, John Skelton Williams of Virginia, Clem Shaver of West Virginia, Edward F. Goltra of Missouri, James Kirby Risk of Indiana, Norman F. Mack of New York, Howard Russell of Ohio, Charles F. Douglas of the District of Columbia, Charles

F. Horner of Missouri, and Manton Wyvell of the District of Columbia.

Secretary of State Kellogg sat in the front pew on the right, the official representative of the government. The official representatives of the war and navy departments, in uniform, occupied the famous Lincoln pew. Representatives of the diplomatic corps were just behind the Secretary of State. Two large delegations of war veterans, one of men who fought in the Spanish-American war, the other of members of the American Legion, sat in the body of the church, to right and left of the aisle.

The soft strains of the organ playing "Lead Kindly Light" began the service. The church quartet took up the words. Then organ and singers swept into Mrs. Bryan's favorite hymn:

"One sweetly solemn thought
Comes to me o'er and o'er;
I'm nearer home today
Than I ever have been before."

With the last notes, the procession began its slow march down the aisle. In the lead came a figure in blue, the blue of the policeman, star shining, vizored cap tilted a bit to the back and on one side. It was a figure strangely incongruous in this solemn setting, yet one rightly fitting. Kelso Rice of the Chattanooga police force was keeping his trust. Back in Dayton he had been one of the detail sent to do special duty in the courtroom. On Bryan's death he had come to Mrs. Bryan to offer his services as a guard over the body of her husband, and over her. Appreciatively, Mrs. Bryan had accepted the offer. To Kelso Rice, the man he had met and watched during the Scopes trial was the greatest, the most to be admired and revered figure, he had encountered during his life.

Behind the tall policeman walked the Rev. George R. Stuart of Birmingham, Ala., and beside him the Rev. Dr. Joseph R.

Sizoo, pastor of the New York Avenue Presbyterian church, who conducted the services.

As he approached the dais and the casket upon it, Dr. Sizoo began to intone the service for the dead:

"'I am the Resurrection and the Life," saith the Lord; 'he that believeth in Me, though he were dead, yet shall he live, and whosoever liveth and believeth in Me shall never die.'"

Then followed Mrs. Bryan and William Jennings Bryan, Jr., she in her wheel chair, with a spray of orchids in her clasped hands, he with a reassuring arm placed about his mother's shoulders. Behind them came the other members of the family, Mrs. Ruth Owen and Mrs. Grace Hargreaves, the daughters, with their husbands; Charles W. Bryan, the brother, wearing his black skull cap; Mrs. T. S. Allen and Mrs. J. W. Baird, the sisters. Mrs. Bryan's wheel chair was pushed up to the end of the second pew, which was reserved for the family. Her son sat on the arm of the pew, with the comforting hand still on her shoulder.

The Spanish war veterans who had guarded the casket took their seats as the service commenced. Only one man stood by the still form of the fallen leader, the tall blue figure again, of Kelso Rice.

From the pulpit, Dr. Sizoo read the words of the Twenty-Third Psalm, "The Lord is my shepherd,"—through to, "and I will dwell in the house of the Lord forever." And the Ninetieth Psalm—"For a thousand years in Thy sight are but as yesterday." Next, the fifteenth chapter of I Corinthians, ending with its unforgettable words:

"Behold, I shew you a mystery: We shall not all sleep, but we shall all be changed. In a moment, in the twinkling of an eye, at the last trump: for the trumpet shall sound, and the dead shall be raised incorruptible, and we shall be changed.

For this corruptible must put on incorruption, and this mortal must put on immortality. So when this corruptible shall have put on incorruption, and this mortal shall have put on immortality, then shall be brought to pass the saying that is written, Death is swallowed up in victory.

"O death, where is thy sting? O grave, where is thy victory? The sting of death is sin; and the strength of sin is the law. But thanks be to God, which giveth us the victory through our Lord Jesus Christ. Therefore, my beloved brethren, be ye steadfast, unmovable, always abounding in the work of the Lord, forasmuch as ye know that your labour is not in vain in the Lord."

Then the fourteenth chapter of the Gospel according to St. John, with its words of the Savior: "In my Father's house are many mansions: if it were not so, I would have told you. I go to prepare a place for you," and, "I am the way, the truth, and the life: no man cometh unto the Father, but by me."

Dr. Sizoo offered the invocation; at its conclusion the congregation repeated the Lord's Prayer. In this prayer the pastor called down a blessing upon the policeman standing faithfully at the head of the casket—"this humble man of the hills, who has stood by and watched over this great man, even as our Savior was guarded by Joseph of Arimathea."

From the choir came the chanted words Bryan loved so well, "Faith of our fathers, living still—."

Dr. Sizoo began his funeral address. He told how years before he had been one of a group of midwestern students who had listened to the man who now lay still in death in his coffin. He told how the words of William Jennings Bryan had changed the course of his entire life and had sent him into the ministry.

"Some years ago," he said, "it seems only like yesterday—Mr. Bryan delivered a lecture to a group of some five hundred students in a midwestern college. His theme was, 'The Value of an Ideal.' He spoke with that amazing clarity which so characterized all his addresses not only of the place of an ideal in life, but also of the various ideals which men may hold, and then that highest of all ideals—Christian service.

"How profoundly he moved that group of young men, Mr. Bryan never knew. There was one student in that audience for whom it changed the whole program of his life. This student was a freshman at college that year with the plan of preparing for some professional career. The plea for Christian service made by this great heart of faith never left him and following that urge he later entered the Christian ministry.

"I was that student. That stirring plea marked the beginning of a whole new attitude to life, and I bring my testimony to the memory of a man who never knew how greatly he had changed that life. Surely it is unique that, as he lies here dead among us, I should bear witness to his influence in this most solemn hour.

"How strange are the ways of God, and how otherwise from our desires. Had it been given to us to control the affairs of life, how different would it have been. Earth can ill spare such noble souls. His ability was so striking, his sincerity was so genuine, his personality was so winsome, and his faith so serene that we had hoped to have him longer with us. We seem to need him so!

"But God willed otherwise; and until the daybreak, when shadows flee away, we reverently kneel in submission to pray, 'Father, Thy will be done.'

"To this broken family circle, whose days have so suddenly and sadly turned to sorrow and loneliness, the sympathy and prayers of the nation go out. Somehow you must be sustained by the innumerable prayers of the people of the land who are kneeling today at the hearth-stone of your broken home. When the golden bowl is broken and the silver cord is loosed, we pause, we wonder, we weep; but God doeth all things well and you may abide in the promise that underneath and round you are His everlasting arms.

"We talk about unfulfilled dreams and incomplete lives and broken circles; but with God there is no unfinished life and there are no broken circles. Jesus—dead at thirty-three—cried out exultantly from the cross: 'It is finished.' So is every life that follows God's will.

"When is a life finished, you ask? When the seeds of its influence have dropped into the lives of others, enriching them. A life is finished when other lives are lit up by it and walk in its strength. A life is finished when those around it have caught the splendor of its power and live happier, nobler and truer.

"If that is true, then this great heart lived a finished life. The heritage of that life it may take long to measure. Multitudes have caught the splendor of it and lived by its guiding light.

"It is to rehearse this splendor that we have come today. Praise or blame do not affect him now unto an evergrowing fullness and likeness of his God and our God. They never disturbed his convictions. He was far above all that on earth and he is far beyond all that now. Nothing we say or do can in any way add or detract from him. It is for us to see again the glory of that life and heed its heritage.

"There was a three-fold splendor about this noble man which will ever challenge those who have lived in his day and who are to carry on in the days to come:

"First. He had a capacity for noble living. His life was an open book beyond all possible reproach. His character was unsullied to the very end. You can turn the searching light of a critical publicity on any page of his past, through all manner of personal and political fortunes of later life, and not one page is smutted or soiled or stained. There was no shadow or self-seeking or gain in him. There was no skeleton in the closet. You do not have to tread softly over any episode. Friend and foe call him a man whose great concern was the causes he espoused, and to those causes he came with clean hands and a pure heart. Not only for what he said, but for what he was, will his name be treasured.

"Second. He had a deep capacity for love. He was a great friend and never played fast and loose with friendship. Some men are not big enough to have friends, because they are not big enough to be friends, but not so with him. Political opposition never lost him personal friendships. His love was genuine with rich and poor alike, it knew no border, breed or birth. . . . It may take decades to measure the urge and hope for peace he provided for the nation in his day and generation.

"Third. He had a rich capacity for faith. Any summary of the heritage of his life, however brief, would be utterly unworthy if it did not bear witness to his unfaltering faith in God. You will never know this man until you know him there. He was essentially a religious man.

"He was not disillusioned about the world. He knew its ills and its failures. . . . How often he said that happiness will be restored, prosperity will beat again with its angel wings and peace will come with its eternal abiding, when men come back to the simple elemental forces of life-like honesty, reverence and faith in God. . . .

"Nothing else explains the greatness of the man like the greatness of his faith. That was unchallengeable, irresistible, and burned with a quenchless fire.

". . . Some day, perhaps, we may see his great contribution to life and the final heritage that he has come to leave. He has rebuilt the altar of faith in God and covered that altar with his very life. It was faith that gave such sweep to his helpful service.

"What a challenge is such a life to all who falter; what a comfort to all who believe; what an indictment upon all who reject it; what a prophecy of power to all who make it real.

"We shall see him again, for such a life cannot die. I like to believe that somewhere in that better country where the sun goes not down, where twilight breaks into eternal dawn, where God wipes away all tears from our eyes, where there is no pain and where the flowers fade not away, he is still carrying on with the same sweet faith and same noble spirit."

The benediction was given, and to the strains of Chopin's funeral march the casket was borne out of the church. Just as it reached the outside there was a sudden burst of rain, but the drenched crowd of mourners who could not find a place inside still stood patiently, to watch the casket placed in the hearse and the funeral party get into the waiting automobiles.

They had suggested to Mrs. Bryan a full military funeral, with the body of her husband borne on a caisson and guarded by troopers. But she would not have it so. Her husband was a man of peace, she said, and she would consent only to a semi-military burial.

The cortege turned down 13th street to Pennsylvania avenue, then down 15th street toward Potomac Park and the bridge across the river. At the south gate of Arlington Cemetery waited the band of the 3d cavalry and a battalion of the 16th field artillery, all dismounted and bearing side arms only. The band struck up the funeral march from "Saul" and to its slow cadence the procession moved to the knoll and the grave beneath a great elm. The knoll overlooked the national capital, the city Bryan loved. To one side was the grave of the Unknown Soldier.

Pressed against the dripping ropes which marked off the burial site, thousands stood reverently, unmindful of clothing soaked through by the downpour. Over the grave, a tent of army khaki was stretched. Soldiers bore the casket from the hearse, with Policeman Rice following close behind. He stood at the gravehead as Dr. Sizoo and the venerable Dr. Stuart read the burial service. In their slickers, shiny with the wet, the soldiers stood at "parade rest," then at "present," and finally at "attention," as the notes of taps, the soldier's requiem, solemn, sweet, began.

From the door of the car which she had not left, Mrs. Bryan listened and watched. The rain had slackened and just as the first notes of the bugle were heard, the sun crept out from behind the lowering clouds. Just for a moment; then the clouds drifted close again.

William Jennings Bryan slept.

It was on the day after the funeral that the flag that had draped her husband's casket was brought to Mrs. Bryan. The hands that gave it to her were those of the policeman, Kelso Rice.

She thanked him for the services which had measured the devotion he felt for the leader he had just found, only to lose so soon, and she placed in the hands of the blue-clad son of the hills the silver fountain pen, inscribed with the initials, "W. J. B.", which the Great Commoner had used up to the hour of his death.

And to this young man who had held her husband so dearly, the widow spoke her epitaph for him by whose side she had lived, and loved, and worked for more than two score years.

"You are the representative of the simple people who loved my husband," she said. "In return, he loved you with tender affection."